GW01458542

MIKHAIL GROMOV

CHEKHOV SCHOLAR AND CRITIC

AN ESSAY IN CULTURAL DIFFERENCE

by

Patrick Miles

Catherine,
with best wishes.
Patrick Miles

ÆP ASTRA PRESS ÆP

ASTRA PRESS

1 PARK AVENUE, PLUMTREE PARK, KEYWORTH

NOTTINGHAM NG12 5LU, ENGLAND

tel/fax (0115) 937 2979

ISBN 0-946134-68-5

Photograph:
Mikhail Petrovich Gromov
(taken about 1980)

Cover drawing:
by William Miles

British Library Cataloguing in Publication Data
a catalogue record for this book is available from the British Library

CONTENTS

INTRODUCTION

One of Mikhail Gromov's favourite quotations was Chekhov's words to Bunin: 'Vse slozhitsia, kogda my umrem, – slozhnye chasti, nad kotorymi nado rabotat'. Togda i lichnost' avtora obnaruzhitsia.'[1]

More than likely Gromov knew this would be true of himself. In a moving and informative obituary following Gromov's death in 1990, Peter Henry described the forthcoming biography of Chekhov in the series 'Zhizn' zamechatel'nykh liudei' [**29**] as Gromov's 'last book'.[2] Since then, however, Gromov's edition of 'The Steppe' ('Step'') has come out in the Academy of Sciences series 'Literaturnye pamiatniki' [**30**], with a new, one-hundred-page essay by him on the story; there has been a new, three-volume edition of Gromov's 1984 two-volume selection of Chekhov's correspondence with additions to his long introduction [**31**]; and a completely new work, *Tropa k Chekhovu* [**32**], originally advertised for 1991, is now (2002) ready for publication by 'Detskaia literatura'. Given that only one of Gromov's Chekhov books was published in his lifetime [**26**], we can say that only now is it becoming possible to put together the 'component parts' of Gromov's *oeuvre*, gain an overall view of his achievement, and sense, in Chekhov's words, his personality as an author.

What emerges is, I believe, a more original, more fundamental, and more creatively written contribution to our understanding of Chekhov than any other produced in Russia since 1917. Of course, there have been outstanding, classic articles and books about Chekhov published in Russia since that year. But only Gromov's work – the full corpus of articles and books – seems to me to be that of a major literary critic.

Such a statement clearly requires substantiation. Why do I venture it, what does it mean, and why does it *matter* what Gromov's work is?

This is not the place to describe the history of Chekhov 'criticism' in Russia, a subject that could fill several dozen dissertations. In the 1970s I examined nearly three thousand items about Chekhov's work published in Russia since the 1880s, and had to conclude that very few of them were literary criticism in any accepted European sense. Some perceptive short reviews of Chekhov's works appeared when these were first published, just as Chekhov received many private letters containing authentic literary judgements. But most of the extended writing about Chekhov in Russia before 1917 was strictly *parti pris*. The *parti* might be political – liberal, Populist, Marxist, conservative – or it might be sociological, pseudo-philosophical, religious or plain journalistic. It was exposition of Chekhov set in these authors' own ideological contexts, which were anything but literary. This appropriation of Chekhov became even cruder in the Soviet period. The official line on Chekhov was incanted endlessly in the official press (there was no other). Writing on Chekhov became 'encratic', i.e. a mere function of the state.[3] Marxist-Leninist reductions to absurdity were performed as routine operations. 'Kashtanka the Dog' ('Kashtanka') was expounded to schoolchildren as a story about the status of clowns in bourgeois society.[4]

Of course, the achievements of Chekhov 'scholarship' in the Soviet period are not to be belittled. Scholarship is not literary criticism, however, and very often these *chekhovedy* (Chekhov experts) purposely went to ground in antiquarian research in order to avoid the mortal dangers attendant on literary interpretation. In reality, as in any totalitarian state, perfect *Gleichschaltung* of discourse could not be achieved. Even the Chekhov writing of Stalin Prize winner Vladimir Ermilov contained flashes of brilliance – he did, after all, know his subject quite well. But the censorship could compromise even the early post-Stalin work of a much more critical writer, Zinovii Papernyi. From the 1960s on, new generations of Soviet *chekhovedy* turned to linguistic and historical-comparativist approaches. Although conscientious and useful, these studies are not so much literary criticism as preparation for literary criticism.

Mikhail Gromov (1927–1990) began publishing on Chekhov in 1960 and it would have been astonishing if his work then had been free from censors both external and internal. Nevertheless, the fact that he was not writing in the central press helped, and the focus of even his early work is more literary than most of his contemporaries. By the time of his first book, 1989, Gromov was able directly to demolish one of the principal political-historical myths, the *bezvremen'e*, that underlay the Soviet version of Chekhov. In this and his subsequent publications, developments in Russia enabled him to concentrate on the meaning of Chekhov's writing as literature rather than another thing. Clearly, then, Gromov 'matters' in that he was one of the first since 1917 to be able to write almost freely in Russia on an inalienable part of Russia's cultural and spiritual heritage.

Gromov was not only superbly qualified in terms of knowledge to write about Chekhov, and engaged with his writing predominantly as literary art, he was also 'critical'. I do not mean this in the traditional Western sense of qualitative evaluation and discrimination. In fact Gromov does not usually give the impression of being engaged in the 'common pursuit of true judgement'. The particular sense in which he was critical does, however, in my view qualify him for the name of 'literary critic' (*literaturnyi kritik*) rather than *chekhoved* (which he tolerated), *istorik literatury* (which he rejected), *literaturoved* (which he abhorred), or the looser-fitting, classical *filolog* (which he was partial to).

This essay aims to assess Gromov's achievements and qualities as a Chekhov scholar and literary critic by looking at some key areas of his writing on Chekhov published between 1960 and the present. The numbers cited in bold in square brackets refer to the publication as it appears in the select bibliography; subsequent numbers in plain type refer to pages. The bibliography is 'select' because Gromov published on many other subjects, from poetry to photography. It is offered as a first working bibliography of Gromov's publications for subsequent researchers to build on.

Longer Russian quotations are printed in Cyrillic. Russian quotations within the English text are transliterated according to the Library of Congress system without diacritics, except in the case of *vishnëvyi* since the distinction from *vishnevyi* is material to the discussion. The titles of works of modern Russian literature are given first in an English version accompanied by the transliterated original, after which only the English version is used; the English versions and transliterated originals are also listed in the Appendix. The titles of unpublished works, works of Old Russian literature, and all other works, are transliterated only. Letters are referred to by their Old Style dates. All Russian prerevolutionary dates are to the best of my knowledge Old Style. Chekhov's works are quoted from the Academy of Sciences of the USSR edition: A.P. Chekhov, *Polnoe sobranie sochinenii i pisem v tridtsati tomakh*, edited by N.F. Bel'chikov and others (Moscow, 'Nauka', 1974–83). In references this is cited as PSSP (Works) or PSSP (Letters) plus respective volume number, and in the text it is referred to as 'the Complete Works'. The edition of Chekhov's works prepared by himself and published by A.F. Marks between 1899 and 1902 is referred to as 'the Collected Works'.

My gratitude to Lidiia Dmitrievna Gromova-Opul'skaia for supplying me with copies of many of Gromov's publications and answering my extended inquiries is greater than words can express. This essay simply could not have been written without her unfailingly kind assistance and encouragement.

I am also indebted to Richard Davies, Peter Henry, Gordon McVay, James Muckle, Harvey Pitcher, Donald Rayfield, Garth Terry and Diane Oenning Thompson for consultation.

CHAPTER 1

CHEKHOV'S 'FIRST PLAY'

Gromov's *oeuvre* as we have it at the moment displays an unusual structural elegance (*stroinost'*). His article publications reappear in other contexts and genres verbatim, subtly altered, or developed in new directions. For example, his original article on the play *Fatherless* (*Bezottsovshchina*) [**5**] was published in Rostov-on-Don in 1963, resurfaced in 1978 with refocussing and additions as his commentary to the play in the new Complete Works [**21**], then was enlarged and boldly re-accented in the *perestroika* period for his first book [**26**], and appears to have found its final, most startling form in his posthumous 1993 biography of Chekhov [**29**]. Every fresh article of Gromov's was on a new and usually unexpected subject, but once published it could be absorbed into his subsequent work. His *oeuvre* therefore gives the impression of growth rather than production. It resembles a tree more than a set of furniture. The essential Gromov is probably contained in his two monographs [**26**; **29**], but there is a great deal in them that, like waving branches, overlaps.

Consequently, although this essay proceeds through Gromov's publications chronologically it will run 'ahead' whilst discussing a theme, to consider the later metamorphoses of the first publication on that theme. What seems to have been Gromov's first Chekhov publication [**1**] was on *The Cherry Orchard* (*Vishnëvyi sad*), but since he appears not to have written anything further on this play until the extraordinary chapter in his 1993 book, I shall consider his first publication in the latter context.

Other than [**1**], republished in shortened form as [**3**] in the same year, all Gromov's publications on Chekhov between 1960 and 1970 were about the *early* Chekhov.

This was unusual and original in itself, but had an impeccable logic. Until 1964 Gromov was living and working in Taganrog, where Chekhov spent the first nineteen years of his life. He was in an ideal position to research and contemplate the sources of Chekhov's biography and writing. Moreover, since Chekhov's early writing was officially regarded as 'minor' literature it was possible to write about it more freely than his later works, which were considered 'major' (canonical) literature and therefore presented a Soviet ideological minefield. Paradoxically, the official Chekhov could be subverted through a reinterpretation of his 'unofficial', i.e. early works.

But Gromov did not address this task directly. On the contrary, at first glance his earliest writing about the young Chekhov is purely documentary and scholarly. He puts forward fresh facts and hypotheses. Their implications, however, are far-reaching and he draws his readers' attention to some of these implications. Thus his early publications move imperceptibly from a documentary focus to a more critical one.

Perhaps this is least apparent in the article 'Tsenoiu molodosti' [**4**] of 1962. In the steps of an earlier biographer, Aleksandr Roskin, Gromov described the role played by money in the Taganrog of Chekhov's childhood, summarising: 'Den'gi opredeliali ne tol'ko psikhologiiu obyvatelei, no byt i dazhe arkhitekturnyi oblik goroda. Luchshie kvartaly Taganroga byli zastroeny osobniakami, udachno voplotivshimi ideiu denezhnogo sunduka' [**4**, 127]. He quoted unpublished memoirs from Taganrog's literary museum to give a more vivid picture of Chekhov's peasant roots and the repressive régime at Taganrog's classical grammar school. He was one of the first to draw attention to the schoolboy suicides that were a side-effect of this régime. He also dealt with the traditional subjects of Chekhov's love of the theatre in Taganrog, the proximity of the steppe, and the role of religion, and put forward the plausible theory that in this period 'v bol'shom chekhovskom semeistve budushchii velikii pisatel' tol'ko s mater'iu nakhodil obshchii iazyk' [**4**, 139], later corresponding with her in Moscow 'secretly' through third parties.

None of this may seem of great literary moment. The article, however, was prefaced by an epigraph [**4**, 125] that in the context was explosive:

> Есть дети, с детства уже задумывающиеся над своей семьей, с детства оскорбленные неблагообразием отцов своих, отцов и среды своей, а главное — уже в детстве начинающие понимать беспорядочность и случайность основ всей их жизни, отсутствие установившихся форм и родового предания. Ф.М. Достоевский.[5]

For a literary scholar to quote Dostoevskii at all was rare at this time; to juxtapose Dostoevskii's name with Chekhov's was most unusual; to suggest that there was a link between the young Chekhov and Dostoevskii's *podrostok* was revolutionary. The rationale behind it became clear in Gromov's next article [**5**], in which he suggested that the 'fatherless' theme of Chekhov's first full-length play, written when he was still in Taganrog, was autobiographical. The epigraph to the article 'Tsenoiu molodosti' is the seed of Gromov's unique analysis of the influence of Dostoevskii on Chekhov, which culminated in the chapter 'Chekhov i Dostoevskii: velikoe protivostoianie' of his 1989 book [**26**], discussed in chapter five of this essay. Meanwhile, however, the biographical-literary aim of the 1962 article was to 'poniat' istoriiu gimnazista Chekhova kak istoriiu bor'by s zhiznennym ukladom, vnutrenniuiu vrazhdebnost' kotorogo on ponimal vse iasnee i iasnee po mere togo, kak stanovilsia Chekhovym' [**4**, 126].

Gromov's truly seminal article 'Pervaia p'esa Chekhova' [**5**], of 1963, begins with a dry examination of the date of composition of the play which was usually referred to by earlier Russian scholars as *P'esa bez nazvaniia* because the manuscript has no title page. This introduction establishes, as it were, Gromov's credentials for writing the piece. Like all Gromov's best scholarly 'proofs', it proceeds with the inexorability of a mathematical theorem. The first mention of the play is in a letter to Chekhov from his brother Aleksandr dated 14 October 1878. Considering that it would take some time for Aleksandr to digest the voluminous manuscript, Gromov suggests Chekhov must have been writing it in 1877. Although the 'discoverer' of the play, N.F. Bel'chikov, dated the handwriting to the beginning of the 1880s, 'pri samom pridirchivom slichenii chekhovskikh avtografov 1877–79 godov s rukopis'iu "P'esy bez nazvaniia" sushchestvennykh razlichii obnaruzhit' ne udalos'' [**5**, 9]. Moreover, the manuscript contains Taganrog dialect: 'Podobnye dialektizmy mozhno vstretit' v pis'makh 1877–1879 godov, v pis'makh zhe moskovskoi pory ikh sovershenno net' [**5**, 9]. The death of Nekrasov (27 December 1877) is referred to in the play as a recent event, and a character reads a novel by Sacher-Masoch published in Russian in 1877. 'Razumeetsia, eti daty sami po sebe ni v koem sluchae ne mogut sluzhit' osnovoi dlia tochnogo khronologicheskogo priurocheniia rannei chekhovskoi p'esy. No v p'ese net zato i sobytii, kotorye proizoshli by **posle** 1878 goda' [**5**, 9]. Finally, Gromov convincingly identifies the sources of the names Platonov and Grekova in Taganrog itself. He concludes that, although Chekhov worked on the play after moving to Moscow in 1879, it was originally written in Taganrog in 1877–78, is the *only* full-length play he could have written between 1877 and 1881, and its subject confirms it is the play *Fatherless* referred to by Chekhov's brothers Mikhail and Aleksandr. These conclusions were sensational at the time for Chekhov scholarship and as far as I know have not been refuted since. The play is usually referred to in Russia now as *Bezottsovshchina*, not *P'esa bez nazvaniia*.

Following this, Gromov considers *Fatherless* as a play. To be more precise, in his own words he subjects it to an 'historical-literary analysis' [**5**, 5–6]. It is impossible to know whether he actually believed in the terms of this analysis, or whether he had no choice at that time if he wanted to discuss the play in print *at all*. Whichever, he produced what looked like a model Soviet exposition.

In Act I of the play Glagol'ev senior ('1') expatiates on the *neopredelennost'* of contemporary society: 'Vse kraine neopredelenno, neponiatno... Vse smeshalos' do krainosti, pereputalos'...'. 'V etikh slovakh – smyslovoi kliuch dramy', declares Gromov [**5**, 11], and relates them to the famous lines in *Anna Karenina*, Book III, Chapter 26, beginning 'Vse perevorotilos'' and approvingly quoted by 'V.I. Lenin'. The play, Gromov explains, presents the particularly severe fathers/children divide of the 1870s (hence its title) and he considers the characters at length under the headings ‘fathers’, ‘children’, and ‘Platonov plus women’. The fathers have squandered their patrimony and ransacked their own country during the Crimean War. The children, however, are ‘“bez viny vinovatye”, i kazhdyi iz nikh po-svoemu preodolevaet svoiu “bezottsovshchinu”. Eto preodolenie i prevrashchaet personazhi chekhovskoi dramy v literaturnye tipy’ [**5**, 15]. Platonov himself imitated the literary heroes of the early 1870s: he bought prostitutes out of captivity, dropped out of university, and ‘went to the people’. According to Gromov, he is ‘svoeobraznaia sovest' “Bezottsovshchiny”. Ego poiavlenie podobno kamniu, broshennomu v prud, – **srazu** konchaetsia tish' i glad', i liudi nachinaiut oshchushchat' bespokoinoe techenie zhizni’ [**5**, 19]. The other ‘children’ in the play, especially the four women he has affairs with, look upon him as a ‘bol'shoi, neobyknovennyi chelovek’ [**5**, 19], a hero in fact.

Gromov’s socio-historical treatment of the play complete with ‘Lenin’ quotation; the implication that the ‘children’ are socially determined victims with no personal responsibility for their lives; the focus on literary ‘types’; the status of Platonov and Voinitseva as progressive ‘heroes’ – all this looks impeccably Soviet. It is undercut, however, by Gromov’s ensuing discussion of comedy in the play. As Gritsenko acts it in the theatre, the part of Platonov ‘vosprinimaetsia zriteliami kak komediinaia, i Gritsenko igraet pod nepreryvnyi khokhot zritel'nogo zala’ [**5**, 26]. The play is not romantic, asserts Gromov: ‘Spravedlivee bylo by schitat', chto osnovu dramy sostavliaet **komediinaia** kontseptsiia, sviazannaia s “etim bezumtsem Platonovym” i drugimi personazhami dramy’ [**5**, 26]. If this is true, the ‘serious’ pretensions of Platonov, the play, and its social engagement as earlier adumbrated by Gromov, can hardly be taken ‘seriously’; these pretensions are in fact sent up. Gromov seems to wish us to draw some such conclusion ourselves at this point, although he heavily qualifies it:

> Разумеется, нельзя говорить о том, что уже в "Безотцовщине" произошло то преобразование жанра, которое сделало драматургию А.П. Чехова новым словом в истории мирового театра. Но жанровая новизна ощутима уже и здесь, хотя молодой Чехов, называя "Безотцовщину" **драмой**, по-видимому, не отдавал себе отчета в своем новаторстве. [**5**, 26]

In the remaining pages of this article Gromov attempted to defend the play against its critics (i.e. virtually everyone who had written on it in Russian to date). The completion of the play had been a

> подлинной школой писательства и реализма [...] Чтобы вывести на сцену двадцать действующих лиц, воссоздать сложнейшие человеческие характеры в еще более сложных обстоятельствах социального бытия, подобрать для каждого из них языковые краски, завязать и снова распутать узлы сюжетных интриг, одного таланта было мало: нужно было ощущать под ногами прочную литературную почву, двигаться в русле совершенно определенных литературных традиций. [**5**, 29]

Even in his first play, Gromov claims, Chekhov showed a mastery of telling detail in character and speech. There are obvious organic links between it and *Ivanov*, but Gromov also identifies connections with *Three Sisters* (*Tri sestry*), *Uncle Vania* (*Diadia Vania*), *The Cherry Orchard*, the 'dramatic study' *On the Highway* (*Na bol'shoi doroge*), and Chekhov's so-called 'huntsman's stories' of 1883–87 [**5**, 31–33]. The fact that in *Fatherless* Chekhov revealed the 'protivorechiia mezhdu kharakterom i zhizn'iu, mezhdu tem, chem mog by po svoim zadatkam byt' chelovek i chem stanovitsia on po usloviiam svoego bytiia', showed that 'realizm molodogo Chekhova **byl realizmom kriticheskim**, i v etom smysle Chekhov prodolzhal traditsii velikikh russkikh realistov XIX veka' [**5**, 31].

The latter statement looks so banally orthodox as to suggest it is a parody! Whether Gromov at this time accepted all the terminology of Soviet historical poetics, or not, such a formulation could only facilitate the publication of the article. Clearly more strongly held were the conclusions Gromov put forward in the three short paragraphs with which he ended:

> Принято считать, что А.П. Чехов начинал свой писательский путь как автор юмористических зарисовок, пародий и коротких рассказов, и поднимался от рассказа к рассказу, как по ступенькам высокой лестницы.
>
> Но "Безотцовщина" писалась до "Письма донского помещика..." и пародий "Что чаще всего встречается в романах, повестях и т.п.?". Иными словами, ее автор стал Чеховым до того, как ему пришлось надеть маску Антоши Чехонте.
>
> Анализ первой пьесы А.П. Чехова неизбежно приводит к существенному пересмотру всей концепции его литературного пути. [**5**, 34]

It is impossible to do justice here to the richness – the clash and contrast – of Gromov's perceptions in this classic article. Basically, however conventional some of his referential framework in it may seem, the last-quoted statements were radical indeed. By implication they subverted the whole Soviet (and pre-revolutionary) 'scheme' and 'periodization' of Chekhov's development.

By 1978, when volume 11 of the new Complete Works was published, for which Gromov edited the text of *Fatherless* and wrote its commentary, he was able to express his thesis more explicitly:

> Существование ранней драмы ясно свидетельствует, что Чехов-художник начинал свой писательский путь не с водевилей, не с простеньких юмористических безделушек и мелочишек, не требующих особенного таланта и труда, а с большой четырехактной драмы, которую предполагал поставить на сцене Малого театра в бенефис М.Н. Ермоловой. [**21**, 382]

He even claimed that *Fatherless* was a completely finished play, arguing that both it and *On the Highway* were 'podgotovleny avtorom k postanovke i polnost'iu zaversheny' [**21**, 381]. Whilst this appears to be true of *On the Highway* because it exists in a copy submitted to the censor, it is difficult to believe it of

Fatherless since the fair copy made by Mikhail Chekhov for submission to Ermolova has not been found and on the heavily revised extant manuscript Anton Chekhov has drafted a note to her which suggests the play still needs a lot doing to it ('Vo mnogikh mestakh [text missing] nuzhdaetsia eshche [text missing]' [**21**, 393]). In any case, in what sense could a play text be said to be completely finished that would take eight hours to perform without intervals [**26**, 57]?

The *glasnost'* of the late 1980s and, probably, the international success of Nikita Mikhalkov's 1976 film *Neokonchennaia p'esa dlia mekhanicheskogo pianino* (which Gromov greatly admired), enabled Gromov in his first book [**26**] to expand his treatment of *Fatherless* and express his views more directly. It forms the fifth longest chapter in the book (26 pages) after the centrepiece on 'The Steppe' (51 pages), the chapter on Chekhov's correspondence (45 pages) which was derived from his introductory essay to the earlier two-volume selection of letters [**24**], the seminal one on Chekhov and Dostoevskii (43 pages), and a chapter on Chekhov's *gorod* (42 pages).

In *Kniga o Chekhove* Gromov provides a new piece of evidence that the extant manuscript of *Fatherless* was written in Taganrog: most of the paper bears the watermark of a paper-mill in southern Russia [**26**, 54]. He appears to have changed his mind since 1978 about the text being 'completely finished', as he now describes the manuscript as 'odin iz poslednikh avtorskikh variantov toi "Bezottsovshchiny", kotoruiu v 1878 godu poluchil iz Taganroga starshii brat' [**26**, 55]. Despite Chekhov's draft note to Ermolova on the manuscript, Gromov now doubts whether she ever set eyes on the play. Apropos of Mikhail Chekhov's statement that Anton 'personally' took his play to Ermolova, he expostulates:

> вот слова, заставляющие думать и думать. Ничего невероятного как будто бы нет в том, что Чехов "лично" обратился к Ермоловой: в истории русской культуры их имена сопоставимы, даже связаны. Но это в истории, в итоге жизни, а не в ее истоках: остается величайшей тайной, как этот юный студент, без имени, без всяких связей, смог пробиться к примадонне русского театра — сквозь все заслоны, вопреки обычаям и порядкам, минуя свиту поклонников, которой она была окружена. [**26**, 52]

In any case, Gromov observes, reading new scripts was not 'po ee chasti'; it would be done by 'assistant directors' or 'literary consultants'; one could just imagine what such a person would have said to the 'young dramatist' after 'leafing through' the gigantic script which would have taken 'almost the whole Maly company to perform'; and none of the women's parts in it 'ne imela nikakogo otnosheniia k amplua Ermolovoi!' [**26**, 57].

Gromov defended the play as a work, but in an intriguing way. Whereas in his first article [**5**] he had restricted himself to placing double exclamation marks or a question mark and exclamation mark in brackets after critical Russian opinions of the play, now he countered the Soviet conventional wisdom by contrasting it with the play's theatrical and critical history in the West. He touched on successful German, Polish, French and English productions and claimed:

> В европейском литературоведении как о чем-то само собой разумеющемся говорилось о сценическом новаторстве этой ранней драмы, колеблющей старый традиционный театр в самых его основах [...]
>
> Никто, естественно, не писал о художественной беспомощности "Платонова", никто не рискнул бы сказать, что драма не заслуживала постановки и обречена на забвение. [**26**, 60]

Gromov left it at that; he did not critically refute the Soviet opprobrium.

Gromov's evaluation of the play in this chapter was essentially historical, and in two senses. First, he claimed as before that the play set out to express the *neopredelennost'*, the loss of orientation, in Russian society in the 1870s. He again juxtaposed Glagol'ev 1's words on the subject with those 'of Tolstoi' (actually, the thoughts of Levin, Tolstoi's hero), but dropped the reference to 'V.I. Lenin'. The play, he claimed, 'byla zadumana kak sovremennaia, s glubokim istoricheskim podtekstom o russkoi zhizni' [**26**, 65] and he repeated his examination of the 'fathers/children' conflict, identifying each group with historical realities. An entirely new idea, however, crept in here. After stating, as he had in 1963, that the play was innovative because 'u Platonova net svoego Iago' [**26**, 69], he continued:

> Образы старшего и младшего Венгеровичей и Осипа, которому старик Венгерович всеми правдами и неправдами внушает ненависть к Платонову, рождены, конечно, наступавшим в России историческим хаосом; это фигуры недалекого будушчего, предугаданного, но еще не наступившего. Чехов дал почувствовать, что они страшнее Яго, но раскрыть их до конца не мог. Справедливости ради нужно сказать, что время полного понимания коллизий такого плана не наступило еше и для нас. [**26**, 69]

In *Fatherless* the Vengeroviches are rich Jews (the son could be a Marxist) and Osip is a cut-throat in the Pugachev mould. Gromov's choice of language here seems opaque and I will return to the problem later. Suffice it to say that the idea of the eighteen-year-old Chekhov being an historical prophet is bound to surprise the Western reader.

The other sense in which Gromov's approach was historical is that he was primarily concerned with *Fatherless*'s place in the Russian literary tradition and in Chekhov's own literary biography. He 'places' Platonov in the literary worlds of Chernyshevskii and Nekrasov, but links the creation of 'stol' protivorechivykh i slozhnykh kharakterov' [**26**, 68] above all with Dostoevskii's *The Adolescent* (*Podrostok*). He attempts to show that when Glagol'ev 1 says in Act I, scene 3, 'russkii belletrist chuvstvuet etu neopredelennost'. On stal v tupik, teriaetsia', he is referring to Dostoevskii and a specific passage in that novel [**26**, 68]. Whatever critics might say about the quality of *Fatherless*, Gromov felt that 'historians of literature' must admit that it is far more sophisticated than anything Gogol', Turgenev or Nekrasov produced at the same age [**26**, 63]. Gromov concluded with a much more inflated claim for the play than he had made before: 'Pervaia p'esa byla dlia Chekhova ser'ezneishei shkoloi i znachila dlia ego posleduiushchego tvorchestva nesravnenno bol'she, chem vse, chto bylo napisano im v eti gody dlia iumoristicheskikh zhurnalov' [**26**, 74]. If *Fatherless* as we have it was written, in Gromov's opinion, between 1877 and 1881, it is not obvious to what 'all' the works written 'in these years' for the humorous magazines refers. His general sense, though, is clear: Chekhov was a 'prirozhdennym dramaturgom' [**26**, 74] and his writing for the humorous magazines was actually a digression from his true course.

The interpretative, one might say synchronic, idea that Gromov developed most in 1989 from his 1963 article was that 'Platonov – svoeobraznaia sovest' "Bezottsovshchiny"' [**5**, 19]. He saw this as the second-most important conflict in the play after that of the generations. It was also 'odna iz vazhneishikh i samykh poniatnykh [kollizii] v istorii mirovoi dramaturgii' and a subject that Chekhov's plays shared with ancient drama and Shakespeare [**26**, 70].

Personally, I find it difficult to see Platonov as exemplifying this. He certainly inveighs against the 'evil' around him and makes much of persuading others to behave conscientiously. He himself, however, is notable for abandoning his wife and baby son, seducing and dumping two other women, threatening to 'debauch' a third when he is well again, neglecting his job as an 'idealistic' schoolteacher, and being habitually drunk. The view that Platonov feels 'responsible' for the state of things around him is part of Gromov's general belief that 'V mire Chekhova ochen' vazhna eta giperbola sovesti, prinimaiushchei na sebia ne tol'ko grekhi ottsov, no vsiu nepomernuiu tiazhest' istoricheskoi otvetstvennosti i vekovechnoi boli' [**26**, 71]. He even traces this 'hyperbolic conscience' to Chekhov himself, quoting from a letter to Ol'ga Knipper the words 'a ia vsegda – pravda tvoia – [...] vsegda budu vinovat, khotia i ne znaiu, v chem'.[6] This is unfortunate, because in context these words appear to mean no more than 'it's always my fault'/'I always get the blame' for things such as supposedly not writing to his mother and sister.

Each of Gromov's publications in the Communist period is finely attuned to the limits of self-expression existing at the time; although often he sails as close to those limits as was possible. He clearly wanted in each publication to say something that was relevant to the time of writing. Examples of this in his 1989 treatment of *Fatherless* are his extended discussion of 'conscience', the 'sins of the fathers', the 'burden of historical responsibility', and the need for 'redemption' (*iskuplenie*). Nevertheless, even in this book he is forced to use Aesopic language ('istoricheskii khaos' [**26**, 69] for 'Revolution', 'da malo li kto eshche' [**26**, 350] for Stalin, etc). As before, even here one feels one does not know the 'whole' of what Gromov 'really' thinks.

In Gromov's *Chekhov* [**29**], published posthumously after the fall of communism, there is a sense that the gloves are off. His language is more direct than ever and at times acerbic. We cannot know whether it embodies 'all' that he 'really' thought, but it certainly appears to have been his last word in the chronological sense. His propositions about *Fatherless* expressed in this book will therefore be evaluated particularly closely.

First, however, this is perhaps the moment to deal with the ironical aspersions cast at Gromov by Michael Frayn for not being explicit about how the manuscript of *Fatherless* was discovered. As Frayn rightly suggests, you cannot 'find' something in the deposit safe of someone still living, in the vault of their bank; you are actually breaking into that person's safe and stealing their property.[7] I have absolutely no doubt, from personal communication, that Gromov thought this way too. But for him to attempt publicly to discuss it in print would have been to question the basis of Soviet power (expropriation). He regarded this as a futile aspiration. More to the point, it was a subject that was inappropriate to his discourse on *Fatherless*. N.F. Bel'chikov was an *arkhivarius* charged with 'processing' the documentary contents of people's bank safes 'nationalised' by the Bolsheviks. The rights and wrongs of this were a matter for *Bel'chikov's* conscience. Gromov merely accepted as historical fact the latter's role in the 'discovery' of the play in Mariia Chekhova's safe in 1920, and its subsequent publication in 1923. Moreover, I think Gromov's attitude emerges from a comparison of his descriptions of the 'discovery' in all his publications on *Fatherless*. In 1963 he restricted himself to saying that the manuscript 'byla obnaruzhena N.F. Bel'chikovym pri razbore arkhivov v 1920 godu' [**5**, 5]. In his 1978 commentary in the Complete Works (of which Bel'chikov was chief editor!) he lets Bel'chikov tell the story himself [**21**, 393–94]. Bel'chikov presents it impersonally. The repeated use of reflexive passive verbs places Bel'chikov's hands, as it were, well away from the safes. However, for the first time the latter are referred to as *lichnye*. 'Zdes' byl i seif M.P. Chekhovoi. V nem obnaruzhilas' rukopis' p'esy' [**21**, 393]. In *Kniga o Chekhove* (1989, by which time Bel'chikov was dead) the more explicit sentence 'Ona [rukopis'] khranilas' v lichnom seife sestry pisatelia' appears, but rather unobtrusively at the end of a paragraph [**26**, 49]. In *Chekhov* (1993) the same sentence appears in a declarative position at the start of a paragraph and the very next paragraph begins: 'Tetrad', naidennaia N.F. Bel'chikovym' [**29**, 66]. The juxtaposition, surely, could not be more pointed, although even here Gromov refrains from inveighing against the 'basis' of Soviet power or the careerism of its archival mandarins. Unfortunately, Gromov did not live long enough to become a post-Soviet writer.

In his 1993 book the section on *Fatherless* is the longest (37 pages) after that on 'The Steppe' (52 pages). It contains a number of entirely new expositions, and certain of Gromov's previous opinions are expanded considerably.

His view of the incident involving the play's submission to Ermolova is now more negative. There were, he feels, villains who duped Chekhov:

> Сейчас уже трудно представить себе, кто наобещал этому мальчику из провинции все эти златые горы — и знакомство с Ермоловой, и благожелательный прием в Малом театре, и успешный дебют. [...] вполне могло быть (да так, всего вернее, и было), что кто-нибудь из второстепенных литераторов, шутников со стажем или записных юмористов, кто-нибудь из выпивох, окружавших Александра или Николая, протежировал Чехову, еще не утратившему той простодушной доверчивости, с какой провинция взирает на столицу. И он верил, торопился с рукописью, а потом отчаивался и страдал. [**29**, 69-70]

This is a purely speculative account, for which no documentary evidence is offered; or to be more precise it executes a circular argument. Only such a scenario, according to Gromov ('tak, vsego vernee, i bylo'), could explain the words of Chekhov to Miroliubov in 1903 concerning his literary début and quoted in Gromov's previous paragraph: '"Etogo svinstva, kotoroe so mnoi bylo sdelano, zabyt' nel'zia"' [**29**, 69], and only words as strong as Chekhov's to Miroliubov could endorse a scenario like the one Gromov proposes. Yet we do not even know what the *svinstvo* was that Chekhov was referring to. It could have been, for instance, the very rude comments of editors in their 'postboxes' rejecting his stories; it could have been anything.

The major literary-critical innovation in Gromov's last treatment of *Fatherless* was to offer a unifying interpretation of its 'faults'. He reproduced the usual quotations from Soviet denigrators [**29**, 99], although without attributing them. He again used western theatre directors and writers, especially Daniel Gillès, as a stick to beat these critics with. Again he declined to examine the traditional criticisms of the play and refute them point by point. But he now felt free to exclaim: 'Kak dolgo, s kakoi provintsial'noi neposredstvennost'iu pisali u nas o proschetakh i neopytnosti Chekhova, o nedostatkakh ego "Bezottsovshchiny", s kakoi dukhovnoi slepotoi ne zamechali ee dostoinstv!' [**29**, 100]. The blanket defence he offered was:

> О недостатках же "Безотцовщины" можно сказать одним словом: это не пьеса, а материал для талантливой и смелой постановки. Этот далекий от совершенства юношеский труд не только нуждается в режиссере, но не может быть поставлен на сцене (или экранизирован) без большой режиссерской работы. Иными словами, уже первая пьеса Чехова предвещала появление нового, так называемого "режиссерского" театра. [**29**, 99]

This might seem to be making a virtue of necessity, but Gromov had already developed a cogent argument behind it. On the one hand, he admitted, 'P'esa sozdavalas' s neprostitel'noi, vozmozhnoi lish' v rannie gody rastochitel'nostiu. Eto odnovremenno i drama, i komediia, i vodevil' – ili, vernee skazat', ni to, ni drugoe, ni tret'e' [**29**, 71]. On the other hand, the author's approach to his material was so 'universal', comprising themes ranging from the impoverishment of the gentry to women's emancipation, nihilism, doctors and the latest books, that 'ne prikhoditsia i somnevat'sia v tom, chto on zadumyval entsiklopediiu russkoi zhizni, – v etom sut'' [**29**, 91]. Moreover, Platonov's character consisted of a whole series of 'hypostases' [**29**, 86] from the lover and 'superfluous man' to the 'eternal student' and *narodnik*. Consequently, Gromov maintained, an endless variety of completely different plays could be quarried from *Fatherless*.

He gave some original examples of his own. For the first time, he suggested that the tradition of Ostrovskii's theatre could be 'easily recognised' in the provincial landowners, the boot-licking, borrowing and lending:

> материала подобного рода в пьесе довольно много, его можно выделить и скомпоновать в общей сюжетной раме — тут все будет зависеть от профессионализма и вкуса инсценировки и режиссуры, но глубоких переработок и стилевых подкрасок "под Островского" тут, по-видимому, не потребуется.
>
> Такая пьеса, компактная и ярко сыгранная, с комедийными эпизодами, с характерными лицами, могла бы, пожалуй, не без успеха пройти и на сцене современного Малого театра. [**29**, 75]

Gromov also laid new stress on Platonov's historical topicality: the fact that he had 'gone to the people' as a village schoolmaster, bought a prostitute out of slavery, and practised the 'bookish Nekrasovian idealism' of Russian students of the time [**29**, 76]. 'S Platonovym sviazana tselaia polosa studencheskogo narodnichestva, o kotorom pochti nichego eshche u nas ne napisano' [**29**, 76–77]. The latter fact was a pity, because it meant Russians did not understand the self-sacrifice of these students, which played such an important role in 'Russia's future', or their 'gotovnost' chinit' sud i raspravu' [**29**, 77] – the fateful historical role of their secret societies and ruthless young female assassins like Sof'ia Egorovna in the play. 'Etot istoricheskii material ne iavliaetsia osnovnym v pervoi p'ese', admitted Gromov, 'no on v nei est', on ochen' koloriten i iarok; mozhno, takim obrazom, iskhodit' iz nego, stroia p'esu kak khronikal'nuiu dramu russkoi zhizni 70–80-kh godov, s zhivymi bytovymi stsenami i dostovernym istoricheskim fonom' [**29**, 77]. Another play could be created by focussing exclusively on the fathers/children pairs, another could be based on the 'Platonov-Osip-Vengeroviches triangle', and so on [**29**, 78].

This defence of *Fatherless* is powerful, because it is manifestly true. More and more plays and filmscripts have now been tailored out of the baggy original, and they have been astonishingly well received by audiences and reviewers. But we should not let this obscure the fact that Gromov has shifted his argument onto a purely pragmatic, rather than critical, plane. The works that can be derived from Chekhov's manuscript are successful, but Gromov does not delve into why the original is 'ne p'esa' [**29**, 99], or what it is if it is not a play, or what there might be in it after all that so strangely guarantees life to its mutations. It seems safe to assume that the young Chekhov knew how long a playscript had to be for performance in the theatre of his day. Why, then, did he run on and on? If he had wanted to compress his 'play' to a stageable length, he would surely have attempted that, and on failing have abandoned the script altogether. But he carried on, over 226 manuscript pages, to the bitter end. As Gromov never tires of stating, this was a magnificent act of will for such a young person, but why did Chekhov bother, if he was perfectly aware that what he had produced was, in Gromov's words, 'ne p'esa'?

A fruitful lead here might have been provided by Gromov's own comment: 'ved' eto prostrannee "Rudina" i "Dvorianskogo gnezda" i lish' nemnogim ustupaet v ob"eme "Ottsam i detiam"' [**29**, 71]. If a 'play' is too long to be performed and can only be read, then the genre it most gravitates towards is the novel. Chekhov's 'play' has a cast of characters long enough and socially inclusive enough for a novel; its leisurely pace and conversationally prolix dialogue are reminiscent of the novel; the range of its settings would not be out of place in a novel; in short, the 'chronotope' of *Fatherless* tantalizingly suggests the 'realistic', 'idea-soaked' (*ideinyi*) Russian novel. Moreover, the provincial landscape, the military component, the prominence of the women characters, and the sheer eventfulness of the work, pre-empt descriptions in Chekhov's letters of the 'long novel' that he worked on between 1887 and 1889. We can agree with Gromov that *Fatherless* is 'not-a-play', but for all its novelistic features it is obviously also 'not-a-novel'. Positively expressed, it is perhaps an unintended hybrid of these two genres, from which Chekhov learned a great deal that went into his plays, novel and stories proper.

The language of the play is similarly hybrid. Almost any sentence one cares to examine has, on its own, a directness and expressiveness that make it irresistibly dramatic. It is, I would suggest, these qualities that guarantee life to more or less any abridged version of the play. They do bespeak an innate theatrical genius. Yet their effect is completely undone by the author's determination to pile as many as possible of these admirable one-liners on top of each other. The result is a complete loss of 'play-time' (the 'dramatic' chronotope) and a subsidence into 'reading-time' (a 'novelistic' chronotope). Any speech longer than four or five lines of Russian would demonstrate this overkill and consequent loss of dramatic power. Here is a very ordinary one from the beginning of Act II:

ТРИЛЕЦКИЙ: Хороший, умный ты человек, Тимофей Гордеич, но

большой мошенник! Ты меня извини... Я по дружбе... Ведь мы друзья? Большой мошенник! Для чего ты векселя Войницева скупаешь? Для чего ему деньги даешь?

The speech starts with great impetus, but this is lost by the end of the fourth sentence. It stops 'speaking' and starts to 'read' more like a character in a Dostoevskii novel. Chekhov tries to regain the momentum by repeating the last words of the first sentence, but in vain. To keep it moving as drama, the speech needs shortening by five sentences:

ТРИЛЕЦКИЙ: Хороший, умный ты человек, Тимофей Гордеич, но большой мошенник! Для чего ты векселя Войницева скупаешь?

There is an aspect of language in *Fatherless* that Gromov does mention, but it is not, in my view, sufficiently analysed. He claims that Chekhov wanted to 'explain' Platonov in the play, but 'poskol'ku avtorskie otstupleniia v drame nevozmozhny, kommentiruet Platonova priiatel' ego ottsa Glagol'ev 1' [**29**, 81]. Gromov is referring to the long speech by Glagol'ev 1 in Act I, scene 3, which is heavily cued in by Anna Petrovna's questions 'Kto takoi, chto za chelovek, na vash vzgliad, etot Platonov? Geroi ili ne geroi?' and commences: 'Kak vam skazat'? Platonov, po-moemu, est' luchshii vyrazitel' sovremennoi neopredelennosti'. Gromov could have cited numerous other long speeches that provide critical 'commentaries', for example Platonov's on his own father (PSSP (Works), 11, p. 21, and first version on pp. 336–37). He seems, however, to be oblivious of the fact that as soon as one thinks one hears the author's own voice in a play, it fails; because a real play depends on the wholly convincing creation of *others*' voices. Usually, the 'commentary' speeches in *Fatherless* sound contrived and tendentious, are not wholly in character, and exasperatingly hamper the action. In other words, they – and the young Chekhov's determination to get his 'message' across – demolish the 'play'.

It is surprising that in the course of his interpretation of *Fatherless* as 'ne p'esa, a material dlia talantlivoi i smeloi postanovki' [**29**, 99] Gromov does not mention its very strong sexual dimension. He was well aware that early adaptors had presented Platonov as a Don Juan. In his 1989 book he referred in passing [**26**, 61] to Michael Frayn's version *Wild Honey*, an adaptation that focussed on what Frayn called 'the wayward sweetness of forbidden sexual attraction [...] that pervades the play'.[8] However, when citing in 1993 the characteristics of Russians that Chekhov listed in his letter to Grigorovich of 5 February 1888 [**29**, 93], Gromov without acknowledgement cut the adjective *polovaia* from Chekhov's phrase 'ranniaia polovaia zrelost'', and certainly did not discuss this aspect of the play. This may have been because Gromov in fact regarded Platonov as the 'antithesis' of Don Juan: 'Sobstvenno, on nikogo ne soblazniaet [...]. Soblazniaiut i liubiat ego, on zhe lish' neumelo protivitsia deiatel'nym popytkam zhenshchin perekroit' ego zhizn'' [**29**, 98]. He should surely have tackled the lubricity of the play, however, because it is an obvious mark of its author's immaturity. Few people can have read Chekhov's attempts at sexual reference in *Fatherless* ('Ia, znaete li, otreshaius' ... ot prav muzha', 'Soblaznil kogo-nibud'?', 'Ne doshlo eshche do ... krupnogo' etc) without cringing. The determination of four women to have sexual intercourse with Platonov is so incredible as to suggest the tumid fantasy of a very adolescent author. In any critical examination of *Fatherless* this subject should be addressed, because it is relevant to the issue of the work's artistic balance and veracity.

Instead, Gromov expanded his 1989 remarks on Platonov, Osip and the Vengeroviches into a self-contained section. A play based on this triangle would, he wrote, be 'simvolicheski véshchei' (i.e. 'symbolically clairvoyant') [**29**, 78]. To post-revolutionary Russians, Osip and his arrogated 'right' to exterminate Platonov were all too familiar [**29**, 79]. The words of Vengerovich junior to Platonov 'Gete, kak poet, dal li khot' odnomu nemetskomu proletariiu kusok khleba?' were also 'Voistinu prorocheskimi [...] Takoi iazyk, takoi slovar' sovsem ne svoistvenny literature – da i v tselom literaturnomu iazyku – XIX veka. Potom Vengerovich skazhet, my uslyshim – i slyshali, slyshali, no gorazdo pozdnee, vo vremena razvitogo marksizma, v proletkul'tovskoi proze i poezii' [**29**, 80]. Finally, the 'kolliziia' between Platonov and 'the Vengeroviches' (i.e. both father and son) was 'edva li ne samoe dal'novidnoe i ne samoe strashnoe po real'no sbyvshimsia nad Rossiei neschastiam i bedam iz vsekh prorochestv russkoi literatury XIX veka' [**29**, 80]. According to Gromov, the Vengeroviches lurk behind Osip's back, 'gotovye finansirovat' etot sud nad Platonovym i ego kazn' – da, eti vladel'tsy vsekh piteinykh zavedenii v okruge uzhe poniali, k chemu skloniaiutsia vesy istorii, i gotovy platit'' [**29**, 80].

My objections to the whole of this section are wide-ranging. First, to maintain that a play is valuable because it is 'prophetic' is essentially an extrapolation from saying (as Gromov does) that it is valuable because it is 'historical'. A play as a play cannot be 'historical'. By definition a play is a theatrical experience in real time, i.e. essentially 'live' and synchronic. As plays, Shakespeare's 'history plays' are no more 'historical' than, say, *The Cherry Orchard*. Naturally, the texts of plays may be objects of interest to professional historians, as they may be to other specialists, e.g. neurologists, but plays live or die *as plays* by their human immediacy in performance, not their specialist applications. Gromov's historical exegeses of *Fatherless* appear, therefore, extraneous to theatrical or literary criticism.

Nevertheless, one can hardly deny the role of 'prophecy' in a certain indigenous conception of Russian literature dating from at least Dostoevskii. What Gromov says about the suggestiveness, the historical resonance, of young Vengerovich's language in educated Russians' ears is surely true. It is the language and tone of the future destroyers of the so-called 'old' culture. And one is aware of the awesome ability of art to address contexts, including historical ones, that come after it. But this is not the same as saying that a work of art is prophetic. To be the latter, it would have to set out to be prophetic; which Gromov's phrase '*symbolically* clairvoyant' (my emphasis) presumably recognises Chekhov's play did not.

In any case, it is as difficult to pin Gromov down to *what* Chekhov prophesied as it was in his 1989 book. One can well appreciate that the young Vengerovich and his language hilariously and sinisterly prefigure Bolshevik aesthetics, or that Osip embodies the *bunt* that destroyed the Russian gentry. But to what actual historical facts is Gromov referring when he claims that the 'kolliziia' between Platonov and the 'rod Vengerovicha' [**29**, 76] is so portentous? The destruction of the Russian intelligentsia by Marxist fundamentalists? Does Gromov intend us to read significance into the fact that the Vengeroviches are Jews? It must be said that by not being more explicit he risks being misinterpreted as a conspiracy theorist. Strictly speaking, because he will not tell us why the conflict between Platonov and the Vengeroviches is such a 'far-sighted' and 'terrible' prophecy, we cannot rationally evaluate his argument. It seems to withdraw into a pre-rational darkness.

The other section that Gromov greatly expanded in his 1993 book was about 'conscience'. He introduced it with a discussion of the 'tri osnovnye kontseptsii sovesti' [**29**, 83] that he considered prevalent in Russian literature at the end of the 19th century: Tolstoi's, Dostoevskii's, and Nietzsche's. Chekhov, Gromov considered, 'sozdavaia obraz Platonova, shel ot [...] chisto russkikh idei Dostoevskogo' [**29**, 85], in whose fiction conscience was the 'zybkaia granitsa mezhdu "mozhno" i "nel'zia", otdeliaiushchaia obyknovennogo greshnogo cheloveka, dlia kotorogo desiat' bibleiskikh zapovedei iavliaiutsia zakonom, ot Napoleona, dlia kotorogo zakony ne pisany' [**29**, 84]. According to Gromov, the Christian Dostoevskii saw conscience as an act of personal choice for which the 'I' was uniquely responsible, and if the 'I' did not act in accordance with its conscience it would eventually disintegrate (e.g. Raskol'nikov). Yet this hardly tallies with Gromov's own reading of Platonov. It is a central tenet of Gromov's interpretation that Platonov feels no personal guilt [**29**, 83] and actually is without personal guilt [**29**, 87]. But all through the play Platonov destroys other people's lives. According to Dostoevskii in Gromov's own exposition, this would make him responsible and guilty; a person who had not acted according to his conscience. There is, in fact, evidence in the play that Platonov feels some guilt (e.g. Act II, division 2, scene 4) and one could even claim that Platonov's 'I' collapses for the very reason Dostoevskii posits: he, Platonov, does not behave towards people in accordance with his personal conscience. But Gromov does not seem to conceive of conscience as responsibility for one's own *personal* actions.

For Gromov conscience is in the first instance a physical sensation, an 'ache':

'Platonov ispytyvaet postoiannuiu, sil'nuiu bol', o kotoroi skazano tak: "Platonov bolit". Eto sovest'. Inymi slovami, pered nami nekoe voploshchenie sovesti, "kolokol, zveniashchii sam po sebe"' [**29**, 87]. His main evidence for this is Platonov's occasional anguished generalisations about evil, hunger and unhappiness (e.g. Act II, division 1, scene 18). But these are either totally incidental to Platonov's other effusions, or precisely the speeches that fail by being too 'idea-soaked' or because an authorial 'commentary' seems audible in them. 'Po Chekhovu', claims Gromov, 'sovest' est' vrozhdennaia sposobnost' dushi. [...] Eta sposobnost' otlichaet cheloveka ot necheloveka, delaet ego sushchestvom obshchestvennym, sposobnym perezhivat' "chuzhuiu" bol', obidu ili bedu kak svoiu lichnuiu bol' i obidu' [**29**, 89]. To the western reader this may sound more like 'compassion', or 'social conscience', than conscience in the personal sense. More portentously, Gromov applies to Platonov words from Dostoevskii's *The Adolescent*: 'U nas sozdalsia vekami kakoi-to eshche nevidannyi vysshii kul'turnyi tip, kotorogo net v tselom mire – tip vsemirnogo boleniia za vsekh. Eto – tip russkii... On khranit v sebe budushchee Rossii' [**29**, 90]. He concludes by bracketing Platonov with Ivanov:

> как скажет Иванов ему [Платонову] вослед: "День и ночь болит моя совесть, я чувствую, что глубоко виноват, но в чем собственно моя вина, не понимаю". Но в этом и суть, в этом и загадка этой таинственной роли, что личной вины ни у Платонова, ни у Иванова, ни у "чеховского человека" вообще [...] нет. [**29**, 94-95]

These arguments are difficult to accept. Ivanov treats his wife Sara lovelessly then brutally, and hastens her death. If he does not understand that he is personally responsible for this – that it is his 'fault' – then far from being an embodiment of conscience, he lacks one. He treats Sara as a *man without conscience* would. The same is even more true of Platonov, who sadistically abuses his wife and three other women. If, as would seem to be the case, Platonov could not care less about the pain he causes others, he must be *conscience-less*. Far from being embryonic saviours of Russia, then, both early heroes would appear to exemplify Platonov's words about his own father in Act I, scene 5: 'Byt' podletsom i v to zhe vremia ne khotet' soznavat' etogo – strashnaia osobennost' russkogo negodiaia!'

The trouble is that Gromov appears to conceive conscience as a purely abstract entity. For him its main manifestation is the *bol'* experienced by its possessor, or the latter's 'philosophizing' (as Anna Petrovna calls it) about the ills of society. Yet the point, surely, about a conscience is that you act on it and it is 'seen' in interpersonal relations. What Gromov describes seems more like an inchoate moral sense, at most Kierkegaard's concept of man's inherent 'ethical self'. We do not usually see Platonov (or Ivanov) acting conscientiously, so it is difficult to agree with Gromov that they actually possess the 'giperbolu sovesti' he endows them with [**29**, 95].

To be fair, when Gromov says that these dramatic heroes are 'blameless' he seems to mean primarily blameless for the state of Russia that has produced their own sickness and superfluity. They are not personally responsible, he says, for the fact that their fathers were hypocrites, squandered their patrimony, brutalized Russian society, and left them with no future. They are 'liudi, ch'ia sovest' ne otiagoshchena nikakoi vinoi, liudi s bezvinnoi sovest'iu' [**29**, 88]. But if Platonov and Ivanov are 'typical', then their own moral inadequacy – their inability to act as individuals with a conscience – must be somewhat responsible for the state of Russia, i.e. they must be collectively to blame. It is particularly odd that Gromov should overlook this nexus, since at the end of this section he writes that Chekhov 'znal, chto sovest' – eto svoistvo dushi, soediniaiushchee kazhdogo iz nas s obshchestvom, gorodom, mirom' [**29**, 95]. Gromov even produces the curiously Soviet argument that if anyone is to blame in *Fatherless* it is Vengerovich senior, 'kotoromu prinadlezhat 70 kabakov i neskol'ko pushchennykh s molotka imenii, a vovse ne Platonov, u kotorogo nichego, krome sovesti, net' [**29**, 89–90].

One has only to think of 'Ward N° 6' ('Palata N° 6') to agree with Gromov's description of Chekhov's own understanding of conscience. Moreover, such stories as 'The Duel' ('Duel''), 'Neighbours' ('Sosedi') or 'The Black Monk' ('Chernyi monakh') focus precisely on the self-indulgence and moral apathy of 'idea-soaked' people like Platonov. But these are mature works. I do not think that in *Fatherless* Chekhov was concerned to portray Platonov's moral failure. The young writer appears gripped by much more subjective interests, such as the condition of 'fatherlessness', sex, Platonov's sado-masochism, and especially his (the adolescent Chekhov's) perceived job as a Russian writer to have 'ideas', to create the latest incarnation of the 'superfluous man', and comment on the 'state of Russia'. Even Ivanov, judging by Chekhov's letters, was conceived in terms of national and sociological typicality; although after two years' revision of the play of that name Chekhov's avowed aim was to 'put an end to' the tradition of the 'whining' superfluous man figure who was supposedly a victim of his environment.[9] Chekhov achieved this aim, and largely by showing that Ivanov's 'environment' was himself: that he had constructed a 'self' out of uncritically received ideas, smothered his 'ethical self', acted conscience-lessly, and was morally culpable. None of this features yet in *Fatherless*.

To sum up my reservations about Gromov's interpretation of the play in his 1993 book, I wish he had brought his formidable powers to bear on the specifics of its language and genre; the historicity and 'typicality' that he rates so highly in it do not seem to me dramatic qualities, quite the contrary; he does not seek to identify in what ways it is an 'immature' work (e.g. its sexuality); he is impenetrably Aesopic about the Vengeroviches; and his conception of conscience in the case of Platonov (and Ivanov) seems to exclude the realm of personal action, which would demonstrate that they possess a conscience in any other sense than a nebulous socio-historical one. Yet I must recognise that these objections are characteristically West European, if not peculiarly English. As far as I can tell, there is little tradition in Russia of critically evaluating works of literature through close verbal analysis (although *discourse analysis* of authors has been a Russian forte). Similarly sexuality, whilst not a taboo subject, was never regarded in Gromov's lifetime as literarily relevant. In a country whose history was still suppressed and where the historian's profession was a dangerous one, the historical content of a play might indeed give it a theatrical vibrancy. And I am aware that Gromov's conception of conscience has more in common with Orthodox theology than, for example, with western protestantism.

More important than these differences is the recognition that as a result of his publications on *Fatherless* spanning thirty years, Gromov put this fascinating text on the critical map. Thanks to Gromov's efforts, it became impossible to ignore it. To appreciate the full extent of his achievement, it is necessary to read chronologically all that he wrote on the play. First he established cogently from biographical and textual evidence when the play was written. In his first two publications he discussed the play's language and parallels with Chekhov's later plays in more detail than he did in the *perestroika* and post-Soviet periods. By then he was more concerned to stress that 'Vse, chto bylo napisano pozdnee, vyroslo iz "Bezottsovshchiny"' [**29**, 101] and to show how alive the issues of the play still were. A full reading of Gromov's work on the play demonstrates, then, that he touched on a very wide range of subjects associated with it, and taken together these present a surprisingly balanced view. He unashamedly placed *Fatherless* alongside Chekhov's other plays in the modern repertoire and by exploring Platonov's historical identity and raising the issue of historical blame he did what one theatre critic has suggested all real theatre must: he 'threw open Chekhov's text to the twentieth century'.[10]

CHAPTER 2

THE WORLD OF CHEKHOV'S EARLY SHORT STORIES

Gromov's rhetorical emphasis on *Fatherless* in his books may give the impression that he had a low opinion of Chekhov's early fiction generally and his comic prose in particular. This was not so. We must remember that in the 1960s Gromov was inspired by an utterly unconventional interest in the *whole* of Chekhov's earliest writing. It is no exaggeration to say that in his 1967 article on Chekhov's early non-dramatic writing [**7**] he presented discoveries that were even more sensational than his 'rehabilitation' of *Fatherless* in his 1963 article.

As part of his editorial work on volume one of the Complete Works, Gromov searched 30 periodicals, 22 newspapers, and 35 almanacs for the years 1877–83 – an Herculean task. The prime object was to establish when Chekhov began being published [**11**, 554]. In the editorial 'postbox' of *Budil'nik* for 4 March 1877 Gromov found: 'Ne budut napechatany: stikhotvoreniia Krapivy.' He knew from Chekhov's letter to Leikin of 4 June 1883 that Chekhov had used the pseudonym 'Krapiva' before this date, although Chekhov did not say where. Gromov's searches disclosed that the mention in *Budil'nik* of 1877 was the only occurrence of this pseudonym in the Russian periodical press before 1883. Obviously, this occurrence precluded the 'poems' having been published, at least under this pseudonym, but from it Gromov concluded: 'Rech', stalo byt', idet ob odnoi iz samykh rannikh popytok Chekhova probit'sia v pechat'. Liubopytno, chto popytka eta byla sviazana so stikhami' [**7**, 165].

It had long been known (for example, from Mikhail Pavlovich Chekhov's memoirs) that as a schoolboy Chekhov had written verse. One of his poetic personae, according to Mikhail, was 'Iov pod smokovnitsei', and, parodying his father's religiosity, he had assumed the nickname 'Starets'. In two issues of *Strekoza* for 1878 Gromov discovered two short poems signed 'Iunyi starets'. The tone and metre of one of these were reminiscent of the verse 'Dear Babkino's bright starlet!' ('Milogo Babkina iarkaia zvezdochka!') written by Chekhov in Sasha Kiseleva's album in 1886. However, what suggested most strongly that these 1878 publications were by Chekhov was that they were followed in the same year in *Strekoza* by a short prose piece also signed 'Iunyi starets' that concerned two dandies, Sasha and Kolia, strapped for cash in a restaurant. This could well have been drawn from the life of Chekhov's brothers Aleksandr and Nikolai. Stylistically, the piece, which was entitled 'Who's to Pay' ('Komu platit"), closely resembled a Chekhovian *stsenka.*

In the Complete Works, these three items were published as 'Dubia', with Gromov's commentary. He had been impeccable in his 1967 article in not claiming outright that they were by Chekhov, but the circumstantial evidence seems strong. No-one has come forward with evidence that they are *not* by Chekhov. In his 1982 commentary [**23**, 237–38] Gromov produced what looks like a clinching argument. He pointed out that there is only one example in Chekhov's correspondence of him giving anything but a round number for how long he had been writing. This is in a letter to P.I. Kurkin dated 2 November 1899: 'Ia rabotaiu uzhe 21 god.' The context of 'rabotaiu' is 'as an artist', 21 sounds very precise, and Chekhov was known only as a prose-writer. The *stsenka* 'Who's to Pay' was published on 2 November 1878. Gromov, it seems, had achieved something that had eluded all other Chekhov scholars.

The other discovery presented in his 1967 article was equally extraordinary. There had always been great speculation about why Chekhov's first known collection of stories, usually dated to 1883, had not actually been published. Two incomplete copies in proof have survived and it was assumed that the book was to be called *V dosuge* because a sketch by Nikolai Chekhov existed for the cover of a book with that title. Gromov rejected this title on the grounds that a humorous anthology with the same title had come out in 1878 [**7**, 172]. He went to Moscow's Central State Archive to examine the files of the Moscow Censorship Committee for the relevant years. For 19 June 1882 he found an application from Kodi Printers to submit in proof the book *'Shelopai i blagodushnye.' Al'manakh Antoshi Chekhonte s risunkami [Nikolaia] Chekhova.* Minutes of the censors' meeting that dealt with this application showed that it was rejected on formal grounds – probably it did not contain enough information. For 30 June 1882, however, Gromov discovered a re-application in Chekhov's own hand explaining the mixed published and unpublished contents of the book and referring to it as *'Shalost'' A. Chekhonte, s risunkami N.P. Chekhova.* Minutes of the same day showed that it had been accepted for submission to the censor Fedorov [**7**, 178]. Why, then, had it not been published?

Scholars had known for decades that Chekhov reworked the stories included in this book, between their publication in humorous magazines and the production of the proofs. Gromov took a closer look at the textual differences. He showed that one layer of revisions consisted of dropping all references, however tiny, to the Church, the clergy, Christianity, and the censorship itself. 'Skladyvaetsia vpechatlenie', he wrote, 'chto kto-to razgadal ezopov iazyk chekhovskikh "portugal'skikh legend" i "perevodov s ispanskogo" i proshelsia po knige bditel'nym krasnym karandashom' [**7**, 175]. He did not identify this *kto-to* as censor Fedorov, or an editorial adviser to Chekhov, or Chekhov himself, but the fact that the censoring had been done was indicative of the atmosphere in which Chekhov was attempting to bring the book out (with his own money). Even though some of these works had been published *with* their subsequently cut text in magazines in 1880/81, they could not be published in that form in 1882, Gromov surmised, because on 1 March 1881 Alexander II had been assassinated, Pobedonostsev had ordered a crackdown on the press, and the government department responsible for censorship had carried it out. In fact Gromov could not show why the proofs incorporating the censoring had themselves been rejected by 'censor Fedorov'; perhaps they had not been but the changes he insisted on were beyond Chekhov's financial means, or at this point Chekhov just threw in the towel. But in so far as *Tales of Melpomene* (*Skazki Mel'pomeny*) had been published in Moscow in 1884, Gromov asserted that Chekhov's words to Leikin in a letter of 1 April 1885 could only refer to his 'first' book, *Shalost'*: 'V Moskve nakhodiatsia izdateli-tipografy, no v Moskve tsenzura knigi ne pustit, ibo vse moi otbornye rasskazy, po moskovskim poniatiiam, podryvaiut osnovy.' Gromov concluded that these words explained why the book had not come out: 'tsenzura zapretila ee, ibo otbornye rasskazy Chekhova **podryvali osnovy**' [7, 178].

The limpidity and rigour of this article conceal truly staggering achievements. By searching thousands of pages of journalistic ephemera more thoroughly than anyone before, Gromov had discovered the totally unexpected fact that some of Chekhov's first submissions (and possibly his first ever publication) were poems. The same hard labour in archives had turned up a new Chekhov autograph, demonstrated that the rejected and final titles for Chekhov's first collection were utterly different from the presupposed one, proved beyond doubt that this collection was scheduled for 1882, not 1883, and established the probable date of composition of 'The Flying Islands' ('Letaiushchie ostrova'). Such excavations tend to put Bel'chikov's 'discovery' of *Fatherless* into perspective.

Moreover, the literary-critical implications of Gromov's discoveries are intriguing. The young Chekhov was technically competent as a verse-writer, i.e. he actually understood about metre and the need for original rhyme. If one's appreciation of Chekhov's 'ear' in his lyrical short stories, say, or 'The Steppe', or late stories such as 'The Bishop' ('Arkhierei') and 'The Lady with the Little Dog' ('Dama s sobachkoi'), was already high, it is now interestingly enhanced. Chekhov, it seems, has his own peculiar place in the Russian tradition from Pushkin through Turgenev to Pasternak, of poets 'turning' to prose (hence, perhaps, Chekhov's penchant for Lermontov). Further, if Gromov's explanation of why *Shalost'* was not published is correct, it confirms our impression from *Fatherless* that, for authentic or received reasons, the young Chekhov was much more oppositionally inspired and 'tendentious' than has been previously appreciated. Finally, Gromov's work on Chekhov's earliest lost writing (of which he gives a list of 24 items in [**11**, 555–57]), together with the evidence of *Fatherless*, compelled him to conclude that 'Nachinaia v 1880 g. v peterburgskikh i moskovskikh zhurnalakh svoi professional'nyi pisatel'skii put', Chekhov ne byl novichkom v literature: period uchenichestva i pervonachal'nykh opytov on preodolel v Taganroge' [**11**, 557]. This completely overthrew the Soviet conventional wisdom that Chekhov 'began' with the 'story' known today as 'Letter to a Learned Neighbour' ('Pis'mo k uchenomu sosedu'). Thanks to Gromov, we have more than a glimpse of the wellsprings of Chekhov's writing – his 'Lycée period'.

Given that Gromov knew more about Chekhov's five hundred prose works published between 1880 and 1887 than, probably, anyone in the world, it might be asked why he never wrote a book about them. An answer to this question may become apparent in the next section, where we shall look at some of Gromov's literary-theoretical views. Meanwhile, I would suggest that Gromov achieved more for the better understanding of these early works by producing his own volume of them [**8**] than he could have by writing a monograph about them. His personal selection, first published in 1970 in 300,000 copies, was the most representative and least ideologically contaminated to have been issued in Russia since the Revolution. It was quickly appreciated by readers and a second edition [**12**] came out in 200,000 copies in 1974. The year after, 'Khudozhestvennaia literatura' brought out a third edition [**13**] in 100,000 copies. Incredibly, in the same year two scientific publishing houses also produced editions [**14**, **15**] totalling a further 200,000 copies.

Gromov's preface to his selection was also by far the most original of the scores of such prefaces printed in the Soviet period. Its substance communicated directly with Russian readers of the time. Instead of mind-numbing clichés about 'exposing' and 'castigating' the 'perezhitki proshlogo', about 'reflecting' the 'socio-economic reality' of 'bourgeois-landowning Russia', 'continuing' the 'revolutionary-democratic' tradition of 'satire', and being endorsed by 'Lenin' and 'Stalin' in their speeches, Gromov's preface presented the world of Chekhov's early short stories in existential, almost ontological terms: 'Dialektika vremeni raskryvaetsia u Chekhova v kharakternom paradokse: rozhdaias' na svet, chelovek popadaet v proshloe' [**8**, 9]. This 'past' is so inflexibly structured by rank, uniform, sign, ritual and mindset that it can strangle life in the cradle: 'slovom, proshloe formiruet budushchee po obrazu svoemu i podobiiu' [**8**, 10]. The underlying theme of Chekhov's early short stories, therefore, is human freedom. To change their own lives and the present, his fictional heroes must exert their freedom: 'V chekhovskom povestvovanii sreda perestala byt' vneshnei, postoronnei cheloveku siloi, i personazhi zavisiat ot nee v toi mere, v kakoi sami zhe ee sozdaiut i vosproizvodiat' [**8**, 10]. However, most of them funk it: 'Ogromnoe mnozhestvo chekhovskikh rasskazov [...] sviazano edinoi mysliiu [sic]: eto – epos poraboshcheniia, istoriia, sotsiologiia i psikhologiia rabstva' [**8**, 13]. Gromov's words addressed the foremost spiritual problem for 'Soviet' Russians of the time. In his presentation, the world of Chekhov's early fiction must have seemed like a prototypical totalitarian society; which indeed it was, complete with totems, conformists, victims and escapists.

Gromov was quick, however, to identify a great life-force in these works: laughter. 'Smekh', he wrote in a memorable phrase, 'nesovmestim s zhizn' iu v futliare' [**8**, 17]. These early works, then, contained the medicine for the very sickness that they diagnosed. Here Gromov quoted from Bakhtin's 1965 book on Rabelais. The allusion was enough to link Chekhonte's laughter in the minds of educated readers with the whole tradition of 'unofficial', non-satirical, ludic and regenerative humour that the philosopher Bakhtin celebrated in the French writer. Although Gromov could not say it, Soviet 'critics', propagandists, and illustrators like Kukryniksy, had turned Chekhonte's laughter into 'official' laughter, so-called satire of approved Leninist-Stalinist 'targets' that was 'unfree' laughter. On the contrary, Gromov declared in his preface, 'Stikhiia svobodnogo smekha – eto, byt' mozhet, samoe nuzhnoe, chto dal Rossii Chekhov' [**8**, 17].

There are many indications that Gromov studied Bakhtin closely. For instance, in a particularly original article of 1981 entitled 'Talant i metod' he put forward the thesis that '"khmurost"' Chekhova i ego pessimizm – eto obrashchennyi, travestirovannyi iumor ili, esli mozhno tak vyrazit'sia, iumor s obratnym znakom' [**22**, 36]. Discussing Chekhov's story 'Neighbours' in 1989, he remarked: 'Po terminologii M.M. Bakhtina, Chekhov "karnavaliziruet" khudozhestvennyi mir Dostoevskogo: nizvoditsia s p'edestala ideia, rasshchepliaetsia "slovo" geroia, parodiruetsia stil'' [**26**, 259]. Gromov uses several of Bakhtin's concepts, but nowhere, it seems, does he attempt to graft Bakhtin's vision onto his own, or vice versa. He conspicuously refrains from tacking the early Chekhov onto the end of Bakhtin's historical scheme of 'carnival'. Rather, he associates Chekhonte with a medical philosophy of laughter as old as Hippocrates [**22**, 35]. He concludes:

> Для самого Чехова, смех, веселость, шутка, противостоящие духовной усталости, сумрачности и хандре, — это не просто состояние духа, более или менее случайное и мимолетное, но культура поведения и жизненный принцип. "Если человек не понимает шуток, пиши пропало" — это сказал не столько писатель, сколько врач. [**22**, 35-36]

Gromov incorporated his 1967 article on Chekhov's first publications, his preface to his Chekhov selection, parts of his Complete Works commentaries on Chekhov's early writing, and his article 'Talant i metod', into his first book [**26**], with small but significant alterations. The chapter 'Debiut' [**26**, 84–101], based on the 1967 article, ends not with the previously emphasized '**podryvali**

osnovy' but with a new paragraph: 'Vse eto [The rejection of Chekhov's first book] proiskhodilo v nachale leta 1882 goda, i eto bylo vtoroe krushenie Chekhova na literaturnom ego puti. Pervoe on perezhil godom ran'she, kogda obrashchalsia so svoei p'esoi k M.N. Ermolovoi v Malyi teatr' [**26**, 101]. This was a brilliant new biographical focus. The main new contributions on Chekhov's early fiction, however, were contained in chapters entitled 'Etogo ne mozhet byt' nikogda' [**26**, 102–13] and 'Poetika traditsii (Chekhov i Gogol')' [**26**, 136–52].

For the first, Gromov had taken his title from what was popularly thought to be Chekhov's earliest publication, 'Letter to a Learned Neighbour' (as it is entitled in its 1882 revised form). He pointed out how surprising it was that a phrase from such an early work had become proverbial in Chekhov's own lifetime, especially among scientists. But with this phrase, Gromov explained, 'Chekhov dal nechto bol'shee, chem aforizm, ustanoviv tochnuiu meru nevezhestva, absoliutnyi intellektual'nyi nul', nizhe kotorogo nichego uzhe net – ni logiki v mysliakh, ni smysla v slovakh' [**26**, 102]. This fine description might have served as the starting-point for an examination of the 'monolithic' (and monologic) type of personality which appears to be one of the psychological poles of Chekhonte's fictional world. Instead, Gromov juxtaposed 'aphorisms' and other verbal humour from Chekhov's early prose with similar phenomena from later works up to and including *The Cherry Orchard*, in order to prove his premise that the pre-revolutionary and Soviet 'scheme' according to which Chekhov wrote humoresques only in his 'early period', was crass [**26**, 105–08].

In his chapter on Chekhov and Gogol', Gromov proceeds the other way round. He collates the references to Gogol' in Chekhov's letters, the overt and covert quotations from Gogol' in Chekhov's work, the borrowed Gogolian techniques, but moves towards generalizations. 'Siuzhetnyi stroi prozy Gogolia', he concludes, 'v osobennosti arkhitektoniku "Mertvykh dush", Chekhov gluboko osvoil uzhe v rannie gody, i tselyi riad ego sobstvennykh siuzhetov priamo otvetvlialsia ot etogo rodovogo dreva russkoi literatury' [**26**, 147]. Yet Chekhov parodies and reinterprets these plots. In 'The Death of a Civil Servant' ('Smert' chinovnika'), for example,

> переосмыслен не только сюжетный конфликт, но весь художественный мир гоголевской "Шинели". Башмачкин, по смирению своему, не посмел бы занять место, какое нашел для своего чиновника Чехов: во втором ряду кресел [...]. Суть этой остропародийной сцены в том, что Червяков, это, как сказал бы гоголевский столоначальник, ничтожество, преследует и донимает генерала до тех пор, пока тот не становится уже не "чужим", а настоящим, грозным, гоголевским. [**26**, 147]

As in Gogol', humans in Chekhov's early fiction are reduced to their uniforms, hats, moustaches, honorifics etc. Chekhov, Gromov suggests, takes the metaphorical 'road' and 'town' ('Mirgorod') of Gogol' and develops them in unexpected directions. Startlingly, Gromov even relates this to Chekhov's last completed prose work: 'Kogda v chernovikakh "Nevesty" Chekhov napishet: "Gorod mertvyi, liudi v nem mertvye" – eto budet ne tol'ko zaversheniem literaturnoi traditsii; eto – real'naia razviazka "staroi zhizni", ee istoricheskii konets i final' [**26**, 152].

Much of this material on the early Chekhov was re-used in Gromov's second book ('Stikhiia smeka' [**29**, 273–92]), but to it was added a long chapter entitled 'Chekhov i "malaia pressa"' [**29**, 120–43].

Numerous other scholars have written on this theme, but Gromov's chapter has a claim to be the most exhaustive. Not only did he analyse the social, economic and literary roots of these weeklies, show that 'malaia pressa po prirode svoei fel'etonna' [**29**, 124] and what its stock subjects were, examine the fundamental differences between Chekhov and Leikin as displayed in their correspondence, and list the commonest 'genres' of this ephemeral journalism, he also strove to define Chekhov's real relation to it and its real place in his literary biography. Gromov, of course, had read hundreds of issues of the *malaia pressa* of the 1880s, so he knew well what its norms were.

Through extended quotation of examples of the 'letter genre' and 'holiday essay genre' as handled by Chekhov's colleagues, Gromov demonstrated the differences between them and Chekhovian masterpieces such as 'Letter to a Learned Neighbour' and 'Naden'ka X's Holiday Homework' ('Kanikuliarnye raboty institutki Naden'ki N'). Whereas his colleagues relied on gags and the crudest surface effects, Chekhonte's humour seemed to flow from the 'other' – from a single-minded preoccupation with another's character and psychology. In both of his stories referred to, Chekhov creates within a microscopic space the sense of a whole life behind the words [**29**, 140]. Gromov suggests – rightly in my view – that the reason for this difference is that 'Chekhov bukval'no pogruzhen v bol'shuiu literaturu, nepreryvno napominaet o Gete, Shekspire, Gogole, Pushkine, Dostoevskom, Turgeneve, o starykh tragediiakh i romanakh, o velikoi literature, kotoraia byla dlia nego rodnoiu stikhiei' [**29**, 134]. If Antosha Chekhonte's 'humoresques' (i.e. jokes, captions, 'fragments') resemble everyone else's in genre and form, his *stories* are in a class of their own:

> Здесь все другое: и сюжеты, и приемы создания образов, и стиль, и язык. Это не малая пресса, это большая литература, лишь по случайности, по драматическому стечению обстоятельств оказавшаяся в соседстве с Подуровым и Лейкиным, с безликой и безымянной стихией малой прессы. [**29**, 142]

We must treat with extreme caution, Gromov concluded, Chekhov's own claim that he had blazed the trail for writers from the *malaia pressa* to the *tolstye zhurnaly* and that the route he had opened up would remain when he himself was forgotten: 'Ni do Chekhova, ni posle nego nikto ne shel i ne proshel po etomu puti – prosto potomu, chto u bol'shikh pisatelei svoi dorogi, i ni odnu iz nikh dvazhdy proiti nel'zia' [**29**, 143].

It will have been noticed that Gromov's approach to early Chekhov is dyadic. He seeks to define by juxtaposition and comparison. Nowhere does he give a close reading of one work, and the 'serious' stories that Chekhov was increasingly writing after 1885 are barely mentioned. Moreover, the conceptual framework in which Gromov sets Chekhov's early prose, especially in his 1993 book (a biography), is historical (diachronic). He even claims Chekhov himself saw his writing in such terms: 'V sushchnosti, on i v samye rannie gody soznaval svoe osoboe mesto i svoi udel, poskol'ku bol'shoe darovanie – eto v samom dele istoricheskii udel, osoboe mesto sredi togo, chto bylo sozdano v literature predshestvennikami i ostalos' v pamiati pokolenii' [**29**, 134]. Nevertheless, Gromov's contribution to a modern reading of Chekhov's early narrative fiction is entirely on a par with his efforts on behalf of *Fatherless*. Nobody has done more.

CHAPTER 3

GROMOV'S CATALOGUE AND RUSSIAN 'SYSTEMISM'

Between 1974 and the publication of his first book in 1989, the seven volumes of the Complete Works with Gromov's monumental contributions came out, as well as reprints of his selection (with preface) of Chekhov's early fiction, but he also wrote a series of articles [**9**, **10**, **18**, **22**] that were more abstract and generalizing than anything he published before or after. This was not fortuitous. On the one hand, his editorial work had given him a profound knowledge of Chekhov's writing early, middle and late – Gromov even supplied the twenty-two pages of notes on 'A Man in a Case' ('Chelovek v futliare'), 'Gooseberries' ('Kryzhovnik') and 'About Love' ('O liubvi') for the volume of Chekhov's last stories [**20**] – and the temptation to compare, contrast and draw general conclusions must have been irresistible. On the other hand, at this precise moment there was also a turning to more theoretical disquisition among the group of literary scholars at IMLI working on the Complete Works, and in Russian *literaturovedenie* generally.

Structuralism, of course, was proscribed; but a Soviet version of it existed that might be called 'systemism'. This was well expressed in the opening sentence of A.P. Chudakov's 1971 book *Poetika Chekhova*: 'Vzgliad na literaturnoe proizvedenie kak na nekuiu sistemu, ili strukturu, stal v sovremennom literaturovedenii obshchepriznannym.'[11] The self-assurance of the last word in this statement was thoroughly justified. It was at about this time that Bakhtin referred to *literaturovedy* as 'v bol'shinstve svoem strukturalisty'.[12] There was also a 'linguistic turn' that took its momentum from the school of academician Viktor Vinogradov and the 'rediscovery' of Russian formalism. The younger generation of Russian *literaturovedy* appeared to believe in more 'scientific' methods in literary criticism, and it was precisely the scientism of their structuralism and discourse analysis that made it acceptable to the régime (Marxism-Leninism was 'scientific').

Thus Gromov opened his first article of this sort, 'Povestvovanie Chekhova kak khudozhestvennaia sistema' [**9**], with reference to a work on the general theory of systems by the cyberneticist William Ross Ashby that had just been published in Russian. As in the sciences, Gromov claimed, until recently analysis had prevailed over synthesis in *literaturovedenie*. Yet the fact that Chekhov had produced a *multiplicity* of works – nearly 600 in 25 years – rather than, say, a few large novels, was a direct invitation to study these works as a whole, a system: 'otdel'nye rasskazy tiagoteiut drug k drugu kak fragmenty tselostnoi povestvovatel'noi sistemy, kak elementy mnozhestva, kotoroe matematik nazval by gomomorfnym' [**9**, 308]. It was not that the selective analytical approach in Chekhov criticism was 'wrong', but that the selection could be made on any preconceived basis and the conclusions of the analysis then projected onto Chekhov's art as a whole. 'Togda literaturovedcheskii impressionizm, sluchainost', zalozhennaia v podkhode, v metodike issledovaniia, istolkovyvaetsia kak "impressionizm Chekhova"' [**9**, 308].

Gromov was right that Chekhov criticism in Russia had always tended to focus on a relatively small number of works. His phrase 'monograficheskii analiz otdel'nykh rasskazov, povestei, p'es' [**9**, 307] seems inappropriate, however, if 'monographic' means anything larger than articles. There had been books in the Soviet period devoted to the plays, and some articles devoted to one story. But most of the publications of Chekhov criticism, both before and after the Revolution, had not been 'monographic' at all: articles tended to examine a small selection of stories or plays, and books (of the 'zhizn' i tvorchestvo' variety) tended to chew over the same biographical details, stories, plays and literary-historical *periodizatsiia* ad nauseam. Moreover, these selections were not 'arbitrary' ('sluchainy'), as Gromov put it [**9**, 308: 'sluchainost', zalozhennaia v podkhode']. Both before and after 1917 they were ideologically predetermined and they simply shoved many major works from public view. One could hardly say, then, that the 'monographic approach' had been truly tried and tested in Russian Chekhov criticism; although it was certainly true that in many Russian contributions 'vyvody chastnogo analiza formuliruiutsia v predel'nykh obobshcheniiakh' [**9**, 308]. What was most consistent was precisely the desire of Russian Chekhov 'critics' to 'generalize' (philosophize) from the 'particular'.

In place of this subjective generalizing, Gromov proposed an objective generalization based on systems theory:

> Эта теория утверждает, в частности, что взаимодействующие элементы (в данном случае ряд рассказов, ряд персонажей) не являются нейтральными по отношению друг к другу; "ряд" в системе не есть простой арифметический ряд, содержание ("целое") знаменательнее любого отдельно взятого элемента (или группы элементов — например, группы рассказов) и выражается в категориях синтеза. [**9**, 308-09]

The synthesis, of course, was greater than its parts: 'obshchaia tema, "obshchaia ideia" nakhoditsia za predelami kazhdogo iz [rasskazov] v otdel'nosti i iavlena v tselom mnozhestve ikh' [**9**, 309]. Thus the most significant themes and images of Chekhov's writing could be identified 'lish' pri posledovatel'nom izuchenii vsekh rasskazov v tselom' [**9**, 309]. Systems theory aside, one can see that the fact Gromov himself had achieved the latter feat as an editor of the Complete Works lent his assertion peculiar authority. He now presented the salient results of his study.

If one took the 'sequential series' of the place-identifier, i.e. setting, through the whole of Chekhov's prose, then, Gromov claimed, one discovered that 'vse bol'shie i malye sobytiia zhizni, vse sluchainosti i proisshestviia, voobshche vse, chto proiskhodit v siuzhete Chekhova, proiskhodit v russkom gorode [...]. Gorod – ob"ediniaiushchii tsentr slozhnoi khudozhestvennoi struktury' [**9**, 309]. At first sight, this is a rather trite and improbable assertion. One had heard that Chekhov was an 'urban' writer, but far from all his stories are set in towns, or even parts of Russia where there were towns. Under 'gorod', however, Gromov included suburbs, dacha-lands (which many would call 'country'), and even 'monasteries'. Moreover, he claimed, wherever a story was set its characters were always on their way *to or from* the 'gorod', which was always in their thoughts. So the action never lost touch 's tsentral'nym obrazom – gorodom' [**9**, 309]. Further, by not identifying his towns by name, or by merely assigning them the letters N, S, etc, Chekhov imbued them with a metaphorical, archetypal quality suggestive of Gogol': 'Gorod Chekhova, kak Peterburg ili Mirgorod Gogolia, – esteticheskaia, a ne topograficheskaia real'nost, psikhologicheskoe prostranstvo, ocherchennoe neskol'kimi sil'no aktsentirovannymi detaliami i otrazhennoe v soznanii, dushevnom sklade, vnutrennem mire deistvuiushchikh lits' [**9**, 310]. In his 1989 book Gromov even associated his conception of Chekhov's 'gorod' with Marcus Aurelius' 'world as a single city', or 'world-polity' [**26**, 209–10].[13]

Whilst it is interesting to see the chronological series of references to *gorod* that Gromov quotes, and whilst the notion of a Chekhovian 'universum' [**26**, 209] is attractive, it must be admitted that this super-concept produced by the 'systemist' approach is of limited assistance to interpreting actual stories. In the early fiction the *gorod* (often in one or another diminutive form) tends to be all too concretely specific, whilst in later stories the term may appear to be used more abstractly or allusively, but in reality does it operate as anything more than shorthand for 'a concentration of other people'? In neither instance is the meaning of the word in the text enhanced by knowledge of the 'super-concept'. Similarly, the *gorod* is a potent concept in such stories as 'About Love' and 'In the Ravine' ('V ovrage'), but they are not actually *about* the *gorod*, and to suggest they are because of the supreme position of *gorod* in a systematic/synthetic model of Chekhov's writing would appear perverse. In fact it might be claimed that reference to Gromov's 'synthetic', extra-textual Chekhovian town whilst reading these stories would be a dangerous distraction from their meaning.

From the 'central image' of Chekhov's artistic 'system', Gromov moved to the 'details'. 'Predmetnaia detal' v chekhovskom povestvovanii', he stated, 'iavliaetsia elementom sistemy: ona povtoriaetsia, var'iruetsia, ona stoit pered glazami chitatelia – Chekhov ne pozvoliaet zabyt' o nei' [**9**, 311]. As an example, he took the realistic feature of a grey/not grey fence topped with nails, tracing it from 'The Little Joke' ('Shutochka'; dated here as 1886) via 'Thieves' ('Vory'; 1890), 'Ward Nº 6' (1892) and 'The Lady with the Little Dog' (1899) to 'Betrothed' ('Nevesta'; 1903). If a reader knew only 'The Little Joke', Gromov explained, then he/she would probably just register the 'tall fence topped with nails' as a detail familiar from reality and soon forget it. But 'esli, kak nadeialsia Chekhov, chitatel' budet vnimatelen', then he/she would 'notice' that it occurs in one form or other in the stories listed, and give it a *general* significance: 'Esli detal' povtoriaetsia tak nastoichivo, stol'ko raz, to eto ne "sluchainost'", a sistema khudozhestvennogo ("sinteticheskogo") obraza, imeiushchego glubokii ideinyi smysl: razobshchenie, ot"edinenie, pregrada, zabor, stena – mezhdu liubiashchimi drug druga liud'mi, mezhdu liud'mi voobshche, mezhdu vsemi liud'mi i volei' [**9**, 311].

Gromov's argument here begs many questions. First, the detail of the nail-topped fence did not appear in 'The Little Joke' until 1899, when Chekhov added it during his fundamental revision for the Collected Works.[14] The fact that this detail derives from the same year that Chekhov was working on 'The Lady with the Little Dog' might confirm the view of those readers who regard Chekhov's use of 'leitmotifs' as tedious, heavy-handed and a sign of poverty of invention. Assuming, though, that 'Thieves' (1890) was the first time that Chekhov employed the image, how could he possibly have done so hoping that the reader would 'notice' it and connect it to its next appearance, when he himself presumably did not know whether there would be a 'next appearance'? How many times must a detail recur for it to be no longer 'fortuitous' but imbued with 'glubokii ideinyi smysl'? Is once (1892) enough? But why does a 'detail' have to recur at all for it to become a trope? The 'attentive', i.e. true, reader can perceive the 'long grey [dingy] fence with nails on it' in 'The Lady With the Little Dog' as a cruel partition between lovers – the embodiment, possibly, of 'razobshchenie' and 'ot"edinenie' in human society – without ever having read another story by Chekhov. Or not inflate the significance of the image if he/she prefers. It is a question simply of the reader's imagination and personal priorities. After all, as Gromov's own list beginning 'razobshchenie' shows, the very word *zabor* combines a concrete/literal meaning ('fence') and an abstract/figurative one ('barrier').

Lastly, Gromov applies his systems approach to Chekhov's characters. This inevitably leads him to consider them not as the sets in which they occur in discrete works, but as a 'population' swarming 'through' the entire *oeuvre*. It must be admitted that the conclusions he immediately presents from this consideration appear sweepingly 'inductive':

> Система взаимоотношений характера и среды раскрывается как связь поколений (тема отцов и детей, зарождающаяся в "детских" рассказах); как история порабощения воли и разума (адаптация характера и связанная с ним система уподоблений и метафор, развивавшаяся от "Хамелеона" до "Человека в футляре"); как боль и болезнь души (психология страха, которую Чехов исследовал подробно и глубоко); наконец, как остро социальная, но и глубоко психологическая тема свободы, воплощенная в противостоящем городу лирическом образе степи, сада, в образах вольных людей. [**9**, 311-12]

These 'basic lines' of Chekhov's art were laid down in his very first years, Gromov continues; they subsequently 'evolved', but 'bez korennykh perelomov, v obshchem dvizhenii ot prostogo k slozhnomu' [**9**, 312]. The essential psychological conflict in Chekhov's characters could, moreover, be summed up as: 'natsional'nyi kharakter ne umeshchaetsia v tekh formakh, kakie pridaet emu zhizn'' [**9**, 312]. Thus the 'true subject' of Chekhov's art would, Gromov felt, be most accurately expressed by the Greek word *demos*: 'Eto – "my": my – natsiia, my – narod, v svoem prirozhdennom estestve, v svoem sotsial'no-psikhologicheskom i istoricheskom bytii' [**9**, 312].

In fine, Chekhov's characters presented a kind of national epic. Contemporaneous critics had found that they were 'nepokhozhi na traditsionnykh geroev klassicheskogo romana' [**9**, 312], that they 'blurred into' one another, and were difficult to 'classify'. Contemporaneous readers had not, of course, been in a position to 'okhvatit' povestvovanie Chekhova v tselom' (the canon had not been established) and therefore could not perceive 'vo imia chego sozdavalos' eto tseloe, kakoi v nem skryvaetsia smysl' [**9**, 312]. Now that the *oeuvre* could be read sequentially and in literary criticism analysis had given way to synthesis, 'slozhilos' predstavlenie ob epicheskoi osnove tvorchestva Chekhova' [**9**, 312–13].

I shall return to this question below. Suffice it to say at the moment that *if* one conceives of the whole of Chekhov's writing as a 'system', which means amongst other things ignoring the boundaries of each work and the distinctions of genre, then it will certainly appear to possess epic features. The sheer repetition of images and epithets is a feature of a genuinely epic work, e.g. *The Iliad*. On the other hand, 'epic' time perhaps approximates more to 'historical' time than that of any other literary genre, yet as C.J.G. Turner has pointed out historical time is precisely the form of time least deployed or alluded to in Chekhov's writing.[15] The 'historical' dimension that Gromov perceives in Chekhov's *oeuvre* is therefore not so much implicit in the writing as in the 'epic' perspective that the 'systems approach' entails.

But, Gromov asks, what is the methodology appropriate for studying this 'mnogolikoe mnozhestvo lits, naseliaiushchikh chekhovskii gorod i mir', given that 'metodika literaturovedcheskogo analiza, sviazannaia s tak nazyvaemymi "zamknutymi khudozhestvennymi strukturami", v dannom sluchae neprimenima' [**9**, 313]? The answer he proposes is, I feel, deeply paradoxical and unsatisfactory.

On the one hand, he admits that 'poskol'ku takie terminy, kak "obshchestvo", "naselenie", priniaty v literaturovedenii', it is tempting to 'primenit' k literature traditsionnuiu metodiku statisticheskogo analiza real'nogo chelovecheskogo obshchestva, sozdav perepis' literaturnogo naseleniia' [**9**, 313]. This would, he avers, be too linear and crude a method, because in addition to the protagonists of stories there are all sorts of doppelgängers, animals, collective agents and 'offstage' characters who are highly significant in artistic terms but statistically indefinable. It would make more sense, he says, to examine Chekhov's characters as 'variations' of his 'obshchei, general'noi temy cheloveka i sud'by cheloveka' [**9**, 313] – although Gromov does not explain how 'variation' differs in practice from 'literary character' or why, for example, a 'variation' is statistically more definable than a minor, though artistically vivid, 'offstage' character. Whereas a 'prostoi arifmeticheskii podschet personazhei' would be an oversimplification, redefinition as 'variations' enables one, he reasons, to 'zadat'sia sleduiushchim voprosom: skol'ko takikh variatsii dano vo vsem mnozhestve rasskazov Chekhova? Kak realizuetsia i opredeliaetsia, v kakikh predmetnykh formakh voploshchaetsia v chekhovskom povestvovanii obraz, tip, kharakter cheloveka?' [**9**, 313].

On the other hand, in practice it is difficult to distinguish the results of this inquiry (presented in the rest of the article) from those of a 'census of the literary population'. 'Okazalos'', Gromov announces, 'chto v chekhovskikh rasskazakh sushchestvuet, opisyvaetsia, upominaetsia bolee vos'mi tysiach tipov, portretov, imen, bolee vos'mi tysiach lits vsekh sostoianii i vozrastov' [**9**, 314]. The figure derives from compiling what Gromov calls not a 'census' but a 'catalogue'. Surely this is not a very surprising figure, is of minimal literary-critical usefulness, and its reliability is impugned by the vagueness of the entity ('variation') being counted? Moreover, although Gromov himself describes the catalogue as presenting 'v opredelennom – no ves'ma uzkom i ogranichennom smysle – [...] "znakovuiu sistemu", uchityvaiushchuiu vse sposoby oboznacheniia personazha v povestvovanii (chin, titul, portretnaia detal', poetika tak nazyvaemoi "individual'noi kharakteristiki" i t.d.)' [**9**, 314], the only 'signs' he discusses here are identifiers such as rank, title, class and profession. The abiding impression, therefore, is that the 'catalogue' is primarily sociological.

This is graphically borne out in the section of Gromov's first book [**26**] in which he discusses the 'catalogue'. 'Kartoteka personazhei', he explains, 'razdeliaetsia na gruppy, sootvetstvuiushchie sotsial'nym sloiam i prosloikam', and he lists nine groups with their component ranks/occupations/statuses and, as it were, population figures in his catalogue [**26**, 240]. The variety of these social identities will come as no surprise to anyone familiar with the work of W.H. Bruford, say, on Chekhov's stories as material for socio-historical analysis.[16] But to suggest that 'istorik i sotsiolog obnaruzhat zdes' proportsional'nye sootvetstviia i perebrosiat ot realizma k real'nosti most, pokoiashchiisia na tverdykh faktakh' [**26**, 241] seems to display a fundamental misunderstanding. The statistics Gromov has extracted from his 'catalogue' are self-evidently derived from 'subjective data': the figure for *chinovniki* in Chekhov's *oeuvre*, for instance, is almost twice as great as that for *krest'iane*. By definition, the 'population ratios' in Gromov's statistics will be at variance with 'objective' ones compiled by demographers. It is difficult to see how the Chekhovian statistics could be of more than polite interest to the scientist, therefore, but are they of any more interest to the literary critic or common reader? Only, I fear, if both have already espoused the 'systemist' approach to the multiplicity of Chekhov's work.

To be fair, in his original theoretical article Gromov stressed that the apparently sociographic elements of his Chekhov 'catalogue' were not to be taken too literally: 'Sushchestvenno znat', chto "znak personazha" (naprimer, chin) v povestvovanii Chekhova vsegda pereosmyslen i predstavliaet soboi, tak skazat', metaforu polozheniia personazha v obshchei ierarkhii glavenstva i podchineniia. Eto ne administrativnaia, a psikhologicheskaia ierarkhiia, transformirovannaia v sisteme khudozhestvennykh obrazov' [**9**, 314]. Citing 'The Death of a Civil Servant', 'Fat and Thin' ('Tolstyi i tonkii') and 'The Bishop', he swiftly moved away from the socio-historical 'facts' to a more literary, existential, and impassioned consideration:

> Понятно, что реального тайного советника или архиерея следовало величать их полными титулами, но когда **в чеховском повествовании** [my emphasis] эти формулы произносит друг детства или мать, то это же не "копия жизни", а, говоря словами Чехова, "логическая несообразность", образное раскрытие противоречий между реальным содержанием жизни и футляром, в котором она пегребена, это раздумье, печаль, жалоба, определяющая содержательность и поэтическую тональность чеховского повествования. [**9**, 315]

In his 1989 book Gromov also considerably expands his account of what is recorded on the cards of his 'catalogue'. As well as the 'chin, titul' etc that he described as the 'znak personazha' and concentrated on in his 1974 article, he mentions that the catalogue details 'priemy, opredeliaiushchie polozhenie i mesto personazha v psikhologicheskom prostranstve goroda N, stepen' ego zavisimosti i podchineniia poriadku veshchei' [**26**, 237], and in particular he explains the phrase 'poetika tak nazyvaemoi "individual'noi kharakteristiki"' which he left tantalizingly undeveloped in the original article [**9**, 314]. This 'poetic' determines the

> отношение персонажа к городу N, его собственный душевный уклад, либо

> противоположный общему укладу жизни (душевная боль, стремление к свободе и воле, открытый или подавленный протест, вообще все формы конфликтного состояния), либо, напротив, сливающийся с этим укладом (подчинение, примирение, вообще все формы подавления или распада личности, растворения собственного "я"). [**26**, 237].

Clearly, this section of Gromov's card-system is not socio-historical, but personalistic in focus. A synthesis of all forms of conflict in Chekhov's work, and of his heroes' spiritual suffering, is potentially of real literary-critical interest.

Unfortunately, even in his book Gromov gives us no example whatsoever from this area of his 'catalogue'. One would have been fascinated to learn how he recorded such intangibles as a character's 'dushevnyi uklad', 'dushevnaia bol'', 'stremlenie k svobode i vole' and 'konfliktnoe sostoianie' – how he had expressed them on card, discriminated between them, or even quantified them. Just to have seen this information for one story would have given us a glimpse of Gromov's empirically based interpretation of a specific work. Similarly, if certain realia/images were associated with certain aspects of this psychological area of the 'catalogue' – for instance with 'escape' – he could presumably produce a 'string' of them by selecting them on a particular principle, say chronologically, from his 'index', and this might have had an intrinsic literary value. But he does not. In his 1989 book, at the end of a two-page discussion of the 'fence' image in Chekhov (see above), Gromov quotes Caroline Spurgeon at length on her meticulous indexing, before computers, of all Shakespeare's images [**26**, 215]; but from his own meticulous indexing he cites only the 'fence' in Chekhov. Gromov gives no detailed synthetic 'model' of the psychology of Chekhov's characters, and no specific 'variations' at all. Instead he presents a composite two-paragraph 'definition' of man in Chekhov's 'narrative', starting with children, progressing to adults who have to choose how to relate to the 'oformlenie (futliar)' that 'life' forces upon them, and concluding with a modulation on the sentence on national character that first appeared in the 1974 article [**9**, 312] and was quoted above: 'russkii natsional'nyi kharakter, predstavlennyi u Chekhova vo vsekh myslimykh variantakh, ne umeshchaetsia v tekh formakh, kakie predlagaet emu zhizn'' [**26**, 239].

I am sure I am not alone in my disappointment at the actual results presented by Gromov from the Sisyphean effort of his 'catalogue'. One looks forward to the reproduction of approximately a thousand of the cards in the forthcoming *Tropa k Chekhovu* [**32**], because this will enable us to see the specific data entered on these cards and ourselves construct the 'strings' of variations that I referred to above. In the meantime, however, the conclusions that Gromov drew in print from his 'catalogue' seem disarmingly lame. Generalizations such as 'Obshchestvo personazhei, naseliaiushchikh gorod N, vossozdano v povestvovanii Chekhova v formakh real'nogo russkogo obshchestva i v etom pervonachal'nom, chisto vneshnem smysle predstavliaet soboi, nesomnenno, dostovernuiu i tochnuiu kopiiu deistvitel'nosti' [**26**, 239–40] verge on tautologous vacuity of a familiar 'Soviet' type.

There are, however, other contexts in which Gromov's catalogue should be viewed, for example biographical. It was initially compiled in the three years between Gromov leaving the Literature Department of Taganrog College of Education (1964) and commencing work at the Moscow Printing Institute. During that period he had little paid employment. He was already engaged in a systematic reading of the whole of Chekhov and like anyone else doing that he needed to keep notes. The extra time he had on his hands enabled him to do this in a particularly thorough way. Further, the cards acquired real practical value when, shortly afterwards, Gromov collaborated with the team at IMLI on producing the new Complete Works. Aspects of stories could be more easily cross-referenced for the purpose of writing commentaries, and where the title of a story had been changed in translation it was possible to identify it for the bibliography without translating it back into Russian, by tracing the names of its characters in the 'catalogue'.[17] Also, Gromov's 'catalogue' exemplifies his tendency to apply to his own work what he saw as Chekhovian techniques. He writes that Chekhov's contemporaries could not understand why he went to Sakhalin and subsequently carried out a census of the island, personally filling out ten thousand statistical cards, especially as Chekhov's account of this feat occupies only about ten lines in the book. But without this labour 'ne bylo by knigi: metod analiticheskoi statistiki, strogo nauchnyi, iskliuchaiushchii sub"ektivizm i sluchainost', imel priamoe otnoshenie k tvorcheskomu metodu' [**22**, 33]. Apparently, most of Gromov's contemporaries to whom he showed his Chekhov 'catalogue', including Viktor Shklovskii, did not understand the point of it either.

Lastly, Gromov undoubtedly saw the 'catalogue' as a powerful aid in the polemic with Chudakov that he conducted below the surface of his Chekhov criticism from the 1974 theoretical article [**9**] onwards. Aleksandr Chudakov's ground-breaking book *Poetika Chekhova* (1971) is essentially a discourse analysis of the whole of Chekhov's narrative prose; but at every 'level' of the text he discerns a 'sluchainostnyi printsip' ('fortuitousness principle') at work that he identifies as the hallmark of Chekhov's 'artistic vision'.[18] He certainly did not claim that 'everything' in Chekhov was 'fortuitous', but his book is definitely devoted to showing that Chekhov strove to recreate the 'adogmatic' nature of existence precisely by keeping the 'fortuitous' element always present. Chudakov was, in effect, taking something that Chekhov had persistently been attacked for (as Chudakov copiously illustrated) in the 'old' criticism, and turning it into a virtue. Gromov, however, seems to interpret Chudakov's book as a *perpetuation* of the 'old' critical shibboleths and to argue the other extreme, namely that 'nothing' in Chekhov is dictated by chance.

Thus Gromov's 1974 theoretical article concludes: 'Temy otdel'nykh rasskazov, kak i povody dlia ikh napisaniia, mogut pokazat'sia "sluchainymi", no za dvadtsat' piat' let pisatel'stva Chekhov okhvatil takoe mnozhestvo sluchainostei, chto dlia sluchainostei v ego tvorchestve prosto ne ostalos' mesta' [**9**, 315]. It is tempting, of course, to say that this view is an *a priori* assumption of the 'systemist' method (see the previous quotation from [**22**, 33]). In his 1989 book Gromov made his allusion more explicit, by discarding the conventional word 'sluchainyi' for the neologism favoured by Chudakov: 'Detali, obrazuiushchie predmetnyi mir chekhovskogo povestvovaniia [...] strogo otobrany i svedeny v stroinuiu khudozhestvennuiu sistemu, iskliuchaiushchuiu samuiu mysl' o "sluchainostnosti" tvorcheskogo myshleniia Chekhova' [**26**, 211]. He adduced Chekhov's own words: 'Govoriu Vam po sovesti, iskrenno, eti liudi rodilis' v moei golove ne iz morskoi peny, [...] ne sluchaino' (letter to Suvorin of 30 December 1888), as proof of Chekhov's 'upornoe otritsanie sluchainosti' in all his works [**26**, 238]. Yet this was a quotation woefully out of context, since Chekhov was referring only to the play *Ivanov*. Still without mentioning Chudakov by name, Gromov attacked the latter's conception of a literary system as a 'sootnoshenie neskol'kikh vzaimosviazannykh urovnei, ili sloev',[19] with an ingenious image:

> Разложение содержательного единства на "уровни", которые рассматриваются затем выборочно, друг за другом или независимо друг от друга, — это не ошибка, а скорее утопия, попытка расплатиться лишь одной стороною монеты. Ее, быть может, и приняли бы, да нельзя отделить: остается другая сторона, а кроме того, сама монета заключена между двумя сторонами! [**26**, 314]

In Gromov's last book, Chudakov's 'sluchainostnost'' became, with 'obshchestvennyi indifferentizm Chekhova', one of the 'psevdouchen[ye], trudnoproiznosim[ye] slova [za kotorymi] stoiat prizraki starykh nedorazymenii i obid...' [**29**, 259].

It would not be relevant to adjudicate between Gromov's and Chudakov's conceptions of a literary 'system' and their respective views about the 'sluchainoe' in Chekhov's art – although it is worth noting that neither of them explains what he takes *sluchainyi* to mean in the first place. To consider how Gromov discusses a concrete example of a 'fortuitous detail' in Chekhov is, however, extremely revealing about Gromov as a literary critic. In his last book, within a discussion of contemporaneous critics' incomprehension of Chekhov's writing, Gromov describes the view of one of his favourite pre-revolutionary critics, A.A. Potebnia, that it is a great mistake to 'smotret' na iazyk kak na sredstvo peredachi', to assume that thought can be 'perelozhena, kak nekaia veshch', ot govoriashchego ili pishushchego k slushaiushchemu ili chitaiushchemu', and to identify the object with the image, the word with the thing [**29**, 332]. As his example, Gromov chooses a *locus classicus* from 'The Lady with the Little

Dog': 'Na stole v nomere byl arbuz. Gurov otrezal sebe lomot' i stal est' ne spesha.' 'Pochemu nepremenno arbuz, a, naprimer, ne persiki, ne vinograd ili dynia?' asks Gromov [**29**, 332]. For Chudakov, presumably, this water-melon would be 'sluchainostnyi'; for Chudakov's Central Committee reviewer Berdnikov 'podobnye detali u Chekhova [...] vsegda ostro kharakterologichny';[20] and numerous other 'motivations' could be suggested, e.g. that to this day in very hot weather Russians may buy a water-melon, put it on a plate at home, and cut slices off it as and when they feel thirsty. Gromov gives all these explanations the slip:

> В предметном мире реальной гостиницы это могло быть чистейшей случайностью; но в мире слов, в столь совершенном тексте каждое слово на нужном, на своем единственном месте [...]. На этой странице, в контрастном соседстве с "грешницей на старинной картине", с одинокой свечой, которая "едва освещала лицо", "арбуз" фонетически необходим и не может быть заменен, например, ни "виноградом", ни "дынею", которые звучали бы — звучали в контексте, а не лежали бы на гостиничном столе — не столь контрастно и резко. [**29**, 332-33]

Sidestepping the somewhat academic question of how a real water-melon would come to feature in a real incident like this in a real hotel, Gromov suggests that the word *arbuz* enacts, as it were, its own contextual significance. As a reader, it is difficult not to agree with him. The deep, dark sound of the word must evoke different associations in everyone, and all of these associations will feel 'right' and in this sense not 'fortuitous'. Moreover, phonetically this rather mysterious, 'ripe' word that finishes like a kiss may evoke a vivid visual image which itself triggers other associations, for example exotic, 'forbidden', or sexual. Whatever significances the word evokes, it is its nature as *word* that precedes them.

It is exceptional for a Russian literary specialist to privilege the signifier over the signified in this way. It is not exceptional, however, for Gromov: as his discussions of the young Chekhov's 'word-monsters' [**26**, 106–08], or the epithet *vishnëvyi sad* [**29**, 369–79; see chapter 6 below] demonstrate, his appreciation of literature was in the first place sensual. He relished the very 'material' of Chekhov's works, namely words in themselves. Whatever other dimensions there are to Gromov's writing about Chekhov – historical, scholarly-investigative, systemist or comparative – we can be sure from a passage like the one just quoted that the departure-point of this writing was essentially that of a literary critic in the more recognizable European sense, namely the immediate experience of reading as any common reader in his own culture. His judgements always inspire confidence because one feels they are rooted in reading as a deeply personal experience.

All the more surprising, therefore, is the emphasis on *sistemnost'* in Gromov's 1974 theoretical article. The vast majority of readers do not read Chekhov, or any other author, in a 'systemist' way. The basic unit for the common reader is a 'work'. He/she is absorbed by the significance of the text 'contained' between its start and its finish. This is not to say, of course, that the experience of reading is totally synchronic, because the reader constantly *recalls* (but also forgets) whilst reading, and actually physically refers back when reading a longer work. The 'systemist' approach, however, is by definition diachronic, because the boundaries of discrete works written at different times have been dissolved to make a single 'continuum', 'system', 'world' and so forth, which has chronological extension and whose *raison d'être* for the 'systemist' is the construction of comparative 'series'. The conceptual model behind Gromov's *sistemnost'* seems, in fact, to be spatial, atomic or astronomical: 'Osobennost' povtoriaiushchikhsia podrobnostei zakliuchena v tom, chto vse oni, skol'ko ni est' ikh vo vsem mnozhestve chekhovskikh rasskazov, povestei, p'es, vkhodiat v obshchuiu orbitu universal'nogo obraza – goroda, mira' [**26**, 215]. But what we are presented with is an atomic or solar system without movement. The dynamics of Chekhov's writing derive from the conflicts presented within each work and can only exist within those limits, under that pressure. Once these 'walls' to the work have been dissolved, we are left with a motionless collection of 'data'. This, I believe, accounts for the disappointing usefulness of Gromov's 'catalogue'. The transfer to cards of 'data' from Chekhov's 'system' is a monological, indeed tautological exercise unless conflict can be imported into it from the world of the specific work, or dialogue in the form of critical interpretation. As we have seen, both are largely lacking in Gromov's account of his 'catalogue'.

Equally unproductive, in my view, is Gromov's systemist belief that the 'meaning' of Chekhov's creations is extrinsic to any particular one of them:

> общая тема, "общая идея" находится за пределами каждого из них в отдельности и явлена в целом множестве их. Так в массе рассказов Чехова синтезируются обобщенные темы и образы, само существование которых может быть выявлено лишь при последовательном изучении всех рассказов в целом. [**9**, 309]

Obviously, there will be a tendency for the few critics who *have* read 'the whole' of Chekhov to feel this. The temptation will then arise of suggesting that the 'meaning' of a Chekhov work is actually ineffable, esoteric, known only to these few – and this was a temptation to which, as I shall describe in my final chapter, Gromov was prone. But it would be fatal for any writer if his readers had to read 'all' of him before they could understand a single work by him. Creative writers do not write this way, as Gromov at one point disarmingly admits: 'Chekhov pisal bez zaranee iasnogo plana i, v otlichie, naprimer, ot Bal'zaka, ne dumal o sviaznosti, posledovatel'nosti i edinstve svoikh rasskazov, v kontse kontsov dazhe ne znal im chisla' [**9**, 315]. Above all, though, the common reader – the person for whom Chekhov did write – does not read this way; it is systemist *literaturovedy* who do. One need not agree with Bakhtin that the creative writer 'ne priglashaet k svoemu pirshestvennomu stolu literaturovedov',[21] but in his deliberations about Chekhov's 'system' Gromov seems to have lost sight of the fact that for the vast majority of people a single work of literature is enjoyed as that or not at all.

In his last book, however, Gromov devoted impressive pages to the question of how the common reader reads in general and what Chekhov in particular demands of his reader. He concluded: 'Kniga sozdaet nas, eto tak; no ona i sama sozdaetsia nami; v kontse kontsov, my vynosim iz nee ne bol'she i ne men'she togo, chto sami v sostoianii vlozhit' v ee tekst siloiu nashei pamiati, vdumchivosti i dushevnoi trevogi' [**29**, 337]. It is perhaps relevant that this book was written for a more popular readership than any of Gromov's other Chekhov publications. His emphasis here is on the synchronic, experiential nature of reading rather than a diachronic and systemist mode. Nevertheless, there are aspects of what we might call the Russian 'tradition' of reading that may make Gromov's systemist approach more acceptable to Russian readers. For example, since Belinskii it has been regarded as a positive thing if a Russian writer is 'encyclopaedic'. Gromov himself subscribes to this view in several places in his writing about Chekhov, e.g. '**Entsiklopedichnost'** – vazhneishee i, mozhet byt', redchaishee svidetel'stvo vysokogo i podlinno khudozhestvennogo priznaniia' [**29**, 91]. To read Chekhov's work *a priori* as an 'encyclopaedia' of Russian life is, surely, to be receptive to the 'systemist' approach. In western Europe it is axiomatic that people do not 'read' encyclopaedias.

In the final analysis, as a Russian version of structuralism Gromov's 'systemism' is vulnerable to the classic refutations of literary structuralism, which I shall not rehearse here. It is now fairly widely accepted that empirical and mechanistic categories have limited applications to verbal art. The scientism of Gromov's approach in his 1974 article seems distinctly of its time and of its Soviet context.

Nevertheless, this should not blind us to the heuristic value for Gromov personally of the 'catalogue' and his incursion into 'systemism'. It looks, in fact, as though his 'catalogue' preceded his theoretical speculations. Perhaps his discussion of systems theory and its applications to Chekhov in his 1974 article was exatrapolated from his 'catalogue' to suit the theoretical setting of a *festschrift* for the *literaturoved* Khrapchenko, from whose own theoretical writings Gromov quotes approvingly [**9**, 308, 314–15]. It was virtually inevitable that someone researching Chekhov on the scale that Gromov was as a critic and an editor would have to keep his own aide-mémoire. The evidence is that he developed one that was peculiarly thorough and systematic, but it is tempting to feel that in its origins and development it remained a means rather than an end. It was a means to recall the experience of reading the individual works, but its cumulative effect must have been to facilitate Gromov's overall (systematic) understanding of Chekhov as an artist. In other words, the 'catalogue' had a profoundly catalytic value for him. This may be borne out by the observation that in the theoretical setting of the 1974 article he defined the 'catalogue' as a 'sposob – ili priem – sistematicheskogo issledovaniia poetiki Chekhova' [**9**, 314], but by 1989 this had become the less teleological 'instrument sistematicheskogo issledovaniia tvorchestva Chekhova' [**26**, 237]. In his posthumous 1993 book there is no mention of the 'catalogue' or its sociological statistics, and Gromov's more theoretical speculations about Chekhov's 'system' have been reduced to two short paragraphs [**29**, 319]. One senses that by then the 'catalogue' had served its purpose for him.

Without his exhaustive knowledge of the Chekhov canon, his 'systematic' overview, and the practical tool of his 'catalogue', Gromov probably could not have written the other three fundamental articles published between 1974 and his first book [**10**, **18**, **22**]. 'Portret, obraz, tip' ranged over Chekhov's stories early, middle and late, but its premise was that 'u Chekhova [...] traditsionnoe portretnoe opisanie zameshcheno sistemoi znakovykh detalei i slozhnykh metafor, kotorye pozvoliaiut chitateliu voobrazit', predstavit' sebe oblik personazha, ne predlagaia emu stol' chekannykh i tochnykh, kak eto bylo v romane, portretnykh form' [**10**, 144]. The reason, Gromov suggested, that Chekhov could get away with this was precisely that the classical Russian novel 'already existed' in Chekhov's and Russian readers' memory. Gromov provided an elegant solution to the then rather fashionable and contentious problem of Chekhovian 'prototypes': after convincingly questioning the most commonly accepted 'prototype' for 'A Man in a Case', he argued that Chekhov's stories had grown in the writer's mind from multiple sources over many years, so that they were not so much 'written' as 'written down' in a particular year; and he dispelled the 'prototypical' status of Kuvshinnikova, Mizinova and Iavorskaia, for instance, with the words: 'zemnaia zhizn' etikh zhenshchin, konechnaia i zavershivshaiasia, sovpala s beskonechnym khudozhestvennym vremenem "Poprygun'i", "Ariadny" i "Dushechki"' [**10**, 160]. The article 'Skrytye tsitaty (Chekhov i Dostoevskii)' [**18**] was almost sensational, since the Russian intelligentsia had long regarded the two authors as mutually exclusive and *literaturoved*'s had commonly referred to Chekhov's 'hostility' towards, and ignorance of, Dostoevskii's works. On the contrary, Gromov sought to show by textual juxtaposition that Chekhov had been deeply influenced by his teenage reading of *The Adolescent* and he identified references to other Dostoevskii novels in works as varied as 'A Boring Story' ('Skuchnaia istoriia'), 'The Duel', 'Neighbours' and 'The Black Monk' (this subject will be discussed at length in chapter 5 below in the context of Gromov's 1993 book). Finally, in the six pages of 'Talant i metod' [**22**] Gromov speculated on such questions as the scientific method, authorial objectivity, death, laughter, and the technological revolution, with a fragmentariness and compression worthy of Chekhov himself.

CHAPTER 4

BEZVREMEN'E AND 'THE STEPPE'

> Vol'no li, nevol'no li, no utrata istoricheskikh pervoosnov privodila k obeskurazhivaiushchemu vyvodu o nepolnotsennosti russkoi kul'tury 80–90 godov. [**26**, 123]

Mikhail Gromov's reputation will rest on his books *Kniga o Chekhove* (1989) and *Chekhov* (1993). These are his summae. As I have indicated above, his pre-*perestroika* articles and commentaries metamorphose complexly into his books; but anyone wanting to know Gromov's 'final' thinking on the Chekhovian themes that occupied him all his life need engage with only these two works (between which, again, there are numerous differences of emphasis). Moreover, in the books new themes appear that are dealt with at some length.

This and the following chapter will concentrate on relatively new subjects as presented in Gromov's books. For reasons of space I can look at only two subjects from each book. My choice is, of course, personal and cannot hope to do justice to the richness of these books as a whole. However, in each of the topics I have chosen there is, I feel, a very radical element that is mould-breaking for Russian Chekhov studies but also has an immediate appeal to the Russian reader of the end of the 20th century.

The first topic is termed 'Vremia Chekhova' in the short chapter that Gromov devotes to it in his 1989 book [**26**, 120–27].

He had touched on this for the first time in section 8 of his introduction to the two-volume selection of Chekhov's correspondence produced with Dolotova and Kataev in 1984 [**24**,19–23]. 'V pis'makh, s kotorymi obrashchalis' k Chekhovu raznye po kharakteru liudi', he wrote, 'zvuchala obshchaia tema i kakaia-to edinodushnaia zhaloba: na bezvremen'e, na "nervnyi vek", na sredu, otnimaiushchuiu luchshie sily, molodost', zhizn'' [**24**, 19]. Quoting from Chekhov's replies, Gromov showed that Chekhov countered this 'pessimism' with humour and a more objective, historical view. Further, in his letters of the 1880s and 90s (the so-called 'period of *bezvremen'e*') Chekhov often discussed science, the scientific way of thinking, and the fundamental differences between the latter and 'publitsisticheskoe vyskazyvanie' [**24**, 20]. These letters, Gromov claimed, are vital for understanding Chekhov's 'mirovozzrenie' and 'obshchestvennaia pozitsiia'. 'On byl dal'novidnee bol'shinstva togdashnikh filosofov i publitsistov uzhe prosto potomu, chto luchshe, chem oni, ponimal neizbezhnost' nauchno-tekhnicheskogo perevorota', Gromov elaborated [**24**, 20], and named Lobachevskii, Tsiolkovskii and Mendeleev as contemporaries of Chekhov whose science 'belonged to the future' [**24**, 20–21]. Chekhov also observed that the 'best' young people were not going into literature (or politics), but into industry, 'kotoraia delaet teper' gromadnye uspekhi'.[22]

At this point, reading Gromov's views in an era that would itself shortly be re-classified as the Communist *bezvremen'e*, one became uneasy. Was Gromov suggesting that Chekhov's *mirovozzrenie* was far ahead of not only Mikhailovskii and the left-wing intelligentsia of the day, but of the 'most progressive Party' of all time? How did Chekhov's 'objective' reflection that the 'best' people were going into an industry that was 'making enormous progress' square with the conventional wisdom about this stretch of Russian history purveyed by the Party that was still in power? With perfect timing, Gromov cut short such speculations by quoting 'Lenin' himself to the effect that 'v Rossii ne bylo epokhi, pro kotoruiu by do takoi stepeni mozhno bylo skazat': "nastupila ochered' mysli i razuma"' [**24**, 21]. The plain implication was that like Chekhov 'Lenin' thought of the 1880s and 90s as a period in which 'reason' and the 'scientific way of thinking' produced far more than 'pessimism', the political disillusion of the Russian intelligentsia, or the publicists' obsession with 'ideals' and ideological engagement. Yet the balance of this 1984 presentation seemed uncertain: in the next sentence Gromov asked us to believe that as well as 'Lenin', 'tak ponimal veshchi i Dostoevskii' [**24**, 22]!

The uncertainty was almost entirely dispelled in Gromov's 1989 treatment 'Vremia Chekhova'. In his opening sentence he boldly placed the subject in a wider ideological context: 'So shkol'nykh let my privykaem "vyvodit"' pisatelia iz ego epokhi po metodam istoriko-kul'turnoi shkoly, ostavivshei v nashem otnoshenii k literature zametnyi sled' [**26**, 120]. In case the reader thought this was a reference solely to the Soviet 'historical-cultural school', Gromov quoted a critic's view in 1904 that Chekhov began writing at a time when the 'coryphaei' Turgenev, Dostoevskii, Ostrovskii, Pisemskii and Tolstoi had left the literary field, that this bequeathed a 'zastoi', and that Chekhov's art 'ob"iasniaetsia usloviiami zhizni vos'midesiatykh godov s ikh dukhovnym zatish'em i rasteriannost'iu' [**26**, 120]. The view that Chekhov's writing, his 'sumerki' and 'khmurye liudi', reflected the 'bezvremen'e' of the 1880s and 90s, was well established before the Revolution in liberal and socialist journalism [**26**, 121–22], but in a swingeing footnote Gromov showed that the coryphaeus of Soviet literary scholarship Boris Eikhenbaum had perpetrated the same cliché [**26**, 376]. The latter had 'derived' Chekhov from 'secondary' writers such as Pisemskii and Leskov, other *literaturoved*'s correlated Chekhov with his distinctly minor contemporaries (e.g. Potapenko, Shcheglov, Al'bov), and Gromov found this a natural tendency in the 'historical-cultural' school: 'chem faktografichnee belletrist, chem slabee on kak khudozhnik, tem legche poddaetsia ob"iasneniiu i pereskazu; vsiakogo roda metafory, simvoly, ironicheskie podrazumevaniia tol'ko meshaiut, i luchshe, esli ikh net sovsem' [**26**, 120].

To what extent, in fact, *were* the 1880s and 90s 'vremia Chekhova' and in what objective sense were they a *bezvremen'e* in which 'nothing happened'? Gromov now tackled these questions in earnest.

The 1880s, he wrote, could hardly be called 'vremia Chekhova', because until Chekhov's journey to Sakhalin in 1890 he was regarded merely as a 'promising author', in no sense a 'vlastelin [sic] dum' to rank with Garshin or Nadson. Moreover, Chekhov was a humorist, and 'iumor – ne v dukhe etoi pory, i konechno zhe ne "Sirenu" i ne "Brozhenie umov" podrazumeval M. Gor'kii, skazavshii: "Ia ne znaiu v istorii russkoi momenta bolee tiazhelogo, chem etot"' [**26**, 121]. By the end of the 1880s, when talk of *bezvremen'e* and 'bol'noe vremia' was rife and sections of the intelligentsia were overwhelmed by lachrymose disillusionment, Chekhov had quite clearly dissociated himself from these phenomena, Gromov demonstrated [**26**, 122]. In the 1890s, when his celebrity was more established, he unambiguously rejected the literary-social haruspications of *bezvremen'e* performed by such *intelligenty* as Merezhkovskii. Later still, he exclaimed to Bunin: 'Kakoi ia "khmuryi chelovek" [...]? Kakoi ia "pessimist"?' [**26**, 122, sentences transposed by Gromov]. Of his contemporaries, Gromov maintained, Chekhov had most in common with the spiritual robustness of Tolstoi and Bunin. Chekhov and Tolstoi were very different, but demonstrably very 'close', people, and 'ni pri kakikh obstoiatel'stvakh Chekhov ne nazval by vremia L'va Tolstogo (svoe vremia) "bezvremen'em"' [**26**, 123]. Addressing his own readers, and as if connecting the 'displacement' of the 1880s and 90s with Soviet denigration of the pre-revolutionary decades generally, Gromov remarked: 'v kontse kontsov, ni u kogo iz nas net nikakikh prichin videt' v proshlom svoei strany odin lish' svintsovyi mrak' [**26**, 123].

The 1880s and 90s, Gromov argued, were in fact a period of vibrant activity in the sciences, industry, and technology. Mendeleev's periodic classification and the principia of Lobachevskii's non-Euclidean geometry had been published, Timiriazev was engaged in his classic work on plant physiology, and the physicist Lebedev measured the pressure exerted by a beam of light [**26**, 124].[23] There was, however, a snag with this argument: the engineers and applied specialists

делали все же нечто понятное современникам: строили здания, мосты, железные дороги; оставаясь безвестными, они были нужны. Лобачевский же, Менделеев и особенно Циолковский опережали свое время по крайней мере на полвека, современники думали о них не больше, чем думали мы о теории относительности и А. Эйнштейне, пока не донеслось до нас эхо атомной войны... [**26**, 125]

Indeed, if the work of Tsiolkovskii, who was three years older than Chekhov, achieved general currency and application only in the 20th century, and if the 'osnovopolozhnik abstraktnoi zhivopisi V.V. Kandinskii' was merely, as Gromov informs us, 'born' in Moscow in 1866 [**26**, 124], how can they alter our perception that the 1880s and 90s were, as many contemporaries found them, a *bezvremen'e*?

The answer is that they dramatically expand the framework of readers' historical understanding of the period. Even if the discoveries of Mendeleev, Timiriazev, Lobachevskii, Lebedev, Tsiolkovskii and Kandinskii were not to impact on 'society' until the next century, the mere fact that they occurred in the last two decades of the 19th century implies a reality to those decades outside the socio-political box to which they had been confined by successive left-wing ideologues, including the Bolsheviks. In the *widest* sense, which Gromov was encouraging his readers to imagine, the existence of these creative minds proved irrefutably that the period was not stagnant, not fallow, not dead.

'Russkaia nauka 80–90-kh godov byla obrashchena v budushchee i gotovila budushchee', Gromov wrote, but it would be difficult to 'predstavit' sebe astronoma, biologa, fizika, voobshche khot' skol'ko-nibud' ser'eznogo uchenogo, kotoryi nazval by etu poru "bezvremen'em"' [**26**, 126]. Chekhov, a natural scientist by education and cast of mind, understood these people; as his recorded utterances show, his sympathies lay with them; indeed he was one of them. The only difference was that he was also an artist, i.e. traditionally a 'humanities person'. Yet his art and his thinking, Gromov explained, were also 'oriented to the future' in a similar way to the science of Lebedev and Tsiolkovskii, both of whom were attracted to Chekhov's writing [**26**, 127]. Gromov concluded the chapter by reflecting that in 'Chekhov's time' 'nachinalsia pod"em nauki i tekhniki – to, chto pozdnee nazovut "epokhoiu NTR", – i prodolzhalsia krizis i raspad religioznogo soznaniia' [**26**, 127], but he also quoted from two letters of 1901 and 1902 in which Chekhov stressed the need to 'search for God' [**26**, 126–27].

Russian readers must have found this chapter of Gromov's 1989 book exhilarating. Here was a 'Soviet' critic stripping away the Bolshevik version of this period of Russian history, which had been inculcated in them since childhood, to reveal professions and areas of society that had previously been blanked out. To see Chekhov compared with non-Marxist scientists, engineers, and specialists in the rapidly growing Russian industrial economy of the late 19th century, was to be introduced to an idea of Russia that was far bigger than that purveyed by the Communist ideology which had dominated everybody's lives since 1929. Gromov was, in effect, reconnecting his readers with their pre-revolutionary past. He was intimating to them that in addition to the revolutionaries and reactionaries to which the period of *bezvremen'e* had been shrunk by a relentless Bolshevik orthodoxy, there was what one might call a self-motivated, creative, non-Bolshevik 'middle class', as well as large numbers of 'doers' like Chekhov himself who it was irrelevant to describe in class terms at all. This thrust, it must be said, was fully in tune with the initiative in *perestroika* towards abandoning the Marxist 'class' approach in favour of 'universal human' values.[24] Nevertheless, Gromov was the first openly to question the orthodox view of the *bezvremen'e* and Chekhov's relation to it. His argument was fundamental, brilliantly supported by quotation, and has not been bettered in Russian Chekhov criticism. There is no doubt that Gromov had holed the Soviet received wisdom about 'Chekhov and his times' below the waterline. The chapter must have evoked horror and outrage amongst the Old Guard of Soviet *chekhovedenie*.

It is intriguing to speculate how a western critic might tackle the same subject. He would surely agree with Gromov that the catchword *bezvremen'e* entered left-wing currency soon after the assassination of Alexander II in 1881 [**26**, 122]. He might point out that to the people who used the word it was a period in which 'nothing happened' in a specific *political* sense. He might suggest it was a *bezvremen'e* for those who sought revolutionary change, and that this is what it meant to Marxists. He might object, therefore, that there was never any question of the term having a 'universal human' application to the 1880s and 90s, only a narrow party one. He might take a closer look at the passage of 'Lenin' which even in his 1989 book Gromov claims shows that 'Lenin' recognised these decades as a period of 'burnoe razvitie tekhniki, estestvennykh i tochnykh nauk, filosofii, istorii' [**26**, 124]. He might conclude that in context 'Lenin' says nothing of the sort – that he is still talking specifically of the progress of 'Russian revolutionary thought' in the reign of Alexander III.[25] Moreover, the obsession of Soviet critics and propagandists with the idea of Chekhov's work exemplifying the *bezvremen'e* could be precisely dated to an article by Zil'bershtein in the 1935 commemorative issue of *Pravda* in which he quoted 'Lenin' noting down from a lecture by Lunacharskii in 1904: 'Russkoe bezvremen'e. (Chekhov).'[26] From then (1935) on, the idea was law and the epithet 'chekhovskoe bezvremen'e' entered the language of Soviet political correctness and even dictionaries. Although the western critic might demonstrate documentarily that Lunacharskii had been the chief expositor of 'Chekhov and bezvremen'e',[27] having taken the cliché over from the turn-of-the-century liberal-populist consensus about Chekhov, the critic's main thrust might be that, like the Leninist theory of 'reflection' in literature generally, the idea of Chekhov being merely a reflection of 'russkoe bezvremen'e' was ruthlessly imposed from above during the Stalin *Gleichschaltung* and therefore could not possibly be true in a 'universal human' sense.

These speculations suggest once again how different Gromov looks in a Russian context and 'from outside', i.e. in a western context. We might well expect a western critic's attack on Soviet critical orthodoxy to be 'explicit', as above. In avoiding all discussion of the precisely traceable Stalinist origins of this orthodoxy (and even quoting 'Lenin' in support of his arguments), Gromov may appear timid and excessively 'Aesopic'. But the fact is that Gromov's Russian readers did not *need* to have the sources of the *bezvremen'e* myth explained to them. Russian Chekhov specialists knew only too well the history of this dogma, whilst the common reader instinctively understood the Marxist-Leninist background to what Gromov was saying. Within the Russian context, Gromov's 'implicit' attack on Bolshevik literary historiography and aesthetics was therefore just as effective, and bold, as the full-frontal one might be coming 'from outside'. It will doubtless be a long time, however, before Gromov's heresy achieves wide acceptance, at least in Russia. The century-old political cliché of the *bezvremen'e* persists in Russian cultural histories and journalism, and even after the collapse of Communism Gromov felt it necessary to accentuate aspects of his deconstruction in 'Vremia Chekhova' and bring it forward as the opening chapter of his later book [**29**, 5–14].

The most surprising feature of Gromov's 1989 book, however, was that by far the longest chapter in it was devoted to 'The Steppe'. Gromov had prepared the text of this story for the Complete Works and written the commentary to it [**19**], but he had never published any extended critical views on it before. On the other hand, one might have surmised that a comprehensive new interpretation was maturing in him since his earliest publications. For example, in his 1960 article on the role of landscape in Chekhov's early stories, and personification/animification in particular, he wrote of the story 'Happiness' ('Schast'e'):

> Тема рассказа — человек и природа, человек и земля, на которой он живет.
>
> Со времен "охотничьих рассказов" и "Счастья" эта тема сделалась задушевной для Чехова. Ею ознаменованы начало и конец зрелой его поры — "Степь" и "Вишнёвый сад"; в ее раскрытии Чехов видел главную задачу своего писательства:
>
> "Вся энергия художника должна быть обращена на две силы: человек и природа" [Letter to Grigorovich, 5 February 1888]. [**2**, 79]

In his 1962 biographical essay on Chekhov's Taganrog boyhood, he suggested that the journeys made by the young Chekhov through the steppe were the very source of the 'precious images and pictures' which, in his famous letter to Grigorovich of 28 March 1886, Chekhov said he had 'saved and carefully hidden' rather than 'wasting' on short stories:

> [Он их] прятал от недружелюбного взгляда, берег от прикосновения грубых рук, от людей, которые были не в состоянии понять его святая святых.

> [...]
> Быть может, уже в детские годы Чехов услышал зов, который впоследствии был выражен им с такой поэтической силой: "Певца! певца!" [Words from 'The Steppe']. [**4**, 138]

In his 1963 article on *Fatherless*, Gromov quoted Platonov's line to Osip: 'Nam by s toboi pustyniu s vitiaziami, nam by s toboi bogatyrei so stopudovymi golovami, s shipom, s posvistom!', which is packed with Russian fairytale imagery reminiscent of 'The Steppe', and claimed that Osip was the 'psikhologicheskii prototip Dymova iz "Stepi"' [**5**, 33].

All of these thoughts re-emerge, and are developed, in the 1989 chapter on 'The Steppe', and its subsequent metamorphoses [**29** and **30**]. Above all, though, Gromov himself 'ros, uchilsia i rabotal v kraiakh, opisyvaemykh Chekhovym v "Stepi", vpital prirodu i vozdukh tekh mest, proshel i proekhal marshrutom, kotorym edet po stepi mal'chik Egorushka' [**30**, 166, 'Ot redkollegii']. Thus even in his commentary in the Complete Works, which necessarily concentrates on presenting the textual, biographical and contemporaneous critical history of 'The Steppe', he could not resist pointing out that, although the big river which Egorushka sees for the first time in his life 'is' the Don, and the town on the hill 'is' Rostov,

> но чтобы увидеть Ростов так, как сказано в повести, нужно приближаться к нему со стороны Батайска, переезжая Дон по наплавному мосту с левого на правый берег. Обоз же двигался с противоположной стороны, и если бы Чехов руководствовался реальной географией, Егорушка, подъезжая к городу, не увидел бы ни громадной горы, ни реки, ни железнодорожной ветки с локомотивом: перед ним на той же степной равнине появились бы предместья Ростова, обоз пересек бы речушку Каменку и затем выехал на мощенный булыжником проспект, который во времена Чехова так и назывался — Таганрогский. [**19**, 629]

This passage, too, occurs in all Gromov's subsequent publications on 'The Steppe'. With other 'personal' details he added later [**26**, 162; **29**, 181; **30**, 188] it lends peculiar authority to what he writes about this work. Even in a scholarly commentary, his factual tone enabled him to infiltrate a serious critical point: 'Chekhov, razumeetsia, ne schital "Step'" bytopisatel'nym ili, tem bolee, etnograficheskim sochineniem' [**19**, 629].

As is well known, probably more controversy surrounds 'The Steppe' than any other of Chekhov's works. Is it 'plotless'? What is it *about*? Who is the 'hero' in it? Is it really told from the point of view of a nine-year-old boy? Is it an ethnographic 'sketch' or a kind of poetic allegory? What is the significance of the omnipotent and ubiquitous Varlamov? Why did so many of Chekhov's contemporaries find 'The Steppe' boring and old-fashioned? Is it the first part of an unfinished novel? In what relation does it stand to Gogol', who is so clearly invoked in its opening paragraph and elsewhere? Is 'The Steppe' an experiment that failed? All of these questions have exercised reviewers, critics and *literaturovedy* from the day 'The Steppe' was published, and they periodically exploded on the pages of Soviet thick journals in articles by Nazarenko, Ermilov, Chicherin and others [**26**, 180–81, 187].

In the chapter of his 1989 book, Gromov addresses all of these questions and, in my view, offers convincing answers to them. True to form, however, he does not engage with them all explicitly. Even when, as with the section 'Tsarstvo Gogolia' in this chapter [**26**, 166–71], he directly tackles a subject, he will return to it in other contexts and present fresh insights into it. His approach, although superbly furnished with documentary detail, is rather cyclical. He returns again and again to his own interpretative key themes, modulating them in different ways and implicitly, cumulatively, covering the specific cruxes of 'Steppe' criticism. It is no exaggeration to say that this chapter is the most comprehensive critical examination of 'The Steppe' ever published, but (despite its sub-sections) its thematic structure is almost as difficult to analyse as that of 'The Steppe' itself. Nevertheless, one may identify two central, and almost entirely original, judgements from which most of Gromov's other critical themes in the chapter appear to branch. These judgments concern the *siuzhet* of 'The Steppe' and the literary origins of a vital area of its stylistic register.

One must immediately point out that Gromov does not use the word *siuzhet* in the sense that has been generally accepted in Russia and the West since the Formalists. He does not distinguish it from the latters' *fabula*, i.e. the sequence of 'events' in a literary work or what in English we call 'the plot'.[28] Consequently Gromov never employs the word *fabula* as coming from himself, although he quotes several pre-Formalist reviewers using it. His use of *siuzhet* to mean both 'plot' and 'thematic composition' is definitely a minority one among Chekhov critics, and at first sight confusing.[29] For example, early in the 'Steppe' chapter [**26**, 160] he quotes Ronald Hingley's opinion that 'The Steppe' is 'hardly a story at all' and 'has no plot',[30] rendering the last word as *siuzhet*. This naturally makes one wonder whether Gromov has really understood what Hingley is saying, since even a biographer, presumably, would not claim that 'The Steppe' is 'about nothing'. However, the point about Gromov's 'idiosyncratic' use of *siuzhet* is that, firstly, it harks back to a Russian critical tradition older than the Formalists or Soviet power, a tradition with which Gromov was concerned to re-establish contact, and, secondly, its inclusiveness implies that the relation between 'plot' and 'theme' is indissoluble, symbiotic. In fact, the latter view may be regarded as 'post-Formalist' and particularly *modern*.[31] As we shall see, it is certainly appropriate to 'The Steppe' in Gromov's interpretation of it.

For Gromov the *siuzhet* of 'The Steppe' is, as its sub-title suggests, the road through the steppe rather than the steppe itself. This automatically meant, in

Gromov's view, that the work had an historical dimension, since the road was ancient and there was no such thing as 'new' steppe [**26**, 169; compare **29**, 374]. It also meant that the work was a dynamic, artistic narrative rather than a static, ethnographic sketch. 'Stepnaia doroga – siuzhet v polnom smysle etogo slova istoricheskii, siuzhet bez nachala i kontsa, s prostorom dlia "dorogikh obrazov i kartin", s ostanovkami dlia podrobnogo opisaniia kharakterov, nravov i vstrechnykh lits' [**26**, 167]. This focus on the 'road' was, incidentally, what linked 'The Steppe' to *Dead Souls* (*Mertvye dushi*). Equally, the 'ispolinskaia stepnaia doroga i geroicheskie, bylinnye figury bogatyrei, "kakie mogut snit'sia ili vyrastat' v skazochnykh mysliakh"' in 'The Steppe' were congruous with the poetics of 'Taras Bul'ba' and other *Mirgorod* tales [**26**, 169], although Chekhov's steppe was full of contrasts with that of Gogol': 'na tom gorizonte, gde u Gogolia "po nebu, izgoluba-temnomu, kak budto ispolinskoiu kist'iu, naliapany byli shirokie polosy iz rozovogo zolota" – dym prokhodiashchego poezda' [**26**, 167].

As soon as the britchka leaves the outskirts of the town, Egorushka's mind is assailed by the ancient features of the steppe – its stone idols, burial mounds, skulls, kites and mysterious sounds. A windmill becomes a wizard, a giant strikes a match across the sky, other giants appear walking behind the wool-cart in the thunderstorm. Everything from hills, a poplar tree and the grass, to the camp fire with its two red eyes and the 'distance' with its eyelids, comes alive, or as Gromov puts it, is 'personified' and 'animified'. The effect is to plunge the reader's imagination deep into the Russian and biblical past – even a minor character, an old shepherd, is perceived as a 'sovsem vetkhozavetnaia figura'. Yet the essence of the *siuzhet* for Gromov is the constant juxtaposition of the present and the past that movement along the ancient highway unveils:

> Сопоставление противоположностей, художественное противоречие и контраст — определяющая черта поэтики "Степи".
>
> Вдоль сказочной степной дороги, на которой уместились бы шесть колесниц, какие Егорушка видел на страницах священной истории, поставлены телеграфные столбы, "похожие на карандаши, воткнутые в землю".
>
> Великое и малое контрастирует в образах персонажей повести: степь, олицетворяющая свободу и волю, очевидно, никому не может принадлежать, у нее нет и не должно быть хозяина. Между тем все, что лежит по эту сторону ее горизонта, и, как в свое время показывал Ноздрев, все, что находится по ту сторону, принадлежит Варламову, который оказывается не властелином, какие бывают в страшных сказках, а "малорослым серым человечком".
>
> Фантастические, сказочные образы, богатыри, которые видятся герою в грозовую ночь, соотнесены с портретами возчиков и встречных. [**26**, 170]

Varlamov, then, is not at all the 'glavnyi geroi povesti i ee siuzhetnyi tsentr' that Shklovskii called him and Bialyi and Papernyi were inclined to see him as [**26**, 177–78]; he is these things only in one dimension of 'The Steppe'. Gromov defined this dimension ('plane') as: 'prozaicheskii delovoi trakt, brichka, voobshche vse, chto daet povod dlia "vzroslogo" povestvovaniia o shersti, den'gakh, torgovykh oborotakh, o tserkvi, lavke, postoialom dvore, o millionere Varlamove i nishchem Solomone, ob otarakh ovets i t.d.' [**26**, 183].

It must be admitted that Gromov gives this dimension scant attention. He is interested to link the proto-Bolshevik Solomon, who has burnt the money his father left him and 'do mnogogo eshche dodumaetsia v ne stol' uzh dalekom budushchem' [**26**, 186–87], with the *ozornik* Dymov who 'mnogoe perelopatit i vyrvet s kornem, poka istoshchit svoi sily, kotorykh emu nekuda devat'' [**26**, 187]; he touches on Egorushka's encounter with Countess Dranitskaia; but he hardly discusses the other human participants at all. In particular, he does not mention the world into which Egorushka arrives – the rich events, memorable personalities and secure domesticity of Chapter VIII of 'The Steppe'. This dimension, the one of 'everyday realism', 'local colour', 'psychology' and the 'growth of a boy's mind', happens to be the one that critics East and West have concentrated on. 'Eta "sovremennaia" liniia v povesti est'', Gromov stresses, 'no ona lishena vsiakoi uvlekatel'nosti i, kak vyrazhalas' staraia kritika, "bedna i punktirna"' [**26**, 183]. He believes that the 'vtoroi [...] siuzhetnyi plan' is the fundamental one for Chekhov; and this dimension is 'sviazan ne s traktom, po kotoromu katiat v gorod provintsial'nye del'tsy, ne s postoialym dvorom, ne s poucheniiami staren'kogo sviashchennika ottsa Khristofora, ne s Varlamovym, a s obrazom pokinutoi drevnei dorogi, po kotoroi "teper'" nikto uzhe ne ezdit' [**26**, 183]. In elaborating this idea and himself re-evoking the 'second' dimension of 'The Steppe', which had defeated his critical predecessors, Gromov penned some of his most memorable pages.

The 'second dimension' of 'The Steppe' was where in Gromov's interpretation 'proiskhodit vse znachitel'noe i vazhnoe, vse, chto bylo dorogo Chekhovu i stoilo emu ser'eznogo tvorcheskogo truda: prosypaetsia step', poiut travy, idut svoim drevnim putem velikany. Zdes' sosredotocheny vse olitsetvoreniia i simvoly, vse znaki drevnosti, rodiny i sud'by' [**26**, 183]. As night falls in Chapter IV of 'The Steppe', Chekhov tells us that Egorushka's sleepy brain 'sovsem otkazalsia ot obyknovennykh myslei, tumanilsia i uderzhival odni tol'ko skazochnye, fantasticheskie obrazy', and when 'one' (second person singular) is in Egorushka's place,

> все представляется не тем, что оно есть. [...] мало-помалу на память приходят степные легенды, рассказы встречных, сказки няньки-степнячки и все то, что сам сумел увидеть и постичь душою. [...] душа дает отклик прекрасной, суровой родине, и хочется лететь над степью вместе с ночной птицей. [PSSP (Works), 7, pp. 45–46]

Thus not only did Chekhov 'leleial derzkuiu mechtu pokazat' etomu mal'chiku ego surovuiu, prekrasnuiu rodinu, drevniuiu legendarnuiu step'' [**26**, 160] through Egorushka's experience of the journey, he wanted through symbols and anthropomorphism to 'probudit' u chitatelia pamiat' o detstve, sokhraniaiushchem intuitivnuiu priverzhennost' k iznachal'noi obraznosti i drevneishei khudozhestvennoi pravde' [**26**, 183].

The latter phrase introduces what seems to me the most original and fruitful part of Gromov's interpretation of 'The Steppe'. He is referring not just to the folklore and fairytales that a Russian like Egorushka would have heard at his mother's or nanny's knee, but to the genres of Old Russian *written* literature:

> Среди наших исторических символов едва ли есть что-нибудь более древнее, чем степь, и если искать сходство и проводить параллели, то не с литературой 80-х годов, а с гораздо более древними горизонтами нашего художественного сознания; искать среди сказочных преданий и былин, среди "дорогих образов и картин", в жанровых руинах древнерусской литературы, где повесть выступала в своем естественном прототипе, как хождение, как рассказ о далеком пути через степь с ее курганами, каменными истуканами, охраняющими могилы печенегов и половцев. [**26**, 184]

It is difficult to conceive of a better description of the bulk of 'The Steppe''s narrative, i.e. after Egorushka has joined the wool-carts, than a 'khozhdenie' in the Old Russian literary sense. From this point the narrative itself moves at a walking pace and Egorushka's cart is accompanied by a barefooted Old Believer who could have stepped out of the Middle Ages. The *khozhdenie* provides the perfect chronotope for the evocation and contemplation of the historical symbols, 'animified' creatures, and personified natural phenomena, that according to Gromov Chekhov wanted to display to both Egorushka and us. These symbols, the use of spatial hyperbole, and the whole 'animist' way of looking at the world are in fact contemporaneous with the Old Russian 'genre' that 'The Steppe' harks back to. Not surprisingly, therefore, Gromov sees the overarching 'sokrovennyi i slozhnyi khudozhestvennyi zamysel' [**26**, 182] of 'The Steppe' as historical:

> Приемы повествования столь же историчны, как поэтика в целом; обращаясь к олицетворениям, писатель возращает нашу память к временам, когда они были привычны. В этом, собственно, и заключен художественный замысел "Степи": контрастное сопоставление обыденного и вечного, быта и бытия; можно предпочесть одно другому, можно не понимать ни того, ни другого, но нужно знать, что замысел Чехова заключен в сопоставлении, помнить о метафорическом двуединстве повествования и войти в него. [**26**, 187]

With this work, Gromov believes, Chekhov brought back into Russian literature the sense of history, and so powerfully that it is 'prezhde vsego chuvstvo, oshchutimoe fizicheski, kak dushevnaia bol'' [**26**, 184]. This strange feeling, a mixture of 'sostradanie i chuvstvo viny', was felt by Garshin, Repin, and 'even' Shchedrin on reading 'The Steppe' [**26**, 184], and we will probably experience it ourselves. But who, Gromov asks, is it a feeling of guilt *towards* – 'pered [...]

Step'iu? Rodinoi? Samim soboi?' [**26**, 184]. He relates it to a theme familiar from our discussion of *Fatherless*: it worries us 'kak napominanie o neproshchennoi vine, kak obrashchenie k sovesti' [**26**, 184].

Once again, to the western mind it may seem that Gromov's conception of *sovest'* is disembodied and undirected. In several separate places in this chapter on 'The Steppe', however, he suggests that the action which this work urges our conscience to carry out is to commit ourselves to the lifelong search for truth, which among other things means connecting with the deep past of our country, the continuum of its history and culture:

> Правильная постановка древнего безответного вопроса — что есть истина — сводилась к исканию истины, к художественной идее пути, протянувшегося из незапамятного прошлого в далекое будущее, поскольку истина по сути своей есть искание, бесконечно возникающий и ежеминутно, шаг за шагом решаемый вопрос. Или, говоря языком художественных знаков и поэтических образов, это — дорога пращуров, которую важно найти в детстве, чтобы в юные и зрелые годы не сбиваться с пути. [**26**, 190]

Through its form as a journey across an ancient landscape and through its links with the artistic sensibility of Old Russian literature, 'The Steppe' re-enacts this commitment to the 'search' and this connection with Russia's past, every time it is read.[32] Yet even now, Gromov says, we know very little about the connection between Old Russian and modern Russian literature. Many Russians wonder what the two can possibly have in common. 'Kak chto? Da to, chto oni russkie!' [**26**, 188].

Finally, Gromov relates the actual language of the 'poetic' passages of 'The Steppe' to certain works of Old Russian literature, especially the *Slovo o polku Igoreve*:

> Плач травы в "Степи" — известный не менее, чем плач Ярославны, обращен в глубину поэтической памяти; у него есть далекое прошлое, какая-то славная историческая родословная. [...] плач травы — когда это было у нас в последний раз? "Ничить трава жалощами, а древо с тугою к земле преклонилось..." [**26**, 185]

The complex sentences of this part of 'The Steppe's' register, broken into clauses between semi-colons, the groups of two and often three adjectives or phrases, the use of anaphora, and other features, do indeed resonate with the *byliny*, with 'nature passages' in certain Old Russian prose works, and the *Slovo o polku Igoreve* itself. In particular, the *Slovo* looks like prose on the page but undoubtedly is poetry, with 'a rhythm far more complex than that of any metrical pattern'.[33] The parallel with 'The Steppe' was not lost: '"Step'", chto ni govori, kak ee ni chitai, vse zhe ne povest', tem bolee – ne zhurnal'naia povest' kontsa stoletiia: v ee poeticheskoi glubine razlichimy zhanrovye ruiny drevnikh povestei i skazanii, eto zapovednik polurazrushennoi poeticheskoi rodiny, drevnei russkoi zemli' [**26**, 188].

Implicitly or explicitly, the above view of 'The Steppe' offers answers to its century-old cruxes. In a *khozhdenie*, which is a *povest'* about a journey, the physical movement is 'the plot' (*fabula*). It may be a 'primitive' plot in the sense that it is predetermined for the artist as the 'way' between two points, but it is neverthless a true plot since every stage of physical movement generates fresh 'events' in the form of new encounters. In 'The Steppe' the 'way' is saturated with history, poetry and metaphysics – all the things that Gromov rightly says the work is 'about'. The *stepnaia doroga* is therefore *both* the 'plot' and the 'subject', and Gromov is right to apply to it the word *siuzhet* in the sense of both. Further, if the narrator's vision and language in his 'poetic' passages (often apparently free indirect speech) are a throwback to Old Russian literature, this explains the perennial difficulty critics have had with the 'point of view' of 'The Steppe'.[34] The narrator's language is highly sophisticated, yet retains the 'child-like' imagery, animism and immediacy of its literary sources; Egorushka actually is a child. The narrator's and Egorushka's points of view are therefore quite distinct but in passages such as the 'plach travy' in Chapter II seem linguistically to overlap. The literary tradition from which 'The Steppe' hails (including earlier 19th century 'steppe-writers' such as Gogol') also accounts for the incomprehension with which it was met by its contemporaries. 'Ne nuzhno udivliat'sia', wrote Gromov, 'chto "Step'" pokazalos' staromodnoi i skuchnovatoi, naprimer, N.K. Mikhailovskomu. Ne emu odnomu: privychno bylo chitat' ob emansipatsii zhenshchin, o nigilizme ili khozhdenii v narod, a step', doroga, poeziia zor' i groz – vse eto davno uzhe vyshlo iz mody' [**26**, 156]. In fact Gromov devoted some pages to examining the kind of prose by Mamin-Sibiriak, Salov, Shatilov and Machtet that featured in *Severnyi vestnik* and *Russkaia mysl'* at the time when 'The Steppe' was written [**26**, 171–74, 176]. It was artistically threadbare stuff of impeccable political correctness. It addressed its authors' conception of the *bezvremen'e* and its favourite genre was the didactic magazine novel. The vast majority of reviewers therefore came to 'The Steppe' seeking the wrong content and the wrong genre [**26**, 183]. Yet as a modern experiment in the poetic *povest'* of ancient lineage it was a brilliant success. In Gromov's eyes there could hardly be, for instance, what Nils Åke Nilsson calls a 'collision between the two themes [Chekhov] tried to tie together – the story of Egoruška, and the story of the steppe',[35] since they were inseparably fused in the *siuzhet* of the *stepnaia doroga* from which Egorushka learns so much.

As with any really creative hypothesis, Gromov's reading of 'The Steppe' is fertile in suggesting to the reader his/her own interpretations. For instance, despite their realistic particulars all the lower-class figures who accompany Egorushka through the steppe have one feature writ larger than the rest, in the manner of epic, folkloric, or medieval characterisation: Vasia is the 'far-sighted' man, Dymov the 'silach', Kiriukha 'stupidity itself', Zvonykh the 'happy' man, and so on. The tales they tell epitomise them as though they are Old Russian *povesti* recounted on a pilgrimage. Seen in this way, these tales need no further justification. Similarly, although Gromov does not mention it, there is a strong current of Old Testament religion in 'The Steppe' ('God', 'Lord God of Sabaoth' rather than 'Jesus' or 'Christ'). Egorushka's imagination is greatly influenced by his upbringing. Yet when we read in Chapter VI that at sunset 'angely-khraniteli, zastilaia gorizont svoimi zolotymi kryl'iami, raspolagalis' na nochleg' we seem to be seeing things the narrator's way too. This would certainly be appropriate to the narrator's 'Old Russian' persona, just as it is tempting to see Father Khristofor as embodying the homiletic dimension of the 'old' literature, especially in the last chapter.

The closing emphasis of Gromov's interpretation of 'The Steppe' is on what may be termed 'genetic memory'. It would be wrong, he says, to think that Egorushka has nothing to 'remember' merely because his personal past is short:

> В детстве сказка вернее правды, былина вернее были, воображаемое и олицетворяемое достовернее реальности — поэтому подлинно историческое и поэтическое прошлое есть только у него. Повествование идет так, будто степь, холмы, ночные грозы, страхи и зарева скорее припоминаются, чем переживаются заново; Егорушка словно бы сохранил в памяти и сам видел все, что видели его предки со времен Тьмутаракани и Соловья-Разбойника. [**26**, 198-99]

If this seems far-fetched, Gromov reminds us that in his 1886 story 'Dreams' ('Mechty') Chekhov himself alluded to 'tu prapamiat', kotoruiu chelovek poluchaet "vmeste s krov'iu i plot'iu ot dalekikh vol'nykh predkov" i kotoruiu teriaet, povzroslev' [**26**, 198]. Although speculation about the 'gene-bank' of the Russian nation and the incalculable damage inflicted on it by the Communist holocaust was widespread by the time *Kniga o Chekhove* appeared, one can only wonder what the effect of Gromov's aeonian vision of 'The Steppe' and Russia's history and culture was upon literary-minded Soviet readers raised on State Prize Winner *chekhovedy* such as Ermilov and Berdnikov.

The core of Gromov's interpretation of 'The Steppe' as expressed in *Kniga o Chekhove* was carried over into his second, posthumous book, *Chekhov* (1993) [**29**], where it also formed the longest chapter, and to the long essay accompanying his 1995 edition of 'The Steppe' in the Academy of Sciences series 'Literaturnye pamiatniki' [**30**]. In both cases, however, Gromov made important additions.

In his 1993 book Gromov associated the Old Russian substance of 'The Steppe' with Chekhov's reading for his 1884/85 research project 'Vrachebnoe delo v Rossii'. Chekhov assembled for this a bibliography of over 150 titles on Russian history from a medical angle, and the long extracts that he copied out (see PSSP (Works), 16) show that he read them. As well as historians like Karamzin, the list included several famous *letopisi* in 19th-century editions, *Povest' vremennykh let*, *Domostroi*, *Pouchenie Vladimira Monomakha*, folk-songs and collections of folklore, and Chekhov owned a copy of the Musin-Pushkin first edition of *Slovo o polku Igoreve*. Gromov commented: 'Ne tol'ko sredi sovremennikov Chekhova, no i vo vsei nashei literature trudno nazvat' pisatelia, kotoryi v stol' rannie gody obladal by takoi shirokoi nachitannost'iu i takoi sklonnost'iu k izucheniiu istoricheskikh istochnikov i otechestvennoi stariny' [**29**, 188]. Drawing on Likhachev's classic *Poetika drevnerusskoi literatury* (1967), Gromov pointed out that the Old Russian *povest'* (with which he grouped *Khozhdenie za tri moria* and the *Slovo*) was always based on historical material and its specific genre was defined in its title ('povest' dushepolezna', 'povest' chiudna [sic]', 'povest' strashna' etc [**29**, 189]). 'The Steppe' ('Istoriia odnoi poezdki') shares these features with the Old Russian *povest'*, whereas 'v novoi literature zhanroobrazuiushchim faktorom okazyvaiutsia obrazy, ili, govoria tochnee, tot labirint stseplenii, o kotorom pisal L. Tolstoi' [**29**, 190]. If Chekhov had 'continued' the tale of Egorushka, then, he would have created not a novel, but an 'epic' rather like Korolenko's *My Contemporary's History* (*Istoriia moego sovremennika*). Chekhov knew this, so even in his correspondence with Grigorovich, who urged him to write a novel, Chekhov assiduously avoided the word 'novel' when discussing Egorushka's literary future [**29**, 192]. The idea that 'The Steppe' is an unfinished novel is consequently a 'literaturovedcheskaia legenda' [**29**, 191]. Gromov then devoted some pages to discussing Grigorovich's proposal that Chekhov write a novel about the suicide of a seventeen-year-old boy [**29**, 192–97]. He convincingly traced the idea to Dostoevskii's 'Dnevnik pisateliia' for 1876 [**29**, 193–94], analysed Chekhov's approach to the theme as elaborated in his letter to Grigorovich of 5 February 1888 [**29**, 194–96], and concluded that in Chekhov's hands such a novel would have been 'incomprehensible' to his older, socially-minded contemporary: 'v osnove ego konfliktov lezhali by mify russkoi istorii i russkoi sovesti, mify rokovoi neoplatnoi viny' [**29**, 197]. Finally, Gromov introduced Jung's concept of the 'archetype' to describe the historical and metaphysical images evoked in 'The Steppe' [**29**, 221–23].

In his 1995 essay on 'The Steppe' (which incorporated most of the above) Gromov raised the question of the extraordinary speed with which it was written. He suggested this was made possible only by extensive preparation in early notebooks that have not survived [**30**, 168–69]. He also discussed the traditional placing of 'The Steppe' in the 'obshchaia kontseptsiia tvorcheskoi evoliutsii Chekhova' [**30**, 175] which, of course, was distorted because it overlooked the 'big bang' of *Fatherless* [**30**, 174–77]. There was more emphasis on the spiritual/religious dimension of 'The Steppe' [**30**, 190, 194] and a new paragraph interpolated: 'S obrazom ottsa Khristofora sviazana zhanrovaia liniia poucheniia, "slova", potrebovavshaia, kstati govoria, dovol'no slozhnogo kommentariia' [**30**, 198]. Gromov related the imagery and themes of 'The Steppe' to Chekhov's last play, *The Cherry Orchard* [**30**, 239, 266–67], and under the new freedoms was able to cite his fellow exile from the Philological Faculty of MGU, Andrei Siniavskii, to expand the section on Jungian archetypes [**30**, 263–65]. The presence of text on themes other than 'The Steppe', ranging from *Fatherless* and Antosha Chekhonte to the nature of artistic language and *The Cherry Orchard*, means that the 1995 essay on 'The Steppe' really contains the quintessence of Gromov as a Chekhov critic. It perhaps deserves to be called his masterpiece.

CHAPTER 5

CHEKHOV, DOSTOEVSKII, AND 'THE BLACK MONK'

As its title suggests, Gromov's first book on Chekhov [**26**] is more of a selective thematic composition than a biography; whereas his 'last' book [**29**] ostensibly deals with every stage of Chekhov's life and career in chronological order. Even so, at first one is surprised to discover that in his 'last' book Gromov's treatment of the theme 'Chekhov and Dostoevskii' has been reduced from forty-three pages to twenty-two. For this was a subject that Gromov had spent much of his critical life exploring and his investigation of it is undoubtedly on a par with his revaluations of *Fatherless* and 'The Steppe'.

The reason for the more 'balanced' presence of Dostoevskii in the 1993 book is probably that Gromov was able to restrict himself here to the essential *results* of his life-time examination of the subject. This was because (a) the full 'workings' (expanded from his 1977 article [**18**]) had been presented in his 1989 book, and (b) the 1989 book had removed the last taboo from the subject 'Chekhov and Dostoevskii' and thanks to political developments this taboo was unlikely to return. To put it bluntly, in 1977 Gromov had written: 'Bylo vremia – i ne stol' uzh davnee – kogda dazhe otdalennaia vozmozhnost' sopostavleniia Chekhova s Dostoevskim predstavlialas' strannoi. [...] Tema "Chekhov i Dostoevskii" eshche tselikom v budushchem: vremia iasnosti i ponimaniia eshche ne nastupilo, vremia polnogo otritsaniia uzhe proshlo' [**18**, 40]; in 1989 he was able to modify this to 'eshche v budushchem' [**26**, 246]; by the time of his death the theme was well on its way to acceptance.[36] This must have been a source of amazement and quiet satisfaction to Gromov. It meant that he could present the topic in his 'last' book with less advocacy and in its most focussed form. In order fully to understand Gromov's 1993 dicta on the subject, however, we must take them together with his 1989 'workings'.

The magnitude and subversiveness of what Gromov was undertaking by tackling the question 'Chekhov and Dostoevskii' need to be appreciated. There were few references to Dostoevskii in Chekhov's correspondence compared, say, with references to Pushkin, Gogol', or Turgenev. The most famous quote on the subject was Chekhov's statement in a letter to Suvorin of 5 March 1889 that he found Dostoevskii 'khorosho, no ochen' uzh dlinno i neskromno. Mnogo pretenzii'. A close second was Nemirovich-Danchenko's memory of Chekhov telling him that he, Chekhov, had not read *Crime and Punishment* (*Prestuplenie i nakazanie*) and was saving the pleasure for 'when he was forty'; on attaining that age, Chekhov remarked that he had read the novel but 'bol'shogo vpechatleniia ne poluchil'.[37] Such utterances were taken at face value. What could the 'objective', sceptical, agnostic Chekhov have in common, it was thought, with the 'subjective', passionate, militantly Russian Orthodox Dostoevskii? Many of the latter's admirers believed that in fact Chekhov and his art were deeply *hostile* to Dostoevskii and his: 'on khotel ubit' v nas Dostoevskogo', Innokentii Annenskii winced.[38] The 'enmity' was doubtless aggravated by the rivalry between the St Petersburg and Moscow intelligentsias. Finally, after 1917 much of Dostoevskii was regarded as ideologically unacceptable, whereas a version of Chekhov was fabricated that enabled him to be promoted to the Soviet pantheon; after which it would have been reckless, indeed perverse, to inquire into any 'connections' between them. There were thus triple and quadruple bars on examining the subject. It was a non-starter. From every point of view, it was thought, Chekhov and Dostoevskii were opposites, hence the title of Gromov's chapter in his 1989 book: 'Chekhov i Dostoevskii: velikoe protivostoianie' [**26**, 246].[39]

Gromov's approach was avowedly empirical and deductive. Instead of concentrating on Chekhov's letters, he would look for 'skrytye tsitaty' in the works themselves. But for these to be genuine allusions to Dostoevskii, he explained, the latter's name had to appear somewhere in the text. Vlasich's extraordinary throwaway line to Ivashin in 'Neighbours', 'Esli tebe kogda-nibud' ponadobitsia moia zhizn', to pridi i voz'mi ee', can be regarded as a portentous quote from 'The Village of Stepanchikovo and its Inhabitants' ('Selo Stepanchikovo i ego obitateli') or *Crime and Punishment* [**26**, 259], because Vlasich's life is conducted in imitation of 'idea-soaked' literature and Dostoevskii is explicitly mentioned in this context. Such a textual conjunction, Gromov argued, excluded the arbitrary factor:

> Дело в том, что, например, слова Власича "Если тебе когда-нибудь понадобится моя жизнь..." довольно обычны; нечто похожее можно обнаружить, вероятно, у Писемского, Тургенева или, скажем, у Диккенса, Бальзака — особенно если искать увлеченно, с желанием и азартом. Если такое случится, нужно перечитать чеховский текст (от строчки до строчки, а не отдельную строчку) и найти в нем имя Диккенса, или того же упомянутого выше Писемского, или Бальзака. Если имени нет (а оно должно быть в тексте, поскольку является знаком скрытой цитаты), то можно считать, что открытие не состоялось. [**26**, 260]

In fact, two explicit references to *Crime and Punishment* in humorous stories of 1883 enabled Gromov promptly to suggest that Chekhov had been fooling Nemirovich-Danchenko [**26**, 249–50]. As well as 'Neighbours', Gromov located 'hidden quotes' in his defined sense in other, chronologically contiguous works, for instance *The Wood Demon* (*Leshii*) and 'Ward N° 6'. Here, he suggested,

Chekhov could be seen as 'carnivalising' Dostoevskii's 'artistic world': 'nizvoditsia s p'edestala ideia, rasshchepliaetsia "slovo" geroia, parodiruetsia stil'' [**26**, 259]. Chekhov's attitude to Dostoevskii in these works was not only 'objective', it was 'historical': 'Dostoevskii byl vlastitelem dum; on ostavil glubokii sled v soznanii i kharaktere tselogo pokoleniia russkikh liudei, kak teper', po istechenii vremeni, vkhodil v khudozhestvennyi mir Chekhova v kachestve "geroev"' [**26**, 261].

However, in the case of the text which Gromov considered had the deepest and longest-lasting impact on Chekhov – *The Adolescent* – he does not seem to apply the same standards of proof.

It will be remembered that in 1962 Gromov began his article on Chekhov's Taganrog childhood with an extended epigraph from Dostoevskii's novel (actually, in its manuscript version), which implied that Chekhov himself was one of the generation of Dostoevskian 'adolescents'. There was no other allusion to Dostoevskii in the article. Similarly, in his 1963 piece on *Fatherless* he coupled Dostoevskii's name once with Tolstoi's [**5**, 11], mentioned Dostoevskii once in passing [**5**, 18], and in discussing Glagol'ev 1's 'neopredelennost'' speech, which contained the 'smyslovoi kliuch dramy', related it only to *Anna Karenina* [**5**, 11]. It was another fourteen years before Gromov linked in print a specific passage of *Fatherless* with a specific passage in *The Adolescent*. Quoting Platonov's speech to Glagol'ev 1 in Act I, scene 5, about the death of his (Platonov's) father, which concludes in first draft with the words 'Byt' zavziatym podletsom i v to zhe vremia ne khotet' soznavat' etogo – strashnaia osobennost' russkogo podletsa!', Gromov commented: 'V monologe – skrytaia tsitata iz "Podrostka" Dostoevskogo' [**18**, 41], and 'identified' the latter as Dostoevskii's narrator's words in the first paragraph of Part III, Chapter 3, Section I ending 'Shirokost' li eto osobennaia v russkom cheloveke, kotoraia ego daleko povedet, ili prosto podlost' – vot vopros!'. It was a further twelve years, however, before Gromov could make the relationship that he perceived between *Fatherless* and *The Adolescent* startlingly explicit.

In his 1989 book he took Glagol'ev 1's 'neopredelennost'' speech from Act I, scene 3, and focussed on the words:

> Это [Платонов] герой лучшего, еще, к сожалению, ненаписанного, современного романа... (**Смеется**.) Под неопределенностью я разумею современное состояние нашего общества: русский беллетрист чувствует эту неопределенность. Он стал в тупик, теряется, не знает, на чем остановиться, не понимает... Трудно понять ведь этих господ!

Instead of discussing the *neopredelennost'* as such and relating it to Tolstoi (and 'Lenin'), Gromov was now able to address the more obvious question: who was the 'Russian novelist' Glagol'ev 1 and the young Chekhov were referring to? Since Gromov's reply is at the heart of his conception of the 'Chekhov and

Dostoevskii' theme, it deserves to be quoted in full:

> Вот страница, предвещающая характернейшие черты Платонова, его чудачества и его судьбу:
>
> "Внук тех героев, которые были изображены в картине, изображавшей русское семейство средневысшего культурного круга в течение трех поколений сряду и в связи с историей русской, — этот потомок предков своих уже не мог бы быть изображен в современном типе своем иначе, как в несколько мизантропическом, уединенном и несомненно грустном виде. Даже должен явиться каким-нибудь чудаком, которого читатель с первого взгляда мог бы признать как за сошедшего с поля и убедиться, что не за ним осталось поле. Еще далее — и исчезнет даже и этот внук-мизантроп; явятся новые лица, еще неизвестные, и новый мираж; но какие же лица? Если некрасивые, то невозможен дальнейшии русский роман. Но увы! роман ли только окажется тогда невозможным?" [*The Adolescent*, Part III, Chapter 13, Section III]
>
> Создание столь проторечивых и сложных характеров невозможно без опоры на традицию: у Платонова должно быть прошлое, лежащее в историческом прошлом русской литературы. В "Подростке", например: "У нас создался веками какой-то еще нигде не виданный высший культурный тип, которого нет в целом мире — тип всемирного боления за всех. Это — тип русский" [*The Adolescent*, Part III, Chapter 7, Section III]. [**26**, 68]

Note that the first passage from *The Adolescent* quoted here by Gromov comes from the pen of the character Nikolai Semenovich, not the narrator-adolescent, let alone a first-person Dostoevskii journalist-critic. So the answer to the question of which 'russkii belletrist' Glagol'ev 1 is referring to is not 'Dostoevskii', but a putative, metaphorical one *as is the case in the first passage Gromov quotes* (the speaker of the second passage is the character Versilov). In a short section later in his 1989 book, Gromov collated the 'hidden quotations' from *The Adolescent* and *Fatherless* [**26**, 247–49] and drew a general stylistic conclusion: 'Sama slozhnost' zadachi, mnogolineinyi avantiurnyi siuzhet, kakoi v dal'neishem vstretitsia razve chto v "Drame na okhote", tselaia tolpa deistvuiushchikh lits, takaia putanitsa intrig, konfliktov, isterik, kakoi v dal'neishem ne budet, – vse zdes' ozareno iarostnymi otsvetami Dostoevskogo' [**26**, 247].

Having established to his own satisfaction the intertextuality of *The Adolescent* and *Fatherless*, Gromov perceived a far wider influence of the novel on the rest of Chekhov's writing career. Referring to the character Kraft's words 'Nyne bezlesiat Rossiiu, istoshchaiut v nei pochvu [...]. Iavis' chelovek s nadezhdoi i posadi derevo – vse zasmeiutsia: "Razve ty do nego dozhivesh'?" [*The Adolescent*, Part I, Chapter 4, Section I]', he concluded:

> Многое в чеховском творчестве восходит к этому художественному зерну, к этому предельно сжатому, бесконечно содержательному конспекту. Здесь не только экологическая карта доктора Астрова и далее все, что в драматургии и прозе Чехова сказано о вырубленных лесах и пересыхающих реках, об одиноких чудаках, упрямо сажающих свои берез-

ки, и о людях с размахом, сводящих под корень старые вишнёвые сады. Здесь все мечты Астрова, Вершинина и Тузенбаха о жизни, которая будет прекрасной через двести, или триста, или тысячу лет [...]. Это близко не просто по смылсу, нет, — это подчеркнуто близко по словарю, это написано так, чтобы у читателя и сомнений не возникало относительно первоисточника. [**26**, 157]

Indeed, if we did not know who was the author of Kraft's words, 'kto usomnilsia by v avtorstve Chekhova?' [**26**, 280]. We all know, maintained Gromov, that Chekhov said each of us should plant at least one tree on the planet whilst we are alive, but these words 'doslovno zhe [...] prinadlezhat Dostoevskomu: "...ia postavil by v zakon ili v povinnost' kazhdomu muzhiku posadit' khot' odno derevo v svoei zhizni vvidu obezleseniia Rossii; vprochem, odnogo-to dereva malo budet, mozhno by prikazat' sazhat' i kazhdyi god po derevu" [Versilov, *The Adolescent*, Part III, Chapter 8, Section I]' [**26**, 280]. More broadly, Gromov thought that

"Подросток" — не просто один из романов Достоевского, но его завещание, обращение к молодому "будущему художнику", которому придется писать о сыновьях и потомках — наследниках минувшего беспорядка и хаоса. Художник этот, — предсказывал Достоевский, — отыщет новые литературные формы, потому что "невозможен дальнейший русский роман". [**26**, 249]

Chekhov, in Gromov's view, was that 'future artist'. The 'classical' Russian novel was grounded in 'types' and in the historical significance of what it portrayed, but in *The Adolescent* Dostoevskii had already questioned the future of this: 'Tekushchaia, neustoiavshaiasia, "sluchainaia" zhizn' – vot granitsa, pered kotoroi ostanovilsia i sam Dostoevskii: "No chto delat', odnako zh, pisateliu, ne zhelaiushchemu pisat' lish' v odnom istoricheskom rode i oderzhimomu toskoiu po tekushchemu? Ugadyvat' i...oshibat'sia" [Nikolai Semenovich, *The Adolescent*, Part III, Chapter 13, Section III]' [**26**, 297].

Such statements in *The Adolescent* were the historical departure point for Gromov's interpretation of Chekhov's relation to the 19th-century novel, most fully argued in the chapter 'Novye formy' in his 1993 book: 'Smysl chekhovskogo novatorstva sleduet, po-vidimomu, iskat' v tom, chto, opiraias' na khudozhestvennyi opyt klassicheskogo romana, on sozdal povestvovatel'nuiu sistemu, stol' zhe tekuchuiu, kak sama zhizn', nashel sposoby tipizatsii mimoletnykh chert povsednevnogo bytiia, pered kotorymi, ugadyvaia i oshibaias', ostanovilsia roman' [**29**, 310]. Similarly, Gromov juxtaposed with his reading of 'The Steppe' passages from Dostoevskii's journalism that dealt with 'dorogi prezhnie', 'dorogi konem', and childhood. He asserted: 'Dostoevskii, chei zamysel i byl, po-vidimomu, realizovan v "Stepi", luchshe drugikh ponial by Chekhova, ego "dorogu konem" i ego Egorushku' [**26**, 156].

Clearly, Gromov derived a very wide significance indeed from the adolescent Chekhov's reading of Dostoevskii. But how justified was he in doing this?

On the face of it, his identification of 'skrytye tsitaty' from *The Adolescent* in *Fatherless* and from Dostoevskii's journalism in 'The Steppe' fails by his own criterion: neither of these texts contains the name Dostoevskii. This might seem particularly surprising in the case of *Fatherless*, where Chekhov eagerly indulges in literary name-dropping. Where 'The Steppe' is concerned, Gromov himself had emphasized the importance of *named* authors, such as Petr Mogila, for recognising that work's 'skrytye tsitaty' [**26**, 260]. Nor did he offer documentary (i.e. extra-textual) evidence that Chekhov had ever read these works of Dostoevskii. 'Roman "Podrostok", pechatavshiisia v "Otechestvennykh zapiskakh" v techenie vsego 1875 goda i vyshedshii otdel'nym izdaniem v 1876 godu', Gromov wrote, 'Chekhovym byl prochitan, konechno, eshche v gimnazii', and he explained his 'konechno' by saying that a 'new novel' by Dostoevskii was an 'event' that no contemporary reader could let pass [**26**, 247]. 'Naprasno sprashivat' sebia, znal li Chekhov "Dnevnik pisatelia", chital li "Podrostka", poskol'ku ne znat' Dostoevskogo v Rossii tekh let mog razve chto kruglyi nevezhda' [**26**, 157]. Logically, Gromov's 'could not not have' argument looks dubious. It is tempting to infer that he is 'reduced' to it by the absence of affirmative facts. There is a similar problem with the importance he ascribes in Chekhov's writing career to Dostoevskii's speech on the inauguration of Pushkin's statue in Moscow in 1880. Unpublished magazine sketches exist by Nikolai Chekhov entitled 'Rech' Dostoevskogo v Blagorodnom sobranii', Anton Chekhov 'byl svidetelem sobytiia' [**26**, 77], 'slushal Dostoevskogo' [**26**, 78], 'veroiatno, videl' Dostoevskii [**26**, 156], and 's etogo vremeni nachalos' vliianie Pushkina i Dostoevskogo – odnovremennoe, dvoistvennoe' [**26**, 78]. Absolutely no documentary evidence is produced for the last four statements. In Gromov's 1993 book Chekhov no longer 'heard' and 'saw' Dostoevskii, he was a 'witness' only in the sense that he was in Moscow at the time. Chekhov 'read' the author's speech a few days later in *Moskovskie vedomosti* [**29**, 104], although no source is given for this either.

In terms of objective proof, then, the whole edifice of Gromov's sub-textual dialogue between Chekhov and Doestoevskii appears shaky. Even its foundation, the 'profound' influence of *The Adolescent* on *Fatherless*, cannot be said to have been 'proven'. Essentially, only two short passages from each work are produced as the main evidence; corroborative evidence in the form of Dostoevskii's name is missing; the circumstantial evidence of stylistic influence (multiple plot, wealth of characters, picaresque elements, hysterical behaviour etc) is impressive, but still only circumstantial.

However, perhaps the model for appraising Gromov's statements on the subject should be less judicial than scientific. His claims cannot be proven true with the documentary evidence that we have, but they have not been proven false either, although it seems perfectly possible to envisage the kind of evidence that could refute them. The parallels that Gromov perceives between *The Adolescent* and *Fatherless* are intriguing enough to suggest an hypothesis of 'profound' influence, and there may be more concrete evidence to support it than he himself produces. Some speech patterns of Chekhov's characters in *Fatherless* – and definitely their volubility – seem closer to Dostoevskii's heroes than to those of any other contemporary Russian classic. They could repay a computer analysis comparing them with *The Adolescent*, which might provide 'harder' evidence for Gromov's claim. Further, it is not sophistical to suggest that the number of times an author names another author in print may be in *inverse* proportion to the profundity of the latter's influence on him. This may not be a matter of 'embarrassment', or fear of being thought derivative, it may be because the dialogue between the two is so intimately pervasive that it would be 'profaned' by being made explicit. One thinks of Bernard Shaw's or Mikhail Bulgakov's reluctance to refer to Chekhov himself in a way that would suggest they were very familiar with his work (which they were). Finally, positive proof can appear from unexpected quarters. For example, in 1898 Chekhov helped Merpert with a lecture on Dostoevskii that Merpert was going to deliver at the Sorbonne, and made the seemingly very personal, pondered comment that Pushkin 'ved' imel na nego [Dostoevskogo] gromadnoe, podavliaiushchee vlianie'.[40]

Altogether, then, it could be claimed that Gromov's unrestricted generalization of the influence on Chekhov of *The Adolescent* and Dostoevskii's journalism approximates more to a scientific hypothesis than a literary-scholarly proof. Like an innovative scientific theory, this generalization was suggested by certain concrete observations (which might be powerfully corroborated by computer analysis), but in its wider applications (which are plausible) it cannot yet, to use Popper's terminology, be conclusively verified, but one can at least imagine how it could be 'falsified' (i.e. refuted). In Gromov's case the analogy may be peculiarly apposite. As we have seen, his approach to literature was affected by the scientism of the time. He also appreciated Chekhov's own practice of the 'scientific method'. Popper's name was largely taboo in the Soviet period because of his critique of Marxism and closed societies, but Gromov appears to allude to him in his discussion of Chekhov's 'synthesis' of the 'scientific and artistic methods': 'Chekhov ob"iasnial to, chto bylo metodologicheski poniato lish' v nauke XX v.: dlia ser'eznoi nauchnoi mysli otritsatel'nye rezul'taty tak zhe sushchestvenny, kak i polozhitel'nye' [**22**, 34; **26**, 131].

At this point, in his 1989 book, Gromov presented a brief argument for what Dostoevskii and Chekhov *share* as writers, which must have been as astonishing to his Soviet readers as it is welcome for being synchronic rather than intertextual/historical [**26**, 250–53]. First, Gromov set out very clearly Dostoevskii's understanding of 'realism in the higher sense'. 'Realizm, ogranichivaiushchiisia konchikom svoego nosa', opined the narrator of *The Adolescent*, 'opasnee samoi bezumnoi fantastichnosti, potomu chto slep' (Part I, Chapter 8, Section II). For Dostoevskii, Gromov wrote, 'realizm est' prozrenie vnutrennikh protivorechii zhizni, dvoistvennogo konflikta mezhdu "pervoi" (estestvennoi) i "vtoroi" (vospitannoi) naturami otdel'nogo cheloveka i vsei natsii v ee istoricheskom bytii. Eto protivorechie raskryvaetsia v zazerkal'e zauriadnoi i budnichnoi zhizni' [**26**, 250]. What, in Dostoevskii's view, could be more fantastical, unexpected, and even improbable, than reality itself? A similar thought is expressed in specific passages of *Fatherless*, 'The Steppe', and Chekhov's notebooks, and underlies the whole story 'Fear' ('Strakh') [**26**, 251]. A similar model of reality and the self is at the heart of Chekhov's most mature work:

> Воспоминания Мисаила Полознева, "человек с молоточком", статистика "Крыжовника", Беликов из "Человека в футляре", да, наконец, и сама возможность жизни в футляре — это, несомненно, фантастические порождения русского быта; нет смысла спорить, что страшнее — "бездны" Достоевского или затаенный, медлительный ужас жизни в чеховском городе N. [**26**, 252]

The classic statement of the dichotomy, which Gromov quoted in full, was the passage in 'The Lady with the Little Dog' describing Gurov's 'dve zhizni: odna iavnaia, [...] drugaia – protekavshaia taino'; but 'vsia "malen'kaia trilogiia", proza zrelykh let ot "Palaty No. 6" do "Arkhiereia", no dazhe, naprimer, i "Dvoe v odnom", "Nevidimye miru slezy", "Otkrytie", "Razgovor cheloveka s sobakoi" ['Early' stories] vkhodiat v obshchuiu sistemu i zakliuchaiut v sebe predstavlenie o dvoistvennosti bytiia' [**26**, 253].

It would be difficult to imagine a more cogent rapprochement of Chekhov and Dostoevskii in purely metaphysical, synchronic terms; although Gromov recognised that 'v to vremia kak Dostoevskogo zanimala lish' vnutrenniaia storona, lish' dukhovnoe podpol'e, u Chekhova predstavleny obe storony v ikh tragicheski protivorechivom edinstve' [**26**, 253]. This *tour de force* of Gromov's was entitled, with admirable ambiguity, 'Dvoiniki'. In 1962, when he first alluded to the theme, it would have been an act of certifiable literary-critical madness. In 1993 it was absent from his last book altogether, perhaps because the death throes of state historicism rendered it superfluous: Gromov had already 'made his point'.

Setting aside the somewhat simplistic issue of Dostoevskii's named appearance in Chekhov's texts, I feel that it was Gromov's exhaustive tracing in these texts of the 'mnozhestv[o] namekov, perefrazirovok i vsiacheskikh podrazumevanii' *vis-à-vis* Dostoevskii [**26**, 253] that yielded most fruit in literary-critical terms. His essays on 'A Boring Story' and 'The Black Monk' examine these stories precisely from the point of view of a dialogic relationship with Dostoevskian antecedents. This produces fresh, mind-expanding readings that have a clear ring of truth.

In both cases Gromov's reinterpretation evolves from discussion of the fundamental role of 'ideia' in Dostoevskii's mature works. The Populist journalist Mikhailovskii took the conclusion reached by the hero of 'A Boring Story' that he lacked '[to], chto nazyvaetsia obshchei ideei, ili bogom zhivogo cheloveka', identified it as the message of the story, and presented it as an autobiographical confession by Chekhov too:

> С тех пор — и до наших дней — "общая идея" понимается по Михайловскому — вне всяких исторических соотнесений и связей: старый профессор из "Скучной истории" — рупор "общей идеи", сами же эти слова принадлежат Чехову, как символ и печать ограниченности и "путаницы понятий" 80-х годов, но также и личной ограниченности и ущербности Чехова. [**26**, 254]

But, Gromov counters, in terms of his contemporaries, his culture and his attitudes Nikolai Stepanovich is demonstrably a man of the 1860s and 70s; '[on] sudit o sovremennosti po starinke, pozhinaia plody svoei molodosti...' [**26**, 253]. The famous statement about 'obshchaia ideia' at the end of 'A Boring Story' should therefore also be seen in historical perspective – as a 'symptom' rather than an assertion of direct ideological import for the story. The most likely source of it, historically, is Dostoevskii, whose novels would have been the professor's essential reading as a younger man: 'V "Skuchnoi istorii" slova "obshchaia ideia" chitaiutsia ochen' kontrastno i, kazhetsia, podrazumevaiut kakoi-to pervoistochnik: "to, chto nazyvaetsia" – v rechevom obikhode chashche vsego nechto obshcheizvestnoe, raskhozhee, kak poslovitsa. U Dostoevskogo eti slova: "obshchaia", "rukovodiashchaia ideia" – obychny' [**26**, 255]. Gromov produces five excellent examples of the latter, from *The Adolescent* to *The Karamazov Brothers* (*Brat'ia Karamazovy*), and it must be admitted he could have given dozens more. Gromov continued:

> Достоевский, сделавший идею "предметом художественного изображения", "великий художник идеи" (М.М. Бахтин), утвердил в русском сознании тревогу и беспокойство, стремление утвердить идею — "бога живого человека" — прежде всего, поскольку жить без нее невозможно [...]
>
> В "Скучной истории" важна не только формула "общей идеи", но в особенности слова: "А коли нет этого, то, значит, нет и ничего". Они-то и удостоверяют, что Николай Степанович не только "когда-то" знал и читал, но и правильно понял Достоевского. [**26**, 255-56]

In other words, the narrator's diagnosis of his own spiritual malaise is simply another of his received ideas. Instead of the story being teleological – moving to its 'solution' in the 'obshchaia ideia' as Mikhailovskii and after him Soviet *chekhovedy* held – its 'unfinished', heuristic qualities were sustained throughout.

The fact that Gromov places Nikolai Stepanovich's obsession with 'obshchaia ideia' in a Dostoevskian context produces a fundamentally different view of the story. As a studiously objective realization of an old man's consciousness, the work reaches no authoritative, epiphanic conclusion. Nothing could display the differences between Chekhov and Dostoevskii more starkly than the fact that 'sredi knizhnykh slov i tsitat, zapomnivshikhsia chekhovskomu personazhu, net edinstvenno toi, k kotoroi nepremenno obratilsia by geroi Dostoevskogo: net Evangeliia, evangelicheskogo slova ili legendy – naprimer, stol' umestnoi zdes' legendy o voskresenii Lazaria' [**26**, 257]. Nevertheless, we may be struck by the irony that a man who supposedly yearns for an 'obshchaia ideia' already possesses a comprehensive *method*, the 'scientific method', that he has presumably believed in all his life and still does. Nikolai Stepanovich's desire for certainty, for dogmatic knowledge rather than an epistemological search, then appears more like another symptom of his ageing. Gromov's reading of this work returns it to its proper existential genre (the 'fragment'), and suggests a somewhat ethical context of self-other relations that may be authentically Chekhovian:

> Мало сказать, что профессорские мысли и мнения не имеют для Чехова "никакой цены". Сам образ старого медика был ему неприятен: "Мой герой — и это одна из его главных черт — слишком беспечно относится к внутренней жизни окружающих, и в то время, когда около него плачут, ошибаются, лгут, он преспокойно трактует о театре, литературе; будь он иного склада, Лиза и Катя, пожалуй бы, не погибли" [Letter to Pleshcheev, 30 September 1889]. [**26**, 254-55]

The reading is richly challenging and appeals directly to our experience of the text, rather than to extraneous issues.

Gromov's much longer essay on 'The Black Monk' [**26**, 262–80] opens with an extended analysis of Chekhov's handling of the concept 'ideia' in works up to 'Ward N° 6' (1892). He shows how in the very earliest stories, and not always humorously, '"ideia" – to est' samo slovo "ideia", nezavisimo ot ego smysla i soderzhaniia – vosprinimaetsia kak narushenie poriadka i ereticheskoe otstuplenie ot normy' [**26**, 263]. The environment that feels threatened by ideas – any ideas – reacts with its own ideology, which Gromov terms 'ideologiia "futliara"'. The latter is 'agressivna i beznravstvenna, poskol'ku kriterii otvetstvennosti, sovesti i viny dlia nee nesushchestvenny' [**26**, 264]. However, in the 1886 story 'His Sister' ('Sestra'), which was renamed 'Good People' ('Khoroshie liudi') for the Collected Works, Chekhov shows ideas being used as sticks to beat people with, irrespective of the content or worth of those ideas; his interest is as much in the victims as in the ideologues. The 'ideas' in this and other stories are in fact *dead* ideas, shibboleths, the currency of party-minded journalism: 'Slozhnoe, dialekticheski protivorechivoe razvitie idei, kotoroe v sisteme Dostoevskogo opredeliaet i soderzhanie, i poetiku "polifonicheskogo" romana, Chekhova ne zanimaet vovse. Programma ("ideia") izvestna "ot A do izhitsy" do nachala rasskaza i opredeliaetsia obshcheponiatno ("konservativnaia ideia", "liberal'naia programma")' [**26**, 265]. In any case, they are nearly always *received* ideas:

> "Идея" не является личным достоянием персонажа: в отличие от романов Достоевского, где она вынашивается в душевном подполье как сущность героя, как тайна его неповторимой и одинокой личности, "идея" в системе Чехова — знак кружковой ограниченности, часто заурядного, безличного мышления, подчиненного очередному "течению мысли". [**26**, 265]

Yet Chekhov's characters are obsessed with and possessed by these stale ideas:

> [они] воспринимают идейность как вероисповедание; они не "служат идее", а — в духе Достоевского — страдают во имя веры: "Ведь я, сударыня, веровал не как немецкий доктор философии, не цирлих-манирлих, [...] а каждая моя вера гнула меня в дугу, рвала на части мое тело" ['Under Way' ('Na puti')]. [**26**, 267]

In 'The Black Monk' Chekhov 'nashel put' k voploshcheniiu ideinoi oderzhimosti ne v slove personazha, no v khudozhestvennom obraze, pochti zrimom, pochti real'nom' [**26**, 268].

However, there was no hope, in Gromov's view, of understanding this story outside the context of contemporary 'esteticheskikh i filosofskikh iskanii, k kotorym Chekhov otnosilsia daleko ne ravnodushno' [**26**, 269], and in particular the Decadent movement and Friedrich Nietzsche. This context may have been fed for Chekhov by his encounters in Europe with Merezhkovskii and Gippius, who 'osvaivali estetiku i filosofiiu dekadansa u samykh ego istokov. Nedavniaia tragediia Fridrikha Nitsshe (on poterial rassudok v 1889 g.) sdelala ego imia edva li ne samym modnym; o nem pisali i govorili, im uvlekalis'; Evropa chuvstvovala sebia na grani dobra i zla' [**26**, 269]. Decadence theorists like Gippius had, moreover, uncritically adopted the view of some of Dostoevskii's characters that superior insight is inseparable from illness or madness. Although we are not given the names of the philosophers Kovrin studies and 'teaches', Gromov postulates that they lie in that area of contemporary fashion. They are responsible for Kovrin's *ideia* – that he is a genius above the common herd – and this *ideia*, obsessively held, produces the hallucination of the black monk in a manner purposely reminiscent of Ivan Karamazov's conversation with the Devil [**26**, 272]. But what is most important for Gromov is that Kovrin's megalomania leads to the persecution of other people and Kovrin sees this as justified:

> Беда в том, что, выделив Коврина из стада, Черный монах объяснил ему, что все остальные люди — и прежде всех близкие ему люди — есть именно и только стадо; считаться с ними Коврин во имя идеи не должен. Это и освобождает героя от всякой ответственности [...], ставит его по ту сторону добра и зла. [**26**, 275]

Here Gromov quotes Tania Pesotskaia's words to the effect that Kovrin 'killed' her father.

Gromov's cultural-historical, clinical, artistic and human account of Kovrin's disease is highly persuasive. His interpretation of the rest of the story, however, seems schematic. In Gromov's view the 'metaphor' of the black monk is '"pridumana i sdelana" v kontraste s zhivym obrazom velikolepnogo sada' [**26**, 272]; the gardener Pesotskii is a 'chelovek dela, on – chelovek sozidaiushchii, pogruzhennyi v rabotu, kotoraia ne tol'ko kazhetsia zhivoi i prekrasnoi, no deistvitel'no iavliaetsia prekrasnoi' [**26**, 271]; both Pesotskii and his garden are the positive 'counterpoint' to Kovrin's destructive solipsism. This, surely, is to overlook the fanatical aspect of Pesotskii and the anti-Utopian portrayal of much of his 'garden'. His management of his empire is hyperactive and dictatorial. His workmen approximate to 'ants'. The only purpose, it seems, of Tania and Kovrin producing a son is to provide *Pesotskii* with an heir whom, in his words, he could 'make' into a horticulturist. The flowers themselves may be beautiful, but there is a decidedly municipal air to their utilisation; the 'decorative' garden suggests Pesotskii lacks an aesthetic sense; and the vast fruit-growing area is literally regimented, 'tochno sherengi soldat'. As Donald Rayfield has written, not only is the garden 'oppressive' and humanity 'subjugated' to it, the 'imagery of smoke, ghosts, tyranny builds up to a Hades by subtle stages'.[41] In fact, at the risk of becoming schematic oneself, it could be said that Pesotskii is shown to be as monomaniacal and tyrannical as Kovrin. Both make Tania's life 'hell'. I find it tempting, therefore, to compare 'The Black Monk' with precisely the earlier stories Gromov mentions, 'His Sister' and 'The Wife' ('Zhena'), and focus on the theme of a woman terrorised and manipulated by male ideologues from whom she has great difficulty escaping. It seems significant, for instance, that Tania's mother and her presumably early death are never mentioned. The fact that Tania accuses Kovrin of killing Pesotskii may be due to her having in the end succumbed to her *father's* particular form of tunnel vision, rather than Kovrin's.

'The Black Monk' has long been a crux of Chekhov criticism and hopefully it will continue to be revalued. Gromov has made an outstanding contribution to our understanding of the story's human protagonist, but he has also related the story as a whole to living concerns, namely 20th-century fascism of the right and left. For what the story shows is embryonic versions of the totalitarian mind. 'Nitsshe byl interesen Chekhovu v kakom-to lichnom plane – mozhet byt', kak chelovek s atrofirovannoi sovest'iu, kak dovedennyi do absurda tip Raskol'nikova, povredivshegosia na idee torzhestvuiushchego ubiistva', Gromov summed up [**26**, 278]. 'U etogo rasskaza byl bolee glubokii smysl – smysl prorochestva i predskazaniia. Chekhov ran'she drugikh ponial, chem grozit ideia sverkcheloveka i kakoi ona budet, zhizn' po tu storonu dobra i zla' [**26**, 279].[42] Whilst we should not, perhaps, take the words 'prorochestvo i predskazanie' literally, but in the specifically Russian sense that I touched on in chapter one of this essay above, Gromov's setting of 'The Black Monk' within the history of 19th-century Russian and European ideas enables us to see the work as a penetrating moral analysis of issues that in the next century would become a matter of life and death to millions. Naturally, in his 1977 exposition of the work [**18**, 47–52] Gromov could not articulate this. In his last book, he compressed the seventeen pages of his 1989 treatment which we have just examined, into two powerful pages concentrating on the story's fascistic core [**29**, 252–53], and later commented explicitly: 'Slovosochetanie "chernyi monakh" ne imeet **nikakikh** polozhitel'nykh znachenii; s nim sviazyvaiutsia lish' rokovye, strashnye, tainstvennye smysly. Zdes' ponevole prikhodiat na um inkvizitory, kostry, gde ispepelialis' knigi, szhigalis' liudi, i eshche zastenki, pytki, bezumnye rechi, bezumnye dela' [**29**, 377–78].

Gromov's study of 'The Black Monk' is the culmination of his lifetime's investigation of the 'dialogue' between Chekhov and Dostoevskii. It is also the apotheosis of his view of the baleful part played by *idei* in Russian life and letters. Obviously, the two topics are not synonymous, but Gromov does identify points of contact between them. From here it is natural for him to proceed to the subject of Chekhov's agnosticism compared with Dostoevskii's religiosity and apparent belief in theocracy ['Krizis very', **26**, 281–88; **29**, 164–72]. Since this discussion is not primarily literary-critical, I shall pass over it and attempt to sum up.

One can scarcely overstate the courage and originality with which Gromov tackled the whole theme 'Chekhov and Dostoevskii', or how far-reaching the implications of his inquiry were. Let us recall that for about a hundred years these writers were regarded by most Russian intellectuals as mutually exclusive – and many still see them that way. But in Gromov's opinion the mere fact that, mainly through *The Adolescent*, Dostoevskii had an 'iznachal'noe vozdeistvie' on Chekhov, 'sushchestvenno oslozhniaet predstavleniia o tvorcheskom razvitii Chekhova' [**26**, 248]. The explicit references, 'hidden quotations', allusions, paraphrases and parodies of Dostoevskii that Gromov collated and examined clearly demonstrate that 'otnoshenie Chekhova k Dostoevskomu vyrazhalos' v formakh iskusstva i bylo otnosheniem khudozhestvennykh sistem, iz kotorykh odna predshestvovala drugoi i predveshchala ee v obshchem dvizhenii literaturnoi traditsii' [**26**, 250]. Simplifying somewhat, one can say that directly or indirectly Dostoevskii invades certain Chekhovian texts because he was the 'vlastitel' dum' *par excellence* of the period in which many of Chekhov's characters grew up. Not only that, specific passages in Chekhov [**26**, 251–52] showed that he shared a vital part of Dostoevskii's conception of realism: 'Dostoevskii i Chekhov vosprinimali deistvitel'nost' kak istochnik fantasticheskogo. [...] Miry, sozdannye imi, – raznye miry. No "krainosti skhodiatsia"' [**26**, 262]. There is little doubt that in a series of mature works Chekhov conducted a subtextual polemic with Dostoevskii about 'obshchaia ideia', the addiction to 'ideas' in Russian intellectual life, and 'bozhestvennaia bolezn'': 'Dolgie gody Chekhov protivostoial Dostoevskomu; eto bylo, byt' mozhet, samaia negromkaia, no i samaia glubokaia i soderzhatel'naia polemika v istorii russkoi literatury rubezha vekov' [**26**, 257]. Further:

> Ко многому у Достоевского — прежде всего к его воинствующему православию, в котором заключалась "общая идея" великого романиста, идея, спасающая мир, Чехов относился со сдержанным протестом, иногда с улыбкой:
>
> "Он [A potential Chekhovian character] пишет о "русской душе". Этой душе присущ идеализм в высшей степени. Пусть западник не верит в чудо, сверхъестественное, но он не должен дерзать разрушать веру в русской душе, так как это идеализм, которому предопределено спасти Европу.
>
> — Но тут ты не пишешь, от чего надо спасать ее.
>
> — Понятно само собой" (*Zapisnaia knizhka*). [**29**, 172]

Nevertheless, when in a famous letter to Diagilev (30 December 1902) Chekhov by implication accused Russian intellectuals of looking for 'the truth' in Dostoevskii, it was intellectuals Chekhov was criticising, not Dostoevskii. Chekhov's profound unease about the future of our planet, which may first have been aroused by his reading of *The Adolescent*, was very close to Dostoevskii's own: 'on tak zhe, kak Dostoevskii, chuvstvoval krepost' tsepi, soediniaiushchei proshloe s budushchim. Nastupaia, ono zastaet ne pervozdannyi mir, a lish' to, chto v nem sokhranilos' ot proshlogo. Rano li, pozdno li, no kogda-nibud' ono zastanet pustyniu' [**29**, 172]. Dostoevskii's hopes of 'averting' the scientific and technological revolution and 'returning' people to the religion of the past may not have been shared by Chekhov, but 'ved' i Chekhov ne dumal, chto nauka prineset vseobshchii mir i garmoniiu, on govoril, chto estestvennye nauki "dvinutsia na obshchestvo, kak Mamai..."' [**29**, 171].

In other words, Gromov's interpretation of the topic 'Chekhov and Dostoevskii' was an overwhelmingly *inclusive* one. The burden of his argument was that it was not a case of 'Chekhov or Dostoevskii', but of 'Chekhov *and* Dostoevskii'. The full significance of this for Russian literary criticism, and even Russian society in the 21st century, will be touched upon in my concluding chapter below.

CHAPTER 6

THE CHERRY ORCHARD

To be deeply rooted in the soil of the past makes life harder, but it also enriches it and gives it vigour. There are certain fundamental truths about human life to which men will always return sooner or later.

Dietrich Bonhoeffer

The most surprising feature of Gromov's 'last' book was a section on *The Cherry Orchard* [**29**, 350–85]. This was completely new. The last time Gromov had written at length on this play appears to have been in 1960 [**1**; **3**]. A comparison of the two essays is startling proof of the critical distance he had travelled in the intervening thirty years.

Gromov's 1960 examination, which was presented as a paper at the celebrations in Taganrog for the centenary of Chekhov's birth,[43] ostensibly focussed on the classic crux of *The Cherry Orchard*'s 'genre' – why Chekhov subtitled it a comedy.

We should recall the leaden atmosphere of those times in Russia. To have anything published in literary 'criticism' at all it had overwhelmingly to conform to the Party's literary-historical dogma. It is with a sinking heart, therefore, that one reads on the first page of Gromov's article that he will 'ob"iasnit' zhanrovoe svoeobrazie p'esy, iskhodia iz esteticheskoi teorii russkikh revoliutsionnykh demokratov' [**1**, 3]. One's heart touches bottom when a few pages later he informs us that 'mysli o komedii, vyskazannye v rabotakh Belinskogo i Chernyshevskogo, ob"iasniaiut komediinuiu prirodu "Vishnëvogo sada" **ischerpyvaiushchim obrazom i do kontsa** [My emphasis]' [**1**, 8].

In fact, however, this article is an intriguing blend of irreproachable orthodoxy and potential heresy. In retrospect, one sees that one should have been alerted to this possibility by the beginning of the sentence on the first page, just quoted: 'V dannoi stat'e **bez vsiakoi pretenzii na ischerpyvaiushchee razreshenie problemy** [My emphasis] sdelana popytka obobshchit' nekotorye nabliudeniia nad "Vishnëvym sadom", naibolee svoeobraznym i slozhnym zhanrovym postroeniem Chekhova, [i ob"iasnit' zhanrovoe svoeobrazie p'esy etc.]' [**1**, 3]. This suggests that what follows actually has two dimensions: an orthodox, exhaustively dogmatic one, and a personal, inexhaustive one. Moreover, the implication is that the 'exhaustive', official, 'explanation' is but a subset of the 'inexhaustive', unofficial, 'observations'.

The article proper opens with an examination of the 'misunderstanding' of the play's genre in pre-Soviet times (beginning with Stanislavskii's and Nemirovich-Danchenko's original production) and a review of accounts of its comedic nature by Soviet critics from Sobolev and Balukhatyi in the 1930s to Ermilov, Reviakin, and Gromov's elder contemporary Berdnikov [**1**, 4–7]. 'Gor'kii's' definition of the play as a 'lyrical comedy' is given an authoritative status. Altogether, Gromov's attitude to these views seems highly deferential and conventional.[44] Nevertheless, he sums them all up with the words:

> Легко видеть, что никто из критиков, исследователей и режиссеров пьесы не был вполне согласен с Чеховым в определении ее жанра — трагедия, драма, пародия на драму, комедия с элементами драмы, трагикомедия, лирическая комедия, но не просто **комедия**, как назвал "Вишнёвый сад" его автор. [**1**, 7]

It is at this point that he appeals to the, in Soviet terms, *superior* authority of Belinskii and Chernyshevskii.

Quoting Belinskii's statement that 'komicheskoe i smeshnoe – ne vsegda odno i to zhe, a smeshnoe dlia tolpy inogda sovsem ne smeshno dlia obrazovannogo klassa obshchestva',[45] Gromov commented: 'Esli nevozmozhno utverzhdat', chto Chekhov znal eti slova Belinskogo, to nel'zia somnevat'sia v tom, chto on razdelial ikh smysl' [**1**, 8]. To be honest, Gromov could offer no direct proof of either. He cited Chekhov's words to Ol'ga Knipper: 'p'esa [...] budet nepremenno smeshnaia, ochen' smeshnaia, po krainei mere po zamyslu',[46] and if we take the last two words to mean in English 'by intention/in conception' then they do imply a detachment in Chekhov's approach that contrasts with the immediacy, the physicality, of the word *smeshno* ('funny/risible/laughable'). Yet Chekhov still uses the word *smeshnaia* here, not *komicheskaia*. Could his understanding of *smeshnaia* be so detached and intellectual as to exclude actual laughter? It seems unlikely. Belinskii's statement 'komicheskoe i smeshnoe – ne vsegda odno i to zhe' surely implies that the 'comic' and the 'funny/risible/laughable' usually *are* the same. Gromov, however, rewrites Belinskii to assert: 'Komicheskoe i smeshnoe – ne odno i to zhe. Chekhov znal ob etom i [...] nazval komediei, ochevidno, ne smeshnuiu p'esu' [**1**, 8]. Whereas Belinskii had not said that the 'comic' and the 'funny/risible/laughable' were mutually exclusive, Gromov polarised them. He suggested that *The Cherry Orchard* was a 'high comedy' in the 'classic' tradition of Griboedov, Gogol' and Turgenev; by which he seemed to mean a play rooted not in laughter, but (quoting Berdnikov) 'v pafose razvenchaniia i osmeianiia opredelennykh obshchestvennykh iavlenii' [**1**, 9].

With the passing of the Soviet Communist system, we need not dwell on these arguments. Grotesque though it sounds, Berdnikov's cited views that *Woe from Wit* (*Gore ot uma*) or Turgenev's comedies had nothing at all to do with laughter closely corresponded to the reality of Soviet productions of these 'classics'. In claiming that *The Cherry Orchard* was not funny, Gromov was perhaps influenced by the theatre he knew. Even so, it is disappointing that in this article he appears to base himself on the Soviet politically correct notion of 'serious' humour. The mere fact that Chekhov described the play as a 'komediia, mestami dazhe fars' should have restrained Gromov from presenting it as an homogeneous, laughter-free 'high comedy'.[47] In any case, it is widely accepted in European culture that people find different things funny, i.e. that laughter is individualistic and comedy subjective.

This is precisely what Gromov could not accept in his 1960 article. He posits an 'objective' definition of comedy, based on Belinskii and Chernyshevskii:

> Комическое, по Белинскому, объективно, оно свойственно действительной жизни в определенные эпохи и времена. [...]
>
> [...]
>
> Высокая комедия возникает тогда, когда люди по логике событий утрачивают смысл своего бытия, сохраняя до времени прежнюю форму жизни.
>
> В этих условиях комическое проявляется как "несообразность, противоречие идеи с формою или формы с идеею", или, как писал, развивая эту мысль, Н.Г. Чернышевский [...]: "комическое есть перевес образа над идеею, иначе сказать: внутренняя пустота и ничтожность, прикрывающаяся внешностью, имеющею притязание на содержание и реальное значение". [**1**, 10]

This, Gromov maintained, is actually the 'source' of the comedy in *The Cherry Orchard*. The reform of 1861 cut the 'historical ground' from under the feet of the Russian gentry. All the characters 'ponimaiut, chto sluchivsheesia nepopravimo, chto nikakimi lekarstvami spastis' ot nakhlynuvshei novizny nel'zia' [**1**, 10], yet they continue to behave as though their social form still had content. This is conspicuously the case with Firs, Pishchik, Gaev and Ranevskaia herself [**1**, 10–15], but the respective Utopias of Lopakhin and Trofimov are also 'comically' out of joint with the increasingly revolutionary times [**1**, 15–21]. The servants 'parody' their masters' comic hubris and are therefore also 'comic', but each of them is 'izurodovan, iskalechen unizhaiushchei chelovecheskoe dostoinstvo sluzhboi' [**1**, 14], and this precludes them from actually being funny [**1**, 15].

Clearly, the socio-historical framework in which Gromov placed *The Cherry Orchard* was absolutely conventional for the times, right down to the extended quotation from 'Lenin' [**1**, 23]. Every official literary textbook would have expounded the same line. However, to argue that it was the 'objective' nature of reality in 1904 that made the play a *comedy*, rather than a drama/tragedy/history play, and to quote Belinskii and Chernyshevskii to prove it, was new or at any rate had not been done with such talent before. To the doyens of

Soviet literary-critical propaganda this must have seemed a considerable enhancement of the official line on *The Cherry Orchard*; which may be why the article was swiftly reprinted in abridged form in an 'All-Union' journal [**3**]. Even so, there are a number of aspects of Gromov's discourse that deserve closer scrutiny.

First, Gromov argues that historical inevitability is so irresistible that no-one is actually 'to blame' for anything in *The Cherry Orchard.* The plot of the play is propelled by 'estestvennyi khod sobytii' and everything that happens to the characters is 'dlia nikh fatum, zloi rok' [**1**, 11]. The source of the comedy is 'samo slozhenie zhizni' in Russia in 1904 [**1**, 12]. Subconsciously or consciously, Gromov even altered Trofimov's words to Ranevskaia in Act III, 'Ne nado obmanyvat' sebia', to 'Ne nado obviniat' sebia' [**1**, 10], supporting his thesis. This attitude to the nobility and bourgeoisie on Gromov's part could hardly be described as the conventional denunciatory one of necrophagous Bolshevism. In fact it enables him towards the end of the article to perform what amounts to an ideological somersault: 'Chekhovskaia komediia besposhchadna po otnosheniiu k usloviiam rossiiskogo bytiia i **polna beskonechnoi zhalosti k liudiam** [My emphasis], poskol'ku stradaiut eti liudi bezvinno' [**1**, 22]. Here he writes finely of the 'podlinnyi i vysokii gumanizm' that inspired Chekhov's 'sochuvstvie i zhalost'' towards his characters, and of the real impact of these Chekhovian values on Soviet audiences [**1**, 22].

Moreover, the article contains passages of such stylistic brutality and political cliché that they could be read as pure parody, e.g. 'V Rossii vremen "Vishnëvogo sada" byla lish' odna deistvitel'no revoliutsionnaia sila – proletariat' [**1**, 19], or (about Trofimov) 'Eta komediinost' ob"ektivno vytekaet iz polozheniia russkoi melkoburzhuaznoi intelligentsii, dolgo plutavshei po putiam revoliutsii pod znamenami gromkikh fraz' [**1**, 21]. In more than one place, Gromov appears to reduce his adopted authorities to absurdity: 'S tochki zreniia materialisticheskoi estetiki, na podobnom zhiznennom materiale Chekhov napisal by komediiu i v tom sluchae, esli by dazhe stremilsia sozdat' dramu' [**1**, 11]. The whole article is stylistically very varied – almost unstable – and this could well be a ploy in the best Aesopic tradition.

Finally, in the closing page and a half Gromov advanced ideas about *The Cherry Orchard* that were actually so un-Soviet that they could be made explicit only in his chapter thirty years later. Immediately after the passages in which he had touched on Chekhov's *zhalost'* towards his characters irrespective of class [**1**, 21–22], he considered the image of the cherry orchard itself. He wrote:

> Этот образ, в котором реализм был поднят Чеховым до одухотворенного символа, своими корнями уходит к самым истокам творчества Чехова.
>
> Идея, какую Чехов связывал с образом леса и сада, росла постепенно — от "Свирели" до "Скрипки Ротшильда", до монологов Астрова, до

> сложной символики, пронизывающей "Вишнёвый сад".
>
> Как "Фауст" у Гете, образ вишнёвого сада — дело целой писательской жизни.
>
> При всей своей сложности чеховский сад воплощает простую и ясную мысль: человек должен быть достоин своей земли, своей родины, своего сада, потому что "вся Россия — наш сад". [1, 23]

The paragraph beginning 'Kak "Faust" u Gete' is an early example of Gromov's highly crafted 'one-liners'. The paragraph that follows may seem bathetic by comparison, but it already intimates that Gromov's understanding of the image is more than 'environmental': his emphasis is on 'chelovek'. In fact he could develop his meaning only through a strained counterpoint with the official ideology. He explained that 'personazhi poslednei komedii Chekhova boleznenno i ostro oshchushchali pered litsom vishnëvogo sada svoiu nedostatochnost', svoe nichtozhestvo' [**1**, 23]. This is a considerable exaggeration, but it achieves its rhetorical purpose of wedding 'chelovek' in ideology-free terms to his 'rodina' or 'earth' in equally de-ideologised terms. Gromov then quotes Lopakhin's words from Act II: 'zhivia tut, my sami dolzhny by po-nastoiashchemu byt' velikanami' and relates them to the epic concept of the steppe, where Egorushka also dreamt of giants. The implication is clear: *The Cherry Orchard* is about the relationship of *people* to their *home* in a perspective of time that greatly transcends Marxist and historiographic notions. In a brilliant act of opportunism, Gromov promptly veiled this meaning again by coupling the image of 'velikan' to 'narod' and associating them both with a passage from 'Lenin' in which the latter talks of Russian history striding forward (to revolution, of course) 'in seven-league boots' [**1**, 23]. In other words Gromov reconnected his 'universal' argument with the narrow, 'class' view of the state ideology. After assuring us that 'Chekhov chuvstvoval, chto revoliutsiia ne za gorami, i radovalsia ee blizosti, ee sile, razrushitel'noi i zizhdushchei' [!], he even proceeded to expound the Party line on Chekhov, 'critical realism' and 'Gor'kii' in paragraphs of ineffable po-facedness [**1**, 23–24]. But all this was undercut by two vibrant sentences. He suddenly quoted the barely tolerated Dostoevskii: 'No uzhe Dostoevskii znal, chto "vsia deistvitel'nost ne ischerpyvaetsia nasushchnym, ibo ogromnoiu svoeiu chast'iu zakliuchaetsia v nem v vide eshche podspudnogo, nevyskazannogo budushchego slova"' [**1**, 24]. The implication was that *The Cherry Orchard* lived by 'that which it is not yet' and its meaning transcended 1904, 1917, 1960, and the whole Soviet fetish of 'history'. The article ended with another 'one-liner': '"Vyshnëvyi sad" – eto povestvovanie o proshlom, napisannoe v nazidanie budushchemu' [**1**, 24]. This and the sentence about Dostoevskii were removed when it was transferred from the provincial to the central press.

Gromov's first essay on *The Cherry Orchard* can be seen, then, as the *nec plus ultra* of the Soviet line on the play, but one that contains charges of such dissidence as to blow it apart altogether. Nevertheless, there is no denying that the piece's approach is essentially historical, or at least diachronic. Gromov's placing of the play in historical time and his view that the characters are 'blameless' reminds us of his interpretation of *Fatherless*. My objections would therefore be similar. A play is the antithesis of 'history' because it is a special experience of fellow humans in real time. To sit through a play 'interpreting' it with a diachronic filter is not to experience it as a play at all. To claim that its characters are 'blameless' appears to deny that they are responsible for their own lives; which is to deny that they are human. In the West, at least, the felt and perceived comedy of productions of *The Cherry Orchard* (i.e. people laughing aloud or to themselves) derives, I would say, largely from the belief that its characters *are* responsible for their own lives. The Bakhtinian concept of 'reduced laughter' might be useful in discussing the range of laughter that *The Cherry Orchard* provokes, but comedy can hardly remain comedy if its laughter is reduced to the point of no return, as the 'revolutionary democrat' and Soviet authorities on the subject adduced by Gromov in 1960 appear to advocate.

The essay by Gromov on *The Cherry Orchard* in his 1993 book is virtually the diametric opposite of his 1960 exercise in that it concentrates on what looks like the *synchronic* impact of the cherry orchard as image/symbol upon the theatre audience (more precisely, as we shall see, the reader). Actually it tells the history of the play's autobiographical sources, social background, MKhT première and first publication with the kind of originality and assurance that come from a lifetime's familiarity with Chekhov research [**29**, 350–61]. But the historicist reading of the play is explicitly denied fairly early on:

> В комедии в самом деле отразились реальные перемены, происходившие в русской пореформенной жизни. Начались они еще до отмены крепостного права, ускорились после его отмены в 1861 году и на рубеже столетий достигли драматической остроты. Но это всего лишь историческая справка, правда, совершенно достоверная, но мало раскрывающая суть и тайну "Вишнёвого сада". [**29**, 356-57]

Subsequently, the *exclusively* historical appreciation of Trofimov's speech to Ania in Act II about the orchard's past, so familiar to Russians (Gromov writes) from their Soviet schooling, is described as a 'dovol'no vul'garnaia [sotsiologicheskaia] [...] kharakteristika uzhasov krepostnichestva' [**29**, 370].

Gromov commences his own interpretation of the poetic resonance of the words 'vishnëvyi sad' by examining Bunin's criticism that Chekhov had 'ves'ma maloe predstavlenie o dvorianakh, pomeshchikakh, o dvorianskikh usad'bakh, o ikh sadakh', that there never were Russian landowners' gardens that were 'all' cherry trees, that if 'parts' of these gardens were cherry trees then these never grew **'kak raz vozle** gospodskogo doma', that cherry trees are not at all beautiful, that it is utterly improbable Lopakhin would order the cherry orchard to be cut down before the previous owner had left, and so on [**29**, 365–66].[48] Such a demand for 'ortodoksal'nyi realizm' is, Gromov notes, 'amazing' in a writer of Bunin's calibre, and he briefly considers how a masterpiece like Bunin's own 'Legkoe dykhanie' ('Light Breathing') falls short of it [**29**, 366–67]. 'Suzhdeniia Bunina o "Vishnëvom sade"', Gromov concludes, 'vedut k pervoosnovam istorii literatury i poetiki: iskusstvo i zhizn', predmet i slovo, simvol, metafora, byl'' [**29**, 367]. Tolstoi was 'right' to denigrate Chekhov's plays in the same breath as Shakespeare's, because both dramatists do not aspire to *that* kind of '**pravdopodobie**' [**29**, 368]. On the other hand, one could adduce pre-revolutionary encyclopedias and gardening books to 'prove' that there were such cherry orchards, even 'vokrug barskikh domov'; but this argument would also be irrelevant to explaining the orchard's poetic power:

> этот "реальный комментарий" ничего, в сущности, не опровергнет и не объяснит: старых барских домов и усадеб в России давно уже нет, нет и садов, которые некогда их окружали и осеняли; а "Вишнёвый сад" по-прежнему ставится — и на русской сцене, и в Англии, и в Японии, где Раневских, Лопахиных, Гаевых, Семеонов-Пищиков не только в наши дни, но и в прежние времена быть не могло и, естественно, никогда не бывало. [**29**, 368]

It would be better to say that the orchard is a '**simvolicheskii sad**' [**29**, 368], but with ironical reference to clotted academic definitions of 'literary symbol' Gromov shows that this too is inadequate: 'Net vozmozhnosti korotko i skol'ko-nibud' iasno skazat', chto v etom slovosochetanii – "Vishnëvyi sad" – ot mifa, chto ot znaka i obraza. No vpolne iasno, chto "Vishnëvyi sad" sut' **slovosochetanie**, vynesennoe avtorom v zaglavie p'esy' [**29**, 369].

Clearly, Gromov has shifted his focus from the cherry orchard as theatrical representation (design) to 'the cherry orchard' as words; and he is surely right. One senses that most of the audience are disappointed by the way the cherry orchard is depicted in any production. For Bunin the cherry trees in MKhT's production were not 'realistic' enough – the blossoms were, he felt, ridiculously big and prolific. Perhaps, though, Stanislavskii had deliberately 'denaturalised' them in order to suggest a more symbolic presence; he could have been influenced by the way cherry blossom is depicted on Japanese theatre prints. As Gromov observes, 'Ob"iasniaia Stanislavskomu, chto na stsene dolzhen byt' ne "vishnevyi", a "vishnëvyi" sad, Chekhov, byt' mozhet, kak raz i predosteregal ot nenuzhnykh konkretizatsii, ot "bytovizma", kotoryi tak meshal Buninu poniat' p'esu, i ne emu odnomu...' [**29**, 370]. Chekhov's distinction accentuates the verbal source of the orchard's potency. Because we *hear* the words *vishnëvyi sad* in a multiplicity of mouths and contexts throughout the play, of course we construct our own mental image and understanding of the orchard. Like 'the Forest of Arden' it becomes, in effect, a private concept. The particular way in which the words have worked upon us will be unique to each of us (the effect will be as personal as poetry), and the chances of a scenic cherry orchard being able to do justice to that are statistically remote.

What, then, does the cherry orchard symbolize, or rather what do the words *vishnëvyi sad* 'designate', or, as Gromov puts it, what are the 'semantic boundaries' of this 'combination of words' [**29**, 369]? In answering this question, Gromov produced some of the most inspired, lapidary, and personal pages he ever wrote.

His immediate answer is: 'Trud i vremia. Meru trudov chelovecheskikh, meru chelovecheskoi zhizni' [**29**, 369]. If a tree is thirty years old, it might have been planted by our father. If another is a hundred years old, it brings to mind our great-grandparents. If another is several hundred years old, if we can say of it, for example, '"eto derevo videlo Petra I"' [**29**, 369], then we think of our ancestors. But according to Gromov we also think of the earth in which these trees are growing; of the care lavished on them to prevent their being destroyed in times of trouble and social upheaval. We think: 'Nuzhna preemstvennost' pokolenii, kotorye smeniaiut drug druga' [**29**, 370].

There is a temptation to regard *preemstvennost'* as an essentially Russian concept that is almost untranslatable into English. It certainly formed one of the deepest-held beliefs of some Russian writers of the 20th century (Mandel'shtam, Pasternak, Bakhtin and others). However, although the idea of 'succession' inherent in it may be peculiarly Russian, its basic meaning appears to be 'cultural continuity', or 'tradition' in Eliot's sense of 'the means by which the vitality of the past enriches the life of the present'.[49] Evidently *preemstvennost'* is peaceful, evolutionary, and predicated on growth, rather than violent, revolutionary, and predicated on chopping down. It was, therefore, a highly subversive concept in the Soviet period (although the régime had its own official version of it). It became almost a byword of the liberal intelligentsia and press in the *perestroika* period. The last sentence of Gromov's that I have just quoted therefore reads as both indirect speech and a personal *cri de coeur*.

If the words *vishnëvyi sad* imply *preemstvennost'*, Gromov continues, then they produce a constant counterpoint between the 'absolute present' of stage events and the idea of the 'flow of time'. This implies during the playing of the play that 'nastoiashchee otnositel'no, ono tsenimo tol'ko na fone proshlogo i v perspektive budushchego' [**29**, 370]. Moreover, the very sounds of the words communicate 'nechto **nasushchnoe** dlia dushi chelovecheskoi, pust' dazhe nedobroi i cherstvoi dushi. Ne zhivopisnost', ne staromodnaia poetichnost', a kakaia-to oseniaiushchaia dukhovnost' i neporochnost', protivopolozhnaia suetnosti i zlu' [**29**, 370]. For a moment, Gromov seems to approach the distinctively Orthodox view of the religious function of beauty. The words *vishnëvyi sad* become a kind of aural icon.

Of course, this discussion is a graphic illustration of untranslatability; of the apparently unbridgeable chasm between the impact of words in one language and in another. The aesthetic qualities of the Russian words *vishnëvyi sad* are very different from those of 'cherry orchard'. Even semantically the latter is impoverished, since 'cherry' would seem to emphasize the fruit of the tree, where *vishnëvyi* on Chekhov's lips speaking to Stanislavskii emphasized the blossom. 'Orchard' suggests agriculture, where *sad* is primarily 'garden'. In English, 'cherryflower garden' might seem the closest that one could get semantically to the Russian, but apart from its quirkiness the word 'garden' here excludes the possibility implicit in the Russian that it could also produce commercially, i.e. double as 'orchard'.

The fact that *sad* means both 'orchard' and 'garden' enables Gromov to set the 'semantic boundaries' of *vishnëvyi sad* far more widely than those of 'cherry orchard'. An orchard, he writes, whether cherry, apple or anything else, is not possible 'bez doveriia k zhizni; zatsvetaia vesnoi i k oseni prinosia plody, on soediniaet proshloe s budushchim' [**29**, 371]. The image of a 'garden', however, 'khranit v svoei serdtsevine ideiu vremeni, tochnee – ideiu chelovecheskoi zhizni, tekushchei iz roda v rod'; in all the world's languages, he surmises, 'garden' (i.e. *sad*!) 'simvoliziruet dolguiu mirnuiu zhizn', idushchuiu ot pradedov k pravnukam, dolgii neustannyi trud, bez kotorogo sovest' ne byvaet spokoinoi' [**29**, 371]. In other words it taps into the meanings and connotations of the very word 'culture'.

In these days of agribusiness, urban gardens and short tenancies, Gromov's conception of orchards and gardens may seem hopelessly romantic. Yet it is undeniable that the concept of the 'garden' has a long, rich, and indeed 'romantic' history associated with humanity's deepest material and spiritual aspirations. At this point Gromov naturally juxtaposes *vishnëvyi sad* with all the other mentions of gardens and orchards in Chekhov [**29**, 371–73]. It is unfortunate, in my view, that one of his prime examples is 'The Black Monk', because, as discussed in the previous chapter, what Gromov regards as the 'gardener' Pesotskii's commitment to economic/cultural achievement strikes the present writer more as frenetic empire-building and an obsession with dynastic continuity. But, discussing 'The Head Gardener's Tale' ('Rasskaz starshego sadovnika'), Gromov is surely justified to claim that

> само неустанное трудолюбие этих чеховских садоводов основано на какой-то древней философии, на идее единства людей, еще свободных от эгоизма, от взаимной подозрительности и вражды — не только друг к другу, но и к земле, на которой они рождаются сами и потом растят своих потомков и свои сады. [**29**, 372].

With evident feeling, he concludes that Chekhov's gardeners possess 'osoboe, pust' utopicheskoe doverie k cheloveku, bez kotorogo ne vyrastish' sad. I ne sokhranish' zhivuiu dushu. A sad u Chekhova – da i v zhizni tozhe – vsegda simvol nasledstvennogo ili potomstvennogo dolga ili truda' [**29**, 373].

Even so, one regrets that he maintains at this point that '"Vishnëvyi sad" edva li vpolne poniaten bez obrashchenii k drugim chekhovskim povestiam i rasskazam, kotorye proiasniaiut i kommentiruiut etu p'esu' [**29**, 372]. By definition, a work of art is never 'fully understood'. One is tempted to say that Gromov's statement is meaningless. It also raises the ghost of 'systemism'. An audience sharing the experience of a play is even less a set of literary critics than readers of a Chekhov short story are, since such an audience is absorbed (one could say 'trapped') in the 'now' of performance and if it is a good performance the audience has no other 'time' in which to be comparative. A play succeeds *as a play* through its own life on the stage, not by reference to extraneous bearings such as history, biography, or the writer's other works.

Gromov's digression is insignificant, however, because for the most part he is so focussed on the universal, one might say synchronic ('live') meaning of the cherry orchard. He excels in producing pithy definitions of this – of what *vishnëvyi sad* actually means to the characters of the play and what it may conjure up for Russian audiences:

> Вишнёвый сад — едва ли не самый сложный из всех символов нашей литературы, обращенный к нашей душевной памяти, ко всем значениям слов и их сочетаний: сад, вишневый цвет, красные вишни на солнце в листве, вишневые сережки (и все, что связывает с ними наша собственная, "личная" память); но также — зори и росы, дожди и радуги, гудение пчел и голоса птиц — вообще все поэтические отзвуки, какие только возможно вообразить или представить себе, до заключительной ремарки. [**29**, 373]
>
> Особенность словосочетания "вишнёвый сад" в том, по-видимому, и заключается, что оно не имеет в нашем языке никаких отрицательных значений; это абсолютный положительный смысловой полюс русского словаря. И, напротив, словосочетания "ударить по дереву топором", "подрубить корни", "сломать ветвь" выражают высшую степень безнравственности и безрассудства.
>
> Вишнёвый сад в пьесе Чехова — меньше всего декорация, на фоне которой философствуют, мечтают о будущем и торгуются персонажи. Сад — олицетворение ценности и смысла жизни на земле, где каждый новый день вечно ответвляется от минувшего, как молодые побеги идут от старых стволов и корней. [**29**, 374]
>
> Вишнёвый сад — не только "краса земная", передающаяся от рода к роду, но еще и купель нравственности, поэтическое лоно, где не проросло еще ни единой былинки скверны или греха. [**29**, 376]

Although the final section of Gromov's essay contains some literary-theoretical speculation on the nature of 'symbols' and the function of titles as keys to whole works [**29**, 375–79], statements such as the above form the heart of this 'last word' about the play. Evidently they address the specific poetic suggestiveness of the words *vishnëvyi sad* in what one might term 'real time', the theatrical or reading present of the receptive individual. They seem to carry great personal conviction.

Nevertheless, whilst Gromov's interpretation of the words *vishnëvyi sad* is synchronic, his conception of the *symbol* and his understanding of the *play* are more diachronic. This is inevitable given that he sees a garden as the expression of *trud* over a long period of *vremia*, i.e. as *preemstvennost'*, a cultural process. Discussing Bunin's criticism of Lopakhin's precipitate chopping down of the trees as 'improbable', Gromov comments:

> Удивительно, что Бунин написал эту страницу уже в эмиграции, в свои поздние, преклонные годы, прекрасно зная обо всех выкорчеванных садах, рощах, лесах, о снесенных усадьбах и храмах; он знал, что в новейшей русской истории, разворачивавшейся на его глазах, ежедневно сбывалось как раз то, что он считал невозможным, "невероятным", и если в последней комедии Чехова было что-либо по-настоящему правдоподобное, так это лопахинское нетерпение, с каким рубили вишни... [**29**, 366]

Trofimov he characterises as one of those 'vechnye studenty, tsel' kotorykh – zhertvennaia iskupitel'naia gibel' vo imia budushchego, a vovse ne terpelivyi trud radi nego' [**29**, 379]. Trofimov's 'bezdomnaia raskhristannost'' contains 'nechto rokovoe, kak [...] pozdnee, uzhe na nashei pamiati – v prezrenii k galstukam, shliapam, tufel'kam na kablukakh, vsiacheskoi kosmetike; zhenshchiny v krasnykh kosynkakh, s korotkoi strizhkoi; bednye shifon'ery v bednykh komnatakh, gde pochti nichego – ni odezhdy, ni bel'ia; bezdomnye deti' [**29**, 380]. In other words, one of the contexts in which Gromov views the play is that of recent Russian ('Soviet') history. As with *Fatherless*, this leads him to regard aspects of it as prescient. To western critics this may seem a strange reason for valuing the play. The link between a businessman chopping down an orchard in 1904 and Bolsheviks devastating the national heritage later in the same century may strike such critics as tenuous. But as Gromov says, 'budushchee Ani i Peti stalo nashim proshlym' [**29**, 380]. For Russians the futurological dimension of the play itself cries out to be tested against what actually happened – their history, the common memory. Diachronically, or perhaps we should say 'metaphorically', Lopakhin's action is indeed 'the same' as that of the Bolshevik destroyers of the 'old' culture. If the cherry orchard symbolises cultural continuity, then Lopakhin's iconoclasm is analogous to what Mandel'shtam called the smashing of the 20th century's 'spine' by Bolshevism. Retrospectively, there *is* a direct link between Trofimov's 'bezdomnaia raskhristannost'' and the aridity of 'Soviet life'.

In this his 'last' book, Gromov went further. After 1917 every character in *The Cherry Orchard* who did not escape from Russia would have suffered a violent death, death from starvation, death from epidemic, or death from forced labour: 'budushchee, v sushchnosti, est' tol'ko u togo rebenka, kotoryi, mozhet byt', poiavitsia u Duniashi. Eto on stanet pisat' v ankete: "iz krest'ian"' [**29**, 380]. Moreover, Chekhov's play rebuts the whole philosophical basis of Bolshevism:

В сущности, по-русски нельзя и сказать: "Мы насадим новый сад" (разумеется, молодой, а не новый), как нельзя заменить свое прошлое иным, обновленным. Это противоречит духу нашего языка, духу живущей в языке совести; это небывальщина, реникса, как говорит в "Трех сестрах" Кулыгин, все равно что "новое" море, "новая" степь... [**29**, 374].

Ania has acquired the idea of a 'new' orchard from Trofimov, whom Gromov describes as 'nesomnenno, "novyi chelovek" v dukhe Chernyshevskogo' [**29**, 379], i.e. the latter's *What Is To Be Done? (Tales about new people)* (*Chto delat'? (Iz rasskazov o novykh liudiakh)*). As history has shown, 'new people' can be produced only by doing the equivalent of destroying trees: denying people's genes, rewriting their past, brainwashing them, uprooting them, or 'liquidating' them altogether. Gromov's concept of *vishnëvyi sad* stands in opposition to the whole history of the Russian radical movement. The futurological fantasies of the play, he says, are akin to the proto-Bolshevik Chernyshevskii's 'Chetvertyi son Very Pavlovny' with its crystal palace [**29**, 380].

Finally, in a manner reminiscent of his approach to 'The Steppe', Gromov relates the image of the orchard/garden to *pre*-historical time. In his essay on *The Cherry Orchard* this happens less explicitly than as a consequence of the essay developing from the previous section in the book, 'Chelovek i priroda', in which Gromov devoted much space to the symbolism of trees. '"Prosto derev'ev"', Gromov wrote there, 'u Chekhova net, oni vsegda oznachaiut nechto gluboko chelovecheskoe i literaturno znachitel'noe' [**29**, 347]. 'Chasto obraz dereva [u Chekhova] khranit v svoei glubine vospominanie o dushe, dolgo skitavsheisia po svetu ili vsego lish' pobyvavshei na svete' [**29**, 348]. Trees are 'obitaemy, i ne samimi soboiu, a proshlym. Otsiuda ikh tainstvennaia zhizn' v nashem soznanii i iazyke, ikh vechnoe ocharovanie' [**29**, 349]. In our consciousness the tree is 'zhivoe sushchestvo, ego i odushevliat'-to ne nuzhno: zhivet, dyshit. I v samom dele olitsetvoriaet zhizn' ("vot eti kleikie, kleikie listochki...") [A version of Ivan's words in *The Karamazov Brothers*, Part 2, Book 5, Chapter 3, also alluded to by Mandel'shtam in his poem 'Ia k gubam podnoshu etu zelen'']. Ono zhivet, khranit proshloe – v samom sebe, v svoei serdtsevine' [**29**, 349–50]. In the essay on *The Cherry Orchard* this became:

есть древности в музеях и сокровищницах, но дерево, сад, лес — это все же совсем иное, **живое** прошлое. Дерево ведет счет своим и нашим годам, наслаивая год за годом кольца вокруг сердцевины, оно в самом реальном смысле **дышит** [...].

Для персонажей пьесы вишнёвый сад — не столько надследственное имение, сколько олицетворенное прошлое, общее для старых и молодых. [**29**, 373]

Trees and gardens, Gromov contends, have a primordial, mythological quality. Thus the play itself is a 'poeticheskii vymysel: v izvestnom smysle eto skazochnyi, polnyi skrytykh podrazumevanii, slozhnykh olitsetvorenii i simvolov mir, sokhraniaiushchii tainy istekshego vremeni, otoshedshei pory. Eto dramaturgicheskii mif, i, byt' mozhet, luchshim zhanrovym dlia nego opredeleniem bylo by sleduiushchee: mifologicheskaia komediia' [**29**, 363].

If the words *vishnëvyi sad* evoke an 'archetypal' image as Gromov suggested *step'* is, then like *step'* one of its chronotopes is *epic* time. The 'garden' stretches back from the present until it is 'lost in time'. The characters have come together, in Gromov's words, 'v kakoi-to **misticheskoi** [My emphasis] [...] nadezhde spasti staryi sad, starinnoe rodovoe imenie, i svoe proshloe, kotoroe kazhetsia im teper' takim prekrasnym, i samikh sebia' [**29**, 362].

Gromov discusses, then, synchronic, historical and epic time in the image of the cherry orchard. Does this imply a confusion on his part? I do not think so. Rather, taken together his treatments of these dimensions imply that the 'cherry-flower garden' trope is *panchronic*: it generates rich meanings in whatever context of time Gromov chooses to see it, starting with the 'absolute' present of the audience/reader and ending with the 'timeless' mythic. 'Est' v etoi p'ese nechto [...] vechnoe' [**29**, 357].

If there is any confusion in Gromov's approach to the time-dimensions of *The Cherry Orchard*, I feel it derives from his previous section, 'Chelovek i priroda' [**29**, 338–50]. There he created the impression that nature in Chekhov has a primarily *historical* significance. Stories such as 'The Reed-Pipe' ('Svirel'') fix the historical fact noted by Dostoevskii and Leont'ev that by the 1880s the Russian environment was in full retreat before industry [**29**, 342]. 'V chekhovskikh opisaniiakh prirody vsegda est' sootnesennost' vremen' [**29**, 344], hence his descriptions are 'always' diachronic. But the example that Gromov chooses, 'The Student' ('Student'), is, surely, untypical of Chekhov's treatment of nature in that the hero specifically relates the landscape he sees in real time to historical times – 'pri Riurike, i pri Ioanne Groznom, i pri Petre' (PSSP (Works), 8, p. 306). To claim that this work has a defining importance because it was Chekhov's own 'favourite story' [**29**, 345] seems spurious.[50] Contrasting Chekhov with his French contemporary Jules Renard, Gromov claimed that the latter 'ne dogada[lsia], chto dlia uspekha eti "malye formy" nuzhno napolnit' istoricheski znachitel'nym soderzhaniem' [**29**, 347]. Quoting a passage from Astrov's ecological speech in Act III of Uncle Vania [**29**, 348], Gromov changed the adjective 'istreblennykh' to 'istoricheskikh' so that it read: 'Da, ia ponimaiu, esli by na meste etikh istoricheskikh lesov [pro]legli shosse, zheleznye dorogi' (there seems to be no textological authority for this). He asserted that 'sobstvenno, opisanie prostranstva, esli ono khudozhestvenno, ponevole metaforichno – ono zakliuchaet v sebe predstavlenie o vremeni i smene vremen velikoi istorii' [**29**, 345]. In his essay on *The Cherry Orchard*, therefore, one expects him to elaborate the orchard's 'historical' connections. Towards the end he declares that 'khudozhestvennaia novizna "Vishnëvogo sada" skryta v ego simvolakh, uvodiashchikh nas v glubiny istoricheskoi pamiati' [**29**, 379], but as we have seen, the only historical context in the strict sense of the word 'historical' that he relates the orchard to is 'recent' (i.e. 20th century) Russian history. In fact he is far more concerned here with the image's *pre*-historical 'womb'. The sentence just quoted concludes: '[uvodiashchikh nas] k drevneishim gorizontam khudozhestvennogo soznaniia', a concept familiar to us from Gromov's 'epic' view of 'The Steppe'.

The overwhelming virtue of Gromov's exposition of the words/symbol *vishnëvyi sad* is that, as I hope my earlier quotations have shown, it proceeds from a belief that the cherry orchard embodies *values*. These values, apprehended in their different ways by all the characters except Sharlotta [**29**, 373], come from the past and imply a culture of non-violent, creative, spiritually fulfilling hard work whose product, in the ancient tradition of Russian 'philokalia', is *beautiful*. Instead of transient historical 'ideas', Gromov posits values in the cherry orchard that are 'absolute'. Many will deny that such values exist, but Gromov's demonstration that the image of the garden/orchard addresses 'all times' is as palpable a proof that these values are absolute as one could ask for in a work of literary criticism. In his 'last word' on *The Cherry Orchard* Gromov has elevated the poetic image at its heart to a moral level that transcends historical 'conditioning'. Whilst sensitive to the image's potential historical contexts, he treats these as functions of its 'panchronic' vitality. In this section of his 'last' book, then, the glimmer of hope ('obraz, v kotorom realizm byl podniat Chekhovym do odukhotvorennogo simvola' [**1**, 23]) discernible through the Soviet murk of his article thirty-three years before, was superlatively fulfilled.

But what of the *people* of *The Cherry Orchard*, who manifestly do not cultivate their garden?

Gromov has very little specifically to say about them. They are 'plokhie khoziaeva' [**29**, 359]; Trofimov suffers from 'infantilism' [**29**, 380]; Ranevskaia does not know the value of money partly because 'dazhe dom ee, sad – ne den'gi, a pamiat'' [**29**, 380] and partly because in Russia 'iz-za deneg, kazhetsia, nikogda eshche ne stradali i dazhe ne rabotali vser'ez' [**29**, 382]. Gromov sees the protagonists as being gripped by 'bespechal'noe otchaianie, chuvstvo rokovoi viny i polneishaia bezzashchitnost' pered siloiu i obmanom: bud' chto budet, i poskoree by v Parizh...' [**29**, 351–52]. They have nothing to do but 'tomit'sia i zhdat'':

> событие, из-за которого они съехались, происходит за сценой, а на самой сцене никакого "действия" в традиционном смысле этого слова, собственно говоря, нет: ждут. В сущности, пьесу нужно играть как сплошную четырехактную паузу, великую паузу между прошлым и будущим, наполненную ворчанием, восклицаниями, жалобами, порывами, но главное — молчанием и тоской. Пьеса трудна и для актеров, и для зрителей: первым играть почти нечего — все держится на полутонах, все — сквозь сдер-

жанные рыдания, полушепотом или вполголоса, без сильных порывов, без яркой жестикуляции. [**29**, 362]

In fact, he writes, they are not so much characters as 'personifications' that 'vosprinimaiutsia kak nastroeniia (tochnee, kak chuvstvo obshchei trevogi)' [**29**, 384]. Firs, Ranevskaia, Gaev and Pishchik 'olitsetvoriaiut proshloe, i chuvstvo sostradaniia k nim smeshivaetsia s chuvstvom styda i boli za proshloe' [**29**, 384]. Moreover, 'edva li ne v kazhdom personazhe "Vishnëvogo sada" est' svoeobraznaia dvoistvennost': oni ne tol'ko vykhodiat na stsenu [...], no eshche i kazhutsia zriteliu znakomymi po knigam' [**29**, 379]. Gaev, Ranevskaia, their house and the orchard remind us of Turgenev, particularly *A Nest of Gentlefolk* (*Dvorianskoe gnezdo*) [**29**, 357]; Trofimov with his rejection of 'proud Man' in Act II recalls 'Gor'kii's' *The Lower Depths* (*Na dne*) [**29**, 380]; Firs is a literary dinosaur [**29**, 366]; and so on.

All of this is far indeed from how the play has increasingly been seen in the West, or at least Britain, by audiences and critics alike. Obviously, unless we are very conscious of the tragedy of recent Russian history, we will not attune ourselves to the *post*-revolutionary historical resonance of the cherry orchard as a symbol. (Britain has, of course, had its fair share of sub-Soviet productions presenting the play as a Marxian model of *pre*-revolutionary socio-politico-economic forces.) Nor are we likely to focus on its 'panchronic' meaning, because the poetic suggestiveness of the English words 'cherry orchard' is feeble compared with the Russian *vishnëvyi sad*. We are more likely to regard the cherry orchard in context as an aesthetically moving symbol of the immediate past and one that is above all a player in the synchronic life – the plot – of the characters. I am tempted to suggest that in Formalist terminology Gromov is so preoccupied with the *siuzhet* of *The Cherry Orchard* as embodied in the symbol, that he overlooks the play's *fabula*, indeed denies that it has one. Strange confirmation of this may be contained in his belief that Ranevskaia was 'deceived' by Lopakhin, who 'promised' her money to buy the orchard but then bought it himself for a song [**29**, 352]. In fact Lopkahin offers to obtain 'about 50,000' venture capital *if* she changes her mind and decides to go ahead with the dachas (Act I). Later he almost screams at her and Gaev that investors would give them 'skol'ko ugodno' if the two of them accepted his plan (Act II). But they will not, and this negative decision is a vital event in the plotline of the play, which can be summarised as the story of how the orchard was abandoned to its fate by *people*. Actors in modern English productions understand very well that this is the story they are telling. Most western directors now realise that Chekhov's plays have a narrative spine of the finest steel and that one of their principal tasks as directors is to give this spine adequate theatrical clarity. The notion that the actors have 'almost nothing to act' [**29**, 362] is the very opposite of my own experience working with English actors on *The Cherry Orchard*. Not only do they believe that as characters they are free agents entirely responsible for the 'story' of the orchard, but the interpersonal stage life of the characters is so replete with possibilities and choices as to be an actor's dream. To take but one example, in rehearsal it is discovered that the amorous/sexual relationships of the characters are endlessly suggestive and open to modulation. The richness and comedy of the synchronic life of the characters, coupled with the actual strength of its storyline, is what has given *The Cherry Orchard* its enormous popularity in the British theatre today.

Again we are aware of substantial cultural difference. Gromov would appear to deny the *fabula* of the play because he cannot accept that its protagonists are self-responsible. He believes that a 'rokovaia vina' hangs over them [**29**, 351], but this is culpability for the past – they are 'defenceless' and 'helpless', he believes, in the present [**29**, 351–52, 363]. There seems little doubt that he is more interested in the play's literary and diachronic life than its life as a theatrical experience in real time.

This is borne out, perhaps, by Gromov's preference for *reading* Chekhov's plays: 'esli chitat' i perechityvat' ikh vnimatel'no i netoroplivo, vsegda est' nechto dostupnoe slukhu, no uskol'zaiushchee ot glaza, nechto bol'shee, chem stsenicheskoe deistvie' [**29**, 364]. One has no difficulty accepting that a play has separate legitimate lives as 'the text for the mind's eye, and [...] the stage as a worthy scaffold',[51] but it would seem inappropriate to privilege reading over performance in the case of *The Cherry Orchard*, since it was written explicitly for MKhT's actors to perform. Again, Gromov's implied assumption that in the Russian theatre one is a spectator rather than a listener (by 'slukhu' he presumably means the 'inner ear' of contemplative reading) has a long cultural history.

The 'nechto' that Gromov believes can be better appreciated from a reading of *The Cherry Orchard* is 'ochen' pokhozhe na tomlenie dukha, na svoeobraznoe neobychnoe nastroenie, kotoroe inache, kak chekhovskim, pozhalui, i ne nazov'esh': nichego podobnogo v mirovoi dramaturgii do "Diadi Vani", "Chaiki", "Trekh sester" i "Vishnëvogo sada" ne bylo' [**29**, 364]. Gromov excels in analysing the origins of this *nastroenie* in *The Cherry Orchard*. 'Mozhno bylo by skazat', chto Chekhov pobuzhdaet nas videt' mir i samikh sebia s elegicheskim razdum'em o proshlom' [**29**, 374–75]; which is to say Chekhov awakens our *conscience* [**29**, 375], just as Ranevskaia's is in Act I ('O, sad moi! [...] esli by ia mogla zabyt' moe proshloe!') and Act II ('Uzh ochen' mnogo my greshili...'). The feeling of yearning for and shame for a past that 'kak-nikak nuzhno iskupit'' [**29**, 384] communicates itself to us from the characters, our compassion wells up, and this 'ves'ma protivorechivaia, neopredelennaia i slozhnaia smes' chuvstv i nazyvaetsia "chekhovskim nastroeniem"' [**29**, 384]. Under Gromov's pen it becomes a heady, almost unbearable mixture:

А жизнь течет своим чередом, и все чувствуют, что она течет, что сад

> будет продан, что уедет Раневская, уйдут Петя с Аней, умрет Фирс. Жизнь течет и проходит — со всеми воспоминаниями о прошлом и мечтами о будущем, с тревогой и сильным нервным беспокойством, которым наполнено настоящее, то есть время сценического действия "Вишнёвого сада" — беспокойством до такой степени напряженным, что на сцене и в зале становится трудно дышать. [**29**, 363]

It would be naive to deny the existence in the play of the angst that Gromov is describing, or the plausibility of his diachronic explanation of it. At the same time, one is apprehensive of indulging such powerful, addictive emotions and one recognises from his description a type of production of *The Cherry Orchard* that has had a long history in Russia but in Britain now seems to be extinct. If the Chekhovian *nastroenie* or *toska* is allowed to combine with a belief that the play's characters are wholly passive or blameless, then again we literally lose the plot of *The Cherry Orchard* and all theatrical quickness dies.

The subject directly impinges on the issue of the play's laughter. Gromov considers here the question of the play's genre, but in a totally different way from his 1960 article. There is no theoretical speculation about the nature of comedy, let alone mention of the 'revolutionary democrats'. Instead, the question is approached entirely empirically, in literary-historical and theatrical-historical terms:

> В идеальной пропорциональности сочетаются традиционные мотивы и образы с художественной новизной, с непривычной трактовкой сценического жанра (комедия), с историческими символами огромной глубины. Трудно найти пьесу, которая была бы до такой степени связана с литературным фоном, романами и пьесами недавних памятных лет — с "Дворянским гнездом" Тургенева, с "Лесом", "Горячим сердцем", с "Волками и овцами" Островского — и в то же время до такой степени отличалась бы от них. Пьеса написана так, с такой прозрачностью литературных соотнесений, что старый роман со всеми его коллизиями, разочарованиями просто не мог не прийти на память при взгляде на Гаева и Раневскую, на старый дом, на декорации вишнёвого сада. "Здравствуй, одинокая старость, догорай, бесполезная жизнь..." [From *A Nest of Gentlefolk*] — это должно было вспомниться и в самом деле вспоминалось, так что К.С. Станиславский и В.И. Немирович-Данченко прочитали и поставили "Вишнёвый сад" скорее как традиционно тургеневскую элегию прощания с прошлым, чем как пьесу во всех отношениях новую, созданную для будущего театра, будущего зрителя. [**29**, 357]

Immediately after this passage, Gromov interpolates with minor changes five paragraphs from his 1960 essay [**1**, 4] that describe Chekhov's annoyance at the play being billed as a 'drama' and Stanislavskii insisting that it was a 'tiazhelaia drama russkoi zhizni' [**29**, 357–58]. Yet the new documentary material that Gromov brings in at this point produces a fundamental paradox. In two letters to Chekhov of April 1904 Knipper recounts that the doyen of theatre critics, Kugel', has told the MKhT company that they 'dolzhny igrat' tragediiu, i ne poniali Chekhova' and 'on nakhodit, chto my igraem vodevil'' [**29**, 358]. The long quotation Gromov reproduces next, from Suvorin's review of 29 April 1904, makes the same point: 'razrushaetsia nechto vazhnoe, razrushaetsia, mozhet byt', po istoricheskoi neobkhodimosti, no vse-taki eto tragediia russkoi zhizni, a ne komediia i ne zabava' as, he complained, MKhT were playing it [**29**, 358]. In other words, whatever the two directors' 'take' on *The Cherry Orchard* and the traditional critical/biographical view that they distorted the play out of all recognition, the evidence is that Chekhov actually got from them much of the 'komediia, mestami dazhe fars' that he wanted.[52]

It is extremely tempting to conclude that the reason Gromov did not resolve this paradox was that he himself was divided on the issue. He appears to have no difficulty in referring to the play in his 1993 essay by the shorthand 'komediia' (in context, 'the comedy'). He was perfectly well aware of Chekhov's own description of the play's genre in his letters, and in fact admitted: 'avtora ne peresporish'' [**29**, 358]. But his own account of the literary ancestry of the play (see above) suggests that he agrees with Stanislavskii and Nemirovich in wanting to direct it as a 'traditsionno turgenevskuiu elegiiu proshchaniia s proshlym' [**29**, 357]. Gromov's own interpretation of the orchard – the centrepiece of his essay – is, as we have seen, 'serious'; in philosophical, spiritual and poetical terms almost agonizingly so. He ends his consideration of the play's comedy early in his essay with words that seem to me indisputable: 'Vozmozhno, zhanr "Vishnëvogo sada" – problema ne formy, a mirovozzreniia' [**29**, 358]. In the thirty or so years separating his first word on the play from his last, he had shifted from an insistence on defining comedy 'objectively' to precisely the subjective understanding that he originally rejected. At the beginning of his 1993 essay he seems happy to leave the question open. Yet this is not his final word on the subject, either. The essay itself ends:

> "Вишнёвый сад" в своем третьем измерении глубоко нетрадиционен, полемичен по отношению к традиции, о которой непрерывно напоминает, погружая зрительный зал в элегическое прошлое русской литературы, так что слезы просятся на глаза... Возможно, "Вишнёвый сад" обращен к иным поколениям, для которых тургеневские ассоциации и мотивы уже не будут значить так много, как для нас, и тогда основное содержание комедии — то, что делает ее комедией — выступит на первый план, и люди засмеются там, где мы до сих пор не смеемся, и сочувственно улыбнутся там, где мы тайком утираем слезы. [**29**, 385]

There seems little doubt from this that Gromov himself found *The Cherry Orchard* not funny 'yet'.

Gromov's 1993 essay addresses far more themes than we have space to discuss here. It is almost as though he set out to touch on the entire 'mnozhestv[o] slozhnykh problem, voznikaiushchikh pri vsiakom obrashchenii k "Vishnëvomu sadu" – inye iz nikh poiavilis' tak davno i reshaiutsia tak dolgo, chto kazhutsia nerasreshimymi' [**29**, 365]. He casts a new light on the autobiographical background of the play [**29**, 351–56] and the biographical frame of its première [**29**, 350–51, 357–61, 382–85], he gives a limpid account of the symbiosis of Chekhov's stories and plays [**29**, 361], and he presents excellent insights into themes ranging from the reception of *The Cherry Orchard* in Japan [**29**, 350] to the stage design of Chekhov productions generally [**29**, 363–64]. The themes are not necessarily dealt with in sections that develop 'logically' from each other: many of them appear unexpectedly and promptly disappear in order to reappear later. Hence the essay is organised more as a piece of music than a prose argument, with statements, developments, rests, recapitulations and variations. An intriguing consequence of this is that one may discover assertions in different parts of the essay that apparently contradict each other but in reality simply reveal Gromov's sense of counterpoint, his ability to look at a question 'both ways'. For example, he may suggest on page 372 (as discussed above) that the play cannot be understood 'fully' without knitting it to Chekhov's *povesti* and *rasskazy*; but much earlier he has made an admirable denial that there can be such a thing as a definitive theatrical reading of the play at all:

> Опыт современных режиссерских трактовок и всяческих театральных экспериментов красноречиво свидетельствует, что не все ясно и для нас, что гениальное творение неисчерпаемо, что сценическое воплощение "Вишнёвого сада" — задача вечная, как постановка "Гамлета", например, и что новые поколения режиссеров, актеров и зрителей будут искать свои ключи к этой пьесе, столь совершенной, таинственной и глубокой. [**29**, 359-60]

It is partly the style and quality of writing in this essay that make one want to return to it again and again. The ostensibly 'fragmentary' manner in which its exhaustive range of topics is presented impels one to re-read it in order to 'compose' these topics, to 'assemble' Gromov's 'arguments'. Yet the net effect of re-reading, I find, is to discover different emphases each time; to see the essay as a whole differently on each reading. There is a sense, indeed, that it has been deliberately written in a semi-artistic manner to make it 'inexhaustible'. It is endlessly challenging and suggestive, so that at every point one feels drawn into a dialogue with its author about a great, shared work of art. It abounds with fresh-cut, aphoristic sentences that flash straight into one's memory ('"Vishnëvyi sad" sogret i oveian osobennym chuvstvom – chuvstvom proshlogo' [**29**, 374]) and I defy anyone to be unmoved by Gromov's explanation of why the two words *vishnëvyi sad* constitute the 'absoliutnyi polozhitel'nyi smyslovoi polius russkogo slovaria' [**29**, 374]. No other writing on *The Cherry Orchard* that I know analyses more profoundly the poetic-iconic meaning of the play and its significance as a national myth. Clearly, Gromov's essay is inspired by personal passion and belief. It is wholly appropriate that he wrote it at the very end of his life and elected to close the literary part of his 'last' book with it.

If such a magnificent achievement can leave one with any sadness, it is that, in acknowledged disagreement with *The Cherry Orchard*'s own creator, even after thirty years Gromov was unable to *laugh* with the play, to accept it as a comedy, in effect to embrace the 'mirovozzrenie' that construed its action as funny. In literary-critical terms I have suggested this was because Gromov overlooked the tensile *fabula* of the play and chose (perfectly legitimately) to focus on the diachronic nature of its *siuzhet*, rather than the play's interpersonal life in real theatre-time.

A more mundane and depressing explanation might be that Mikhail Gromov was born, grew up and died 'v toi zemle, chto ne liubit shutit'', as Gogol' put it.[53]

CHAPTER 7

SCHOLAR, CRITIC, WRITER, MAN

There are important other areas of Gromov's writing on Chekhov's life and works that would have to be considered in a full-length study before a proper appraisal of him as a Chekhov critic could be offered. Nevertheless, it seems reasonable even in a relatively short essay to attempt some answers to the question that has perhaps been forming in the reader's mind over the preceding six chapters: how good a scholar and literary critic is Gromov?

Immediately, I think, we must acknowledge the 'fact of difference'.[54] Gromov writes about Chekhov from within Russian culture and a Russian tradition of what constitutes literary criticism. I have read him with, I hope, as much understanding of that culture and tradition as I can muster. But I need make no apology for reading him also from within my own culture and literary-critical tradition. We must take adequate cognizance of the fact that the two sets of cultures and traditions are *different*. In our attempt at appraisal we must expect, indeed insist on, dialogue between what is understood by scholarship and literary criticism in the one culture and in the other. We should expect a fertile mismatch between the vocabularies used in the two languages, and not be amazed when there simply are not words in one language to express concepts in the other.

A prime example is the word *chekhoved.* I believe Russians would agree that this word has no critical or qualitative content. The suffix *-ved* expresses merely 'knowledge about'. There is no suggestion in the word that a *chekhoved* might be an exponent of the highest standards of academic inquiry, learning, accuracy or truth; so it may not be rendered in English as 'Chekhov scholar'. Equally, the word does not imply that its bearer might be engaged in evaluative literary analysis, so it may not be rendered as 'Chekhov critic'. The most, I imagine, that it conveys in English terms is 'Chekhov specialist' or 'Chekhov expert'. As such, it was perfectly tailored to the Soviet period: the Leninist-Stalinist state did not need 'scholars' wedded to idealistic, individualistic notions of quality and integrity, it certainly did not want 'critics' of anything, it simply needed Chekhov 'specialists' to go with the other 'specialists' that made up the 'Soviet intelligentsia'. The word was therefore applied as a levelling term to anyone 'working on' Chekhov, great or small. In fact it became, and still is, somewhat pejorative. It carries distinct overtones of Soviet vulgarity, since the literate form of the word (as originally used in the early 1920s) is *chekhovoved* and *chekhoved* queerly suggests some kind of 'Czech specialist'.

Yet how might one express the concept 'Chekhov scholar' in Russian? The basic word for 'scholarship' is *nauka*, which usefully also means 'science'; the basic word for 'scholar' is *uchenyi*, which also means 'scientist'; and *filolog* replicates much of the flavour of 'literary scholar'. But it seems that the Russian language does not permit the coupling of these words with 'Chekhov' to produce a form like 'Chekhov scholar', or even 'scholar studying Chekhov'. Of course, longer Russian paraphrases (in effect glosses) of the concept 'Chekhov scholar' are possible, but I have yet to encounter one that either fully conveys the implicit senses of 'scholar' in English or sounds really Russian. *Chekhovist*, on the analogy of *pushkinist*, sounds, surely, as frivolous and pejorative as *chekhoved*. We must recognise the possibility, then, that the concept 'a Chekhov scholar' does not exist in Russian and is not actually expressible in that language, just as the audible Soviet nuances of *chekhoved* cannot be conveyed in English.

In Soviet parlance Gromov was a *chekhoved* and he presumably tolerated this as his Soviet job-title. In English, I believe, we can make a strong case for describing him as a Chekhov *scholar*, in the way that we speak of the most painstaking, knowledgeable and creative editors of Shakespeare as 'Shakespeare scholars'.

Gromov was the only person to edit a volume of Chekhov's fictional prose in the Complete Works single-handed; in fact he edited two (PSSP (Works), 1, 4) and the remaining dozen volumes (PSSP (Works), 2, 3, 5–13, 18) were edited by between three and twelve people, including, of course, Gromov himself. It is a very considerable achievement. For volume 1 he presented 484 pages of verified text for 63 of Chekhov's earliest works, 53 pages of manuscript and published variants, 56 pages of factual notes, and an introduction in which he listed 87 periodical sources that he had searched for the years 1877–83 plus 24 lost works identified by him from a complete survey of Chekhov's letters, contemporaries' memoirs, and editorial 'postboxes 'between 1877 and 1882 [**11**, 553–57]. For volume 4 he performed similar labours single-handedly for 98 stories from the years 1885–86 and wrote a more discursive introduction in which he gave valuable accounts of Chekhov's move from the comic weeklies to the St Petersburg newspapers, and contemporary reviews of the stories [**17**, 456–66]. In between, he collaborated editorially with Dolotova, Sokolova and Chudakov on volume 3, stories of 1884–85 [**16**]. He also edited 'The Steppe', identified its variants and wrote its commentary [**19**], did the same for 'A Man in a Case', 'Gooseberries' and 'About Love' [**20**] and, of course, presented the most complete edition ever published of *Fatherless* [**21**]. He devoted approximately twenty-five years of research to the Complete Works; well over half his working life. His scholarship in these volumes appears exhaustive and exact. If one did not suspect that Gromov would protest at being singled out, one would be tempted to describe him as clearly the leading Chekhov scholar among the group that produced the Complete Works between 1964 (when the group was formed) and 1983.

Yet even Gromov's editorial contribution to the Complete Works is not the summit of his achievement as a scholar. As we saw in chapter 2 above, his relentless searching through libraries and archives, and his Holmesian application of logic, led to him tracking down what are most likely the first three publications and the title of the first planned book by Chekhov. It is given to extremely few scholars to make discoveries of this order about classic writers. Nor was there an element of luck in Gromov's finds: they were the result of years of hard work and rigorous deduction. Taken together with his fastidious investigations of textual correspondences between Chekhov and Dostoevskii, and between Old Russian literature and 'The Steppe', they surely qualify him to be called one of the greatest *filolog*'s, or 'literary scholars' (if that is how we choose to translate the Russian word), that Russia produced in the 20th century.

However, although the quality of Gromov's Chekhov scholarship was an adornment to the Complete Works, one cannot say that he himself was well served by some of its editorial policies. The latter seem inconsistent. They occasionally compromise Gromov's achievements.

To some it might appear admirably rigorous to insist that the first three Chekhov publications Gromov had discovered should be printed in the 'Dubia' section of PSSP (Works), 18; to others, aware of the far less rigorous scholarly standards applied elsewhere in the Collected Works, it might seem severe or even disparaging [**23**, 235–39].

In the case of *Fatherless*, the general editors went to the other extreme. They approved of Gromov describing the manuscript as 'belovaia' [**21**, 393] and explicitly stating in his introduction to volume 11:

> пьесы располагаются в хронологическом порядке (по времени написания), при этом первая драма "Безотцовщина" и драматический этюд "На большой дороге" не отнесены в раздел "Неопубликованное. Неоконченное": не напечатанные при жизни Чехова, они были подготовлены автором к постановке и полностью завершены. [**21**, 381]

Yet the unfinalised nature of the manuscript and the play's running-time of eight hours indicate that Gromov's assertion could not possibly be true of *Fatherless*. Moreover, the general editors presented the text of this play in volume 11 as though it were actually entitled by Chekhov *Bezottsovshchina*. That is, although the word was placed in the equivalent of square brackets in the text and contents, it was given a capital letter *as though it were the title of a play*. In fact, in the only two documented contemporaneous mentions of this 'title' (in Aleksandr Chekhov's letter of 14 October 1878), it is written with a small letter and in one instance without quotation marks at all.[55] To me this suggests in context that it was at most a 'working title', but more likely just jocular shorthand between the brothers for the *subject* of the play. It is, of course, a very good description of the play's over-arching subject; but numerous arguments could be put forward for it being a terrible *title* which Chekhov, like his brother, might never have dignified with a capital letter and quotation marks. Intriguingly, in his introduction to the play in the Complete Works Gromov is scrupulous in punctuating the quotation from Aleksandr's letter accurately [**21**, 396], but in his books he presents it as though in both instances Aleksandr wrote *bezottsovshchina* with a capital letter and in quotes [**26**, 53; **29**, 68].

Another example of Gromov being ill served by the general scholarly standards of the Complete Works is the publication in PSSP (Letters), 10, p. 33, of a letter purportedly written by Chekhov to Lidiia Avilova between May and September 1901 and purportedly signed by him 'Alekhin'. Somewhat unwillingly, the editors of the volume admit that 'tekst vosstanovlen Avilovoi po pamiati i iavliaetsia otvetom na ee shutlivuiu zapisku, pozdravliaiushchuiu Chekhova s zhenit'boi' (PSSP (Letters), 10, p. 304); but they do not mention that Avilova 'reconstructed' the text of her 'congratulatory note' as well. There is no independent evidence that either text existed. It is somewhat unsettling, then, that the general editors did not apply to Avilova's 'letter' the same rigorous scholarly criteria that they applied to Gromov's 1878 discoveries – and publish it, if at all, in their own epistolary 'Dubia' section in the same volume, entitled 'Nesokhranivshiesia i nenaidennye pis'ma' (PSSP (Letters), 10, pp. 532-48). As Gromov put it, 'nuzhno verit'' in the existence of this correspondence [**26**, 306; **29**, 269]. Unfortunately, he meant this phrase positively: despite the gaping hole in the evidence, he felt one *should* accept that Avilova's note and 'Alekhin's' reply really existed. He devoted considerable space in both of his books to the 'liubovnaia taina' [**26**, 309; **29**, 273] that he strenuously believed was shared by Chekhov and a woman whom a recent biographer has described as Chekhov's 'most deluded admirer'.[56]

These instances do not, I think, detract from Gromov's own scholarly standards within the strictly scholarly (*nauchnyi*) context of the Complete Works. However, in the West it is generally expected that the same standards of scholarly rigour will be practised in literary criticism. Here it has to be said that in western terms Gromov seems to fall short.

Naturally, I have not checked the wording and source of every quotation in Gromov's critical writing. Merely in reading, though, I have been alerted by dozens of peculiarities which on checking turned out to be manifestations of what western academics might call misquotation.

These 'misquotations' are of various types. In the first instance, Gromov's publications have perhaps more than their Soviet quota of misprints and ragged footnotes. It is understandable that Firs' word *vrazdrob'* might come out in print as *vrazbrod'* [**1**, 12], that an editor might not know why Chekhov wrote in 'The Little Joke' 'pod navozom eshche sneg' and change it to 'pod zaborom eshche sneg' [**26**, 212], or that even in 1993 the word *polovaia* might have to be cut (without acknowledgement) from a quotation of one of Chekhov's letters [**29**, 93]. It seems less likely that changing 'obmanyvat' 'to 'obviniat'' [**1**, 10], 'bezottsovshchina' to 'Bezottsovshchina' [**26**, 53 etc], 'istreblennykh lesov' to 'istoricheskikh lesov' [**29**, 348], or Pushkin's 'No mramor sei ved' Bog' to 'No kamen' sei ved' Bog' [**29**, 216] is the result of straightforward error, because these modifications fit too well with Gromov's own context – with *what he was trying to prove at the time*. Could he, perhaps, have been quoting from memory? I shall consider this question in a moment. He could hardly, however, have inserted unacknowledged into his own text five verbatim lines from the Soviet *literaturoved* Svetlov 'from memory' [**26**, 93, lines 6–10], or edited and completely rearranged an extended quotation from 'Easter Eve' ('Sviatoiu noch'iu') simply because that is how he remembered it [**29**, 170].

Yet the biggest class of what in western parlance would be misquotations is of a different and much more interesting kind. Let us restrict ourselves to seven examples.

Concluding his interpretation of 'A Boring Story' in his 1977 article and 1989 book, Gromov writes:

> Таким образом обесценивается дело жизни: наука, медицина, тот духовный подъем, который овладевал им в университетской аудитории, где он понимал, что "вдохновение — не выдумка поэтов, а существует на самом деле", — все это ничтожно в сравнении с апокалиптическим видением "общей идеи", заслоняющей его жизнь "как гора, вершина которой исчезает в облаках". [**18**, 46; **26**, 257 with minor changes]

Clearly, the second half of the sentence, from 'vse eto nichtozhno', is crucial to Gromov's argument about the role of the Dostoievskian *ideia* in the story. The last six words in inverted commas are a quotation from Chekhov's text (PSSP (Works), 7, p. 279) and in Gromov's sentence seemingly confirm how 'apocalyptic' the hero's vision of an *obshchaia ideia* is for him. However, in their context in the story they do not remotely refer to this problem: 'v prisutstvii zhe takikh liudei, kak Gnekker [The hero's prospective son-in-law], moi zaslugi kazhutsia mne vysochaishei goroi, vershina kotoroi ischezaet v oblakakh'. The quotation has therefore been appropriated to Gromov's own context, for his own use. It gives a wholly misleading impression of the importance of the concept of *obshchaia ideia* in Chekhov's text. Similarly, when Gromov writes: 'V "Skuchnoi istorii" "chitatel' uvidel...geroev i avtora, kotorye umnee ego"' [**26**, 254] and his reference tells us that the last eight words are from a Chekhov letter (PSSP (Letters), 3, p. 217), we assume they refer to 'A Boring Story'. In fact they refer to Paul Bourget's novel *Le Disciple* and there is not a word about

'A Boring Story' in Chekhov's letter.

Gromov's claim that Chekhov was radically influenced by Dostoevskii and in particular that *The Adolescent* and *Fatherless* are intertextual, is one of his most innovative theses. One is taken aback, however, to discover that what Gromov has presented as a revealing general statement by Chekhov about Dostoevskii as a benchmark of 19th-century Russian chronology, namely '"V 1839 g." – eto malo govorit...i...pozhalui, luchshe bylo by tak: "Kogda Dostoevskomu bylo 20 let"', is in its original context merely a piece of technical advice to someone who had sent Chekhov the draft of a lecture to a French audience on Dostoevskii [**26**, 261] (letter to Ia.S. Merpert of 29 October 1898, PSSP (Letters), 7, p. 315). Numerous times, as we have seen, Gromov identifies as Dostoevskii the 'russkii belletrist' referred to by Glagol'ev 1 in *Fatherless*; but on turning to the last three pages of *The Adolescent*, on which Gromov bases his claim, we note that in context Dostoevskii is not speaking of himself, but of a theoretical novelist ('voobrazhaemyi romanist'[57]). Indeed in context it is not Dostoevskii speaking/writing, nor even the first-person narrator, but a minor character.

When we go to the actual letter in which Chekhov used the words 'eti liudi rodilis' v moei golove ne iz morskoi peny, [...] ne sluchaino' (PSSP (Letters), 3, p. 115) we find they refer to the characters of *Ivanov*, rather than the 8500 inhabitants of Gromov's catalogue with whom he juxtaposes them in his context [**26**, 238]. When, after reading as a personal utterance of Chekhov's an admirable passage about the future of freedom in Russia [**26**, 126], we look up its source, we realise that it is actually the utterance of a character in a draft of 'A Terrorist's Tale' ('Rasskaz neizvestnogo cheloveka') (PSSP (Works), 17, pp. 195, 439). In Gromov's essay on 'The Steppe' we read: 'Nakonets, sama step', dikaia i svobodnaia vol'nitsa – "kuda ono vse devalos'? ... tut i gusi byli, i zhuravli, i utki, i tetereva – tucha tuchei... Poshli prakhom i orly, i sokoly, i filiny ...a novoe ne rastet" ("Svirel'")' [**29**, 198]; yet 'The Reed-Pipe' is set in wooded country and the word *step'* never occurs in it.

There seems little doubt that many western commentators would regard such a use of quotation as 'spin'. But how does it appear in a Russian perspective?

It is a 'fact of difference' that Russians, and especially *filolog*'s, commit large quantities of literary text to memory. They deeply 'internalise' such text. In a sense they make it 'theirs'. Consequently when they have to 'externalise' it again, for example as a quotation in their own text, they do not feel the need to check it against the original. They quite frequently reproduce it in 'their' version, as though it is more important to them that it is now theirs than that it was once someone else's (even Bakhtin did this). We know from third-party accounts that Gromov could recite literary texts from memory for hours. One explanation, therefore, for Gromov quoting inaccurately or 'out of context' could be that in his writing he often quoted 'from memory' in both the narrow and the wider sense: he may well have remembered the word *obmanyvat'* as *obviniat'*, and he may well have recalled a string of words such as the last-quoted from 'The Reed-Pipe' when seeking ways to express *his own* thoughts, then gone to the text and transferred them irrespective of the words' own setting. Either way, it is questionable whether in a western context his approach to quotation would earn the adjectives *bezuprechnyi* and *skrupuleznyi* that have been applied to him by Russian commentators.[58]

In the search for deeper explanations of Gromov's 'misquotations' we should, I believe, relate the latter to other peculiarities of his scholarship as it is practised in his literary criticism.

A special case of misquotation is his tendency to present the direct/indirect speech of literary characters and narrators as utterances of the author personally. Gromov does this throughout his *oeuvre*, but here are three classic examples:

> Случайно, по Чехову, лишь конкретное время "личной" жизни, но не сама жизнь: в ней "ничто не случайно, все полно одной общей мысли, все имеет одну душу, одну цель, и, чтобы понимать это, мало думать, мало рассуждать, надо еще, вероятно, иметь дар проникновения в жизнь, дар, который дается, очевидно, не всем". [**22**, 35]

> Наука в целом и естественные науки в особенности развиваются в конфликте с религиозным сознанием и верой; Толстой и Достоевский понимали это столь же ясно, как Чехов. "... Коли Бога бесконечного нет, то и нет никакой добродетели, да и не надобно ее тогда вовсе... Стоит только религии хоть немного уступить, как сейчас же лезет наука", — сказал Достоевский. [**29**, 171]

> "Русская жизнь, — писал Чехов незадолго до "Степи", — представляет из себя непрерывный ряд верований и увлечений, а неверия или отрицания она еще, ежели желаете знать, и не нюхала. Если русский человек не верит в Бога, то это значит, что он верует во что-нибудь другое". [**30**, 204]

To me as an English reader, the phrases 'po Chekhovu', 'skazal Dostoevskii', and 'pisal Chekhov' mean that these two authors uttered the quoted words in expression of their views as individuals (and not even as 'authors'). The phrases imply 'thought', 'believed', 'was of the opinion that'. Admittedly, at the end of the first and third quotations Gromov gives in brackets their sources – the stories 'On Official Business' ('Po delam sluzhby') and 'Under Way' respectively. But to the English reader this only makes the claim that these are Chekhov's views more paradoxical. In fact, it is quite clear in context that the first Chekhov quote is not even the narrator's view but the thoughts or free indirect speech of the third-person hero Lyzhin, and the last quote is direct speech from another third-person hero, Likharev. In the second example, Gromov does not tell us where Dostoevskii said these words. The first quoted sentence is direct speech of Smerdiakov's in *The Karamazov Brothers*, Part IV,

Book 11, Chapter 8, the second quoted sentence I have been unable to trace.

From the point of view of our appraisal of Gromov as a literary critic, this phenomenon might seem a rather defining flaw. It would hardly occur to an English reader to seize on the views of a character in Jane Austen, say, as Austen's own. In Russia, of course, there has been a long tradition of regarding creative writing as didactic and writers as 'teachers'. Gromov himself attempted to deconstruct this tradition where Chekhov was concerned (most explicitly at [**26**, 5]). He was certainly aware of Chekhov's own impatience with readers who identified him with his characters.[59] It may seem a peculiarly western assumption that a character's views are *not* its author's, but in the 1970s there was lively discussion about this very point among the young *chekhoved*'s toiling with Gromov on the Complete Works. The consensus was perhaps best expressed in print at that time by Bakhtin: 'Avtor – sozdaiushchii – ne mozhet byt' sozdan v toi sfere, v kotoroi on sam iavliaetsia sozdatelem.'[60] It is intriguing, then, that Gromov should regularly fall into the 'trap' of interpreting created utterances in Chekhov and Dostoevskii as monological 'authorial' assertions, or, at least, deploy them monologically for his own purposes.

The subject invites comparison with Gromov's attitude to evidence and proof in his literary criticism. As we saw, his theory of intertextuality between *The Adolescent* and *Fatherless*, and between Dostoevskii's journalism and 'The Steppe', fails to meet his own condition of the name Dostoevskii appearing in Chekhov's texts. In his first book he attached enormous importance to Chekhov having seen and heard Dostoevskii deliver his speech on Pushkin at the 1880 celebrations: 's etogo vremeni nachalos' vliianie Pushkina i Dostoevskogo' [**26**, 78] (why not of Pushkin and Turgenev, since the latter was also there?). Yet by his 1993 book he was forced to admit there was no documentary evidence that Chekhov had been present. Other, potentially fruitful hypotheses/assertions are dropped from later publications with no explanation. For instance, in his first essay on *The Cherry Orchard* Gromov quotes (without bibliographic details) a long passage from N.K. Mikhailovskii which he forcefully concludes was the model for Trofimov's longest speech to Ania at the end of Act II: 'Nichto ne utracheno v monologe Trofimova: ni mysl' o neoplatnom dolge, ni dazhe obraz tsvetka, ni ideia iskupitel'nogo i ochishchaiushchego stradaniia – ochen' trofimovskaia, no sovsem-sovsem ne revoliutsionnaia ideia' [**1**, 19]. As far as I know, this extremely interesting observation was never repeated in Gromov's *oeuvre*. Why not? Similarly, the thought-provoking thesis put forward in Gromov's 1962 article [**4**, 138–39] that the young Chekhov had a special relationship with his mother, rather like D.H. Lawrence's say, is never returned to. Why not? Despite the conviction behind his extended 1962 assertions on the subject, did Gromov subsequently discover that there was insufficient documentary evidence for it? It is forgivable, I think, if one involuntarily speculates along these lines.

In fact, Gromov's work is peppered with highly challenging statements that either seem perverse, or can be easily refuted, or for which he gives no evidence whatsoever. In his 1967 article on Chekhov's first publications he claimed that if all the lost works and letters that Chekhov wrote in his Taganrog years could be gathered together they would form 'po krainei mere odin tom [...] polnogo sobraniia sochinenii i pisem Chekhova', and informed his readers: 'Esli by etot utrachenyi tom byl sobran, kogda ego eshche vozmozhno bylo sobrat', to v nem nashlis' by razgadki dlia vsekh neiasnostei, probelov i tain, nad kotorymi stol'ko let lomaiut golovy biografy Chekhova' [**7**, 163; **26**, 85; **29**, 54]. 'Dlia **vsekh**?' one cannot resist asking. In listing Russian philanthropists who could have helped Chekhov in his own charitable projects if he had wanted them to, Gromov mentioned the 'Morozovy', i.e. the family of Savva Morozov, adding: 'tozhe znakomye, dazhe odnofamil'tsy (Evgeniia Iakovlevna [Chekhov's mother] byla iz Morozovykh, pravda ne stol' bogatykh i znamenitykh)' [**26**, 339; **29**, 255]. Yet 'Morozov' is an extremely common Russian name and it is rather blithe of Gromov to suggest Chekhov's mother was of the 'same' *Morozovy*: although it may be true, where is the evidence? Gromov informs us as fact that 'Chekhov – etogo ne stoit zabyvat' – byl osnovopolozhnikom beskorystnoi russkoi meditsiny' [**29**, 260; **31**, 23], but omits to mention thousands of other *zemstvo* doctors with similar principles. Elsewhere he tells us Chekhov 'liubil dorogu, liubil glukhie lesa, gribnye mesta, no nikogda ne okhotilsia' [**29**, 339]. But what of Chekhov's passion for fishing and his famous shooting expedition with Levitan? How could Nicholas II have been influenced in giving Chekhov a medal by the royal family's visits to 'all Chekhov's plays, from *Uncle Vania* to *The Cherry Orchard*' [**26**, 23], when the tsar's award was dated as early as 28 December 1899? In his last essay on *The Cherry Orchard* Gromov mentions that the play was performed in a bombed-out theatre in Japan in 1945 and 'ego smotreli liudi, perezhivshie atomnyi pozhar Khirosimy, po-svoemu ponimavshie final: "Slyshitsia otdalennyi zvuk, tochno s neba, zvuk lopnuvshei struny, zamiraiushchii, pechal'nyi. Nastupaet tishina..."' [**29**, 350]. This is a moving rhetorical and poetic juxtaposition, but is it based on fact? How does Gromov know that the Japanese audience made this connection? He does not tell us.

I do not think this is nit-picking. Beneath these and other examples there seems to lie a methodological and philosophical problem. Gromov asserts, but he very rarely questions, analyses or debates his own assertions. Even when presenting a major hypothesis, he persists with what he considers confirmations of the hypothesis, but he does not consider the possible refutations. The blatant instance of this is his theory of the influence of Dostoevskii on Chekhov. As we have seen, on closer inspection the biographical-epistolary evidence and the explicit textual evidence in *Fatherless* and 'The Steppe' collapse. This does not seem to worry Gromov. On the other hand, there is good explicit textual evidence in *The Wood Demon*, 'Ward N° 6', 'Neighbours' and 'A Terrorist's Tale', and I have suggested that a close verbal analysis of *Fatherless* by computer might substantiate its intertextuality with *The Adolescent* even though the name Dostoevskii never features in the play (I do not see why this should be a 'condition' anyway). Yet such arguments are not the burden of Gromov's proof either. His evidence mainly takes the form of a series of quotations from Dostoevskii's characters or journalism 'juxtaposed' with sentiments expressed by Chekhov's characters [**26**, 67–68, 156–57, 247–48, 250–52, 255–56, 259, 272–73, 280, 284–85]. These collocations are evidently intended to confirm Gromov's theory of influence; doubts or arguments that might tend to refute them are not considered. In fact it could be claimed that Gromov presents his Dostoevskii theory in such a way as to make it seem incapable of refutation, because his account of the incident with Nemirovich-Danchenko [**26**, 249–250] suggests that the one fact which might be taken as irrefutable proof of lack of influence, namely a documented point-blank denial by Chekhov that he had ever read *The Adolescent* (for example), could never be taken at face value and hence accepted as evidence.

Altogether, I feel that the way Gromov presents his literary hypotheses and interpretations is dogmatic. To name other major examples, Gromov believes that *Fatherless* is absolutely central to any true understanding of 'Chekhov' and he will not seriously address its artistic failure or the possibility that Platonov bears personal guilt; according to Gromov the world of interpersonal life, men's business and women's compassion is not at all interesting in 'The Steppe' [**26**, 183], perhaps because he himself is overwhelmingly interested in its historical dimension; and in his mature view *The Cherry Orchard* is entirely about the contemplative image of the orchard, its characters bear no personal responsibility for the orchard's fate, and Chekhov was misguided to call the play a comedy. This is not to mention the confidence with which Gromov applies the tautologous 'systemist' approach to Chekhov's work. Borrowing the phrase he used when accepting Avilova's account of her 'love affair' with Chekhov, 'nuzhno verit'' in many of Gromov's controversial claims, as they can be neither proved nor disproved.

To western commentators the conclusion may appear irresistible that Gromov modified quotations, appropriated authors' text for his own contexts, or made controversial claims without sufficient evidence, because he possessed a 'certain idea of Chekhov' as a result of the total 'system' approach and consciously or unconsciously adapted his material to this idea. However, the temptation to conclude this must be resisted, as it is purely speculative and itself not capable of refutation.

What I believe we can say is that on the whole Gromov is not critical in a *philosophical* sense. As Karl Popper, for instance, has written:

> the dogmatic attitude is clearly related to the tendency to *verify* our laws and schemata by seeking to apply them and to confirm them, even to the point of neglecting refutations, whereas the critical attitude is one of readiness to change them – to test them; to refute them; to *falsify* them, if possible. This suggests that we may identify the critical attitude with the scientific attitude, and the dogmatic attitude with the one which we have described as pseudo-scientific.[61]

It is particularly interesting that Popper equates 'critical' with 'scientific' here, since the Russian word *kriticheskii* has been so debased in the Soviet period that for most Russians it means only 'attacking', yet *nauchnyi* ('scientific') also means 'scholarly' and approximates more than *kriticheskii* to what Popper understands by 'critical'. It would perhaps make more sense in Russian, then, to say that in his literary criticism Gromov is not *nauchnyi*. He is scholarly (*nauchnyi*) in his editorial work, but not *nauchnyi* (scholarly, philosophically critical, 'scientific') in his literary criticism. He is critical towards other critics, from Shklovskii, Sobolev, Ermilov and Chicherin to Papernyi, Hingley, Chudakov and Kataev, in that explicitly or subtextually he polemicizes with them. He is not critical towards himself, in that he asserts and only confirms his theories, brooks few counter-arguments, and often ignores glaring factual evidence. His 'systemism' is, as we have seen, pseudo-scientific.

Yet we could hardly claim that Gromov is alone, or peculiarly 'Russian' in all this: the phenomenon has been just as prevalent in 20th-century western literary criticism. Northrop Frye, whom Gromov might be thought in some respects to resemble, aimed to 'place [literary] criticism upon what he at times calls a "systematic" and at times a "scientific" basis',[62] yet his 'archetypes' are far less empirically testable than 'the steppe' and 'the garden' in Gromov's hands, for the latter have an historical reality demonstrably embedded in Russian culture, whatever one may think of his linking them to Jung's theory of the 'collective consciousness' [**30**, 263–67]. Was western literary structuralism any less tautologous than Gromov's 'systemism'? Are literary 'gender studies' any more critical in the Popperian sense than Gromov's takes on *Fatherless*, 'The Steppe' or *The Cherry Orchard*?

Further, we may consider Gromov to be *philosophically* uncritical, but why should that preclude his work from being of great value as *literary* criticism? A 'metaphysical' and relatively dogmatic literary interpretation may not be philosophically critical/scientific, but as Popper himself recognised such theories can still have meaning and could be true. Perhaps only 20th-century English literary criticism has made the criteria of philosophical criticism so integral to what it understands by 'literary criticism'? In Russia the philosophical meaning of criticism became so debased in the Soviet period that the concept of a 'literary critic' hardly exists and has been replaced by *literaturoved* ('literary expert/specialist'). Like Bakhtin, Gromov deprecated this Soviet term. However, although Gromov's articles might reasonably be described as *literaturovedenie*, even in a Russian context the non-biographical bulk of his books can only be called *literaturnaia kritika* ('literary criticism'), which confirms that this concept does still exist in Russian. Rather, therefore, than measure Gromov against some personal or cross-cultural definition of what a 'literary critic' is, I propose addressing the question 'how good a critic is he?' by comparing him with major ascertainable constituents of the English and Russian literary-critical traditions. In order to bring out the contrasts more clearly, I shall consider these constituents in parallel rather than in series.

The most basic demand we make of English literary criticism is that it persuade us to 'see' a work in a new way. One could hardly deny that Gromov does this. His hypotheses about the role of the Dostoevskian *ideia* in 'A Boring Story', of Nietzschean proto-fascism in 'The Black Monk', of Old Russian literature in 'The Steppe', or the garden archetype in *The Cherry Orchard*, 'open our eyes' to dimensions in these works that had either been overlooked or greatly under-explored. His 'systemist' presentation of the 'whole world' of Chekhov's early short stories *revealed* them to Soviet readers as works about forms of human suffering and experience that they were very familiar with. And there can be no doubt that Gromov set out to change perceptions of Chekhov in a big way. Let us recall that he concluded his 1963 article on *Fatherless*: 'Analiz pervoi p'esy A.P. Chekhova neizbezhno privodit k sushchestvennomu peresmotru **vsei** [My emphasis] kontseptsii ego literaturnogo puti' [**5**, 34].

Nevertheless, the kind of shift in the way of seeing a work that Gromov achieves is rather different from the concept of 'revaluation' in English literary criticism. He does not so much lead us to revalue the work as a whole as see it wholly in terms of one new idea. 'The Steppe' becomes 'only' about the nine-year-old Egorushka's encounter with his mythical and historical *rodina*, when it is self-evidently at least as much about the real people he meets. Moreover, as has repeatedly been noted in this essay, Gromov's literary-critical hypotheses are most often historical or diachronic in nature. Not only are we to see *Fatherless* as a neglected first-rate *history* play, according to Gromov its existence should lead us radically to revise our 'conception' of Chekhov's literary *development through time*, rather than deepen our understanding of his dramatic art as such or our experience of specific works. The new ways that Gromov proposes we look at 'The Steppe', 'A Boring Story', 'The Black Monk' and *The Cherry Orchard* also derive from an examination of historical ingredients or contexts. It is a basic requirement of Russian literary criticism too that it make us 'see' works differently. That the means to this new seeing should be historical stands, however, in a peculiarly Russian tradition that can be traced back through the Marxist-Leninist 'obsession with history' to 19th-century critics and reviewers who insisted that writers were first and foremost chroniclers of Russian society. Moreover, in both of his books Gromov freely weaves personal history (biography) and literary criticism together, whereas in the English literary-critical tradition 'biographism' has been anathema from at least T.S. Eliot until recently.

In fact it could be claimed that for much of the 20th century English literary criticism was 'obsessed with the synchronic' and that there has been excessive concern with it in this essay too. Eliot, Pound, Leavis, Richards and others were committed to a process of what Leavis called 'feeling into' or 'becoming'; of 'realizing' a 'complex experience that is given in the words'.[63] Apart from a few 20th-century Russian poets' incursions into literary criticism, an interest in the 'synchronic experience' of reading, i.e. in the way works of literary art come alive for us and what they 'mean' to us in the process, has been foreign to Russian criticism/*literaturovedenie*. The Soviet official school of literary criticism was *de rigueur* historical. Gromov also tells us: 'Poetika zhe – esli eto poetika – vsegda i prezhde vsego istorichna' [**30**, 238].

The main strand of English literary criticism since Samuel Johnson has been analysis. Both Eliot and Leavis name it among the two chief tools of the critic.[64] In his key theoretical article [**9**] Gromov explicitly rejects it in favour of a synthetic, 'systemist' approach. Of course, not even Russian 19th-century literary critics and reviewers could dispense with analysis – the father of them all, Belinskii, was at times a fine exponent of it. But the idea that works of literature should be 'encyclopaedic' and mirror an all-inclusive entity called 'society' has been potent in Russian literary criticism from Belinskii and Chernyshevskii to Bakhtin and Gromov. Naturally it has inclined Russian critics to a synthesizing, generalizing and in English eyes over-simplifying approach. Gromov attacked what he called the 'selective analysis' of Chekhov's art in the 'old' and Soviet criticism [**9**, 308], but the latter was far more selective than analytical and certainly contained very little of what in English would be called close *verbal* analysis. It was more concerned with the ideological-political-social interpretation of 'canonical' works and their supposed relation to Chekhov's biography; as Gromov complained, there was a consistent urge to *generalise* about Chekhov's art from the conclusions of 'particular analysis' [**9**, 308]. In fact, though, Gromov's books are themselves highly selective,[65] and his adherence to a 'printsip sistemy, okhvatyvaiushchei ves' material' [**30**, 180] leads him to present over-simplified generalizations about Chekhov's work in the long Russian tradition that he himself deplores.

As I suggested in chapter three above, Gromov is relatively rare among Russian critics in subjecting any text at all to close verbal (as distinct from linguistic) analysis. His meditations on the shape, feel, phonetics, colour and ethical content of Chekhovian language ('Ves'ma zhelal by sochetat'sia uzami igumeneia', 'arbuz', 'Erakin', 'chernyi monakh', 'vishnëvyi sad' etc) would be congenial to Eliot, Leavis and Richards. They certainly qualify Gromov for the title *filolog*, philo-logue, in its literal sense, and give his criticism a fundamental authenticity for Russian and English readers alike. Nevertheless, it cannot be claimed that he practises analysis in any depth as a critical method. He analyses, say, the archaic register in 'The Steppe', or the Dostoevskian origins of *obshchaia ideia* in 'A Boring Story', but if in addition he had analysed these as complete works he might well have come to different, more balanced conclusions. If he had critically analysed 'The Black Monk', rather than projected onto it a single literary-historical hypothesis and a dogmatically positive value for 'garden' from his Chekhovian system, he would have discovered richer meanings in it. He does not present an extended analysis of a single Chekhov story earlier than 1888. Several times in his *oeuvre* he quotes approvingly the narrator's remark in 'Ward N° 6' that the rantings of Ivan Dmitrich amount to a 'besporiadochnoe, neskladnoe popurri iz starykh, no eshche nedopetykh pesen' (e.g. [**26**, 228–29]), but he does not analyse the fact that this 'main hero' as he calls him [**26**, 225] is mentally ill; he does not attempt to relate this fact of madness to the complex meaning of the story as a whole. One could hardly claim that his reading of *The Cherry Orchard* analyses more than the play's central image.

In his theoretical writing, Gromov even denies that analysis can address the full meaning of a Chekhov story, since there is a collective theme, an *obshchaia ideia* or *Gestalt*, to all the stories, that is situated 'za predelami kazhdogo iz nikh v otdel'nosti i iavlena v tselom mnozhestve ikh' [**9**, 309]. This view would surely be unacceptable to most English critics. It suggests that there is some extrinsic, ineffable 'meaning' to a Chekhov work which only the 'systemist' who has read everything Chekhov ever wrote can understand. In locating the 'truth' outside the specific text, or indeed any Chekhov text as such, it approximates more to a metaphysical, quasi-mystical, even pre-critical approach. Gromov's 'systemist' view of Chekhov's writing as a continuum or 'world' comes close to being a *revelation* that only hierophants can share. In this respect some might maintain it is peculiarly Russian.

Whatever the truth of that speculation, Gromov's preference for 'synthesis' over 'analysis' certainly stands in a firm 19th- and 20th-century Russian tradition. As I showed in chapter three above, in practice it is difficult to distinguish the systematic 'world' (or *gorod*) of Chekhov's works in Gromov's interpretation from that of *obshchestvo* in the familiar all-inclusive sense developed by Russian literary journalists in the 19th century and flogged to death by the Soviet literary-critical establishment in the 20th. Indeed, Gromov claims that Chekhov's 'world' is sociologically accurate. Moreover, it is tempting to see connections between Gromov's synthetic/systematic view of Chekhov's art and other totalising tendencies in 20th-century Russia. The idea of a 'system' that had to explain everything was perhaps endemic. Both Formalism and Marxist literary criticism aspired to explaining 'the sum' of a work. Stanislavskii posited a total 'system' for acting. Theatre directors like Meierkhol'd, Liubimov or Efros aimed to present not the single masterpiece by Gogol', say, but 'the whole' of Gogol' through selective compilations made by themselves.[66] In a similar way, the titles of Gromov's books [**26**, **29**] and their mixture of biography and criticism suggest that he saw himself as studying a whole *subject* called Chekhov, understanding what 'Chekhov' was about, penetrating the message of the phenomenon 'Chekhov', rather than comprehensively interpreting specific, 'self-contained' literary works.

The point here is that on the whole 20th-century English philosophy and literary criticism adopted what has been called 'a piecemeal approach – an approach that seems to develop naturally from empiricism', and their achievements were 'more in the way of careful local analysis than the erection of total systems'; there was, indeed, 'something like an assumption that such individual analysis is the only means of achieving truth'.[67] Whatever the origins of Gromov's 'systemist' approach, whether Marxian, Hegelian or in some anterior sense 'Russian', it exhibits, then, considerable difference or otherness from the English tradition. In so far as his belief in his system and some of his literary hypotheses is dogmatic, i.e. in Popper's term 'unfalsifiable', it might also seem to present a species of 'bees in the bonnet' or conspiracy theory. And to the western mind that is precisely what Gromov's concentration on, say, the paramount place of *Fatherless* in Chekhov's writing career, or Chekhov's supposed relation with Dostoevskii, or the 'historically prophetic' status of the Vengeroviches, may appear to be.

Returning to key components of the respective literary-critical traditions, we note that with 'analysis' Eliot coupled 'comparison'.[68] Gromov does employ comparison in a recognisable English sense, for instance when considering the genres of the *malaia pressa* as exemplified by Chekhov's works and those of his colleagues [**29**, 136–42], or when examining the qualities of 'The Steppe' and of 'idea-soaked' stories published in 'thick journals' at the same time [**26**, 171–74]. However, given that comparison has to be based on analysis, the former is also relatively rare in Gromov. More often it resembles what in English we would call 'juxtaposition' – and *sopostavlenie* or *sootnesenie*, rather than *sravnenie*, are the words Gromov most commonly uses to describe it. A quotation from another Chekhov work, from a letter, or another author, is interpolated without comment from Gromov and allowed to speak for itself (examples are too numerous to list). As we saw, Gromov's 'comparison' of Chekhov's stories with Gogol''s, or Chekhov's 'doubles' with Dostoevskii's, is more 'dyadic' than comparative in a discursive sense. In these and other juxtapositions he is more at pains to show what the terms of his 'comparison' share than what differentiates them.

Gromov's compositional, juxtapositional technique could be said to follow in a long tradition of Russian journalism and art. The inlaying of quotations without comment in a text of one's own is a well-established ploy of Russian 'Aesopic' writing and it should be noted that its intention is rather monological (one uses someone else's words less as a 'quotation' than to say something oneself cannot). In icons, poems and fiction the Russian fascination with spatial contrast can have a deeply aesthetic effect; I shall return to the subject in Gromov's case shortly. Suffice it to say, I do not think he practises literary-critical comparison in Eliot's sense. An analytical comparison of 'Ward N° 6' and 'The Black Monk', for example, would surely have radically changed Gromov's perception of both.

Unlike Eliot, Leavis chose to couple 'judgement' with analysis as the tools of the critic.[69] What he meant by judgement was a valuing of specific qualities based on as sensitive as possible a 'realisation' and 'possession' of the work, leading to discrimination and the 'placing' of works in what he called an 'organization of similarly "placed" things, things that have found their bearings with regard to one another, and not a theoretical system or a system determined by abstract considerations'.[70] There is minimal judgement of this kind in Gromov and his skills of juxtaposition do not extend to 'placing' works in the way Leavis means. But then his treatments of *Fatherless*, 'The Steppe', 'The Black Monk' or *The Cherry Orchard* show that he cannot really be said ever to 'realise' or be in 'possession' of a Chekhov work in the round: he examines one aspect of it to the exclusion of most others. Nor is there much of a tradition of qualitative evaluation in 20th-century Russian literary criticism of the 'classics'. Whereas contemporary Russian writers have been more than criticised by reviewers and Party hacks, Soviet/Russian literary critics and *literaturoved*'s have tended to take the perfection of their 'classical' writers for granted. To attempt a critical evaluation of Pushkin's verse, say, or Tolstoi's novels, would have been regarded as sacrilegious and irrelevant in the Soviet period, as Russians were only too grateful to have these texts at all. Even when criticism of a classical writer was officially sanctioned, as in the case of Dostoevskii, it was not, of course, literary criticism of Dostoevskii as a writer, but ideological criticism of him as an 'ideologue'.

One would very much have liked to read Gromov's views on, say, whether 'The Duel' is an artistic failure as many western critics hold, what is 'wrong' with so many of Chekhov's early short stories, or how *as works of verbal art* his middle stories compare with his late and *Three Sisters* compares with *The Cherry Orchard*. Yet almost the only criticism in this sense that Gromov allows himself is of the 'technical' imperfections of *Fatherless*. An English reader might come away from Gromov's books with the impression that Chekhov could not write anything bad, or did not achieve a hard-won qualitative evolution. But as a Russian critic Gromov almost certainly did not regard this exercise of judgement as part of his brief. On the contrary, he wrote about Chekhov because he 'loved' Chekhov.[71] The possible impression of an English reader that his books are inspired by uncritical adulation is not, then, unfounded. Yet this very Russian attitude to 'his' author enables Gromov outstandingly to satisfy what Eliot saw as the *first* requisite of a critic, namely 'interest in his subject, and ability to communicate an interest in it'.[72]

Finally, an area in which English 20th-century literary criticism and the Russian tradition are in surprising agreement is the belief that critics should relate their activity to living literary and social concerns.

Eliot wrote: 'The important critic is the person who is absorbed in the present problems of art, and who wishes to bring the forces of the past to bear upon the solution of these problems.'[73] I have found no sustained example of this in Gromov, but his books are permeated with the sense that both laymen and writers still have a huge amount to 'learn' from Chekhov's art (see, for example, [**26**, 127, 134–35]). He was particularly interested in the cinematographic qualities of Chekhov's writing. He freely quotes recent and living Russian writers from Olesha to Solzhenitsyn as demonstrations of Chekhov's modernity. A startling illustration of the intertwining of Gromov's life with contemporary Russian literature is his correspondence, whilst still a student, with Boris Pasternak, who confided to him that he was writing a novel in which the main hero was 'vrach po professii, no s ochen' sil'nym vtorym tvorcheskim planom, kak u vracha A.P. Chekhova' [**28**]. The last thing one can say of Gromov is that his approach to Chekhov is 'academic': his own creative interests, from writing poetry and prose to taking photographs, ensure that he brings to Chekhov a live concern with 'the present problems of art'. As I shall discuss below, Gromov's own writing is influenced by Chekhovian standards and techniques. In fact it is possible to see Gromov as himself more of a Russian writer than a critic in the scholarly mould. He is closer to Tynianov and Shklovskii, who were original writers as well as Formalists, than he is to the university Chekhov specialists.

Leavis's articulation of a similar requirement is perhaps so unexpected that it merits full quotation:

> to insist that literary criticism is, or should be, a specific discipline of intelligence is not to suggest that a serious interest in literature can confine itself to the kind of intensive local analysis associated with 'practical criticism' – to the scrutiny of the 'words on the page' in their minute relations, their effects of imagery, and so on: a real literary interest is an interest in man, society and civilization, and its boundaries cannot be drawn; the adjective is not a circumscribing one.[74]

This admirably describes Gromov's own interest in Chekhov as what I earlier called an inalienable part of Russia's 'spiritual heritage'. In the 19th century, Russian literary criticism became an established medium for discussing the socio-political issues of the day to the exclusion of what was actually literary; in the 20th, the Communist government dictated to functionaries and journalists the socio-political line they were to project whilst ostensibly discussing literature. Neither variety of superficiality is to be found in Gromov. It would have been all too easy for him to flaunt the words *glasnost'*, *perestroika*, *obshche-chelovecheskii*, *demokratizatsiia* and so forth in his post-1985 books, but he does not. Equally, as I have suggested, the passages of Soviet piety in his earlier writing are so grotesque as to suggest parody through gritted teeth. What Gromov actually sees Chekhov intimately related to is the *deepest* problems and aspirations of the Russia in which he, Gromov, was living.

The 'sins of the fathers' and 'historical guilt', which Gromov identified as the young Chekhov's main focus in *Fatherless*, were the single most burning issue amongst the younger generation of the 1960s when Gromov published his influential article. They account for the Russian theatrical obsession with *Hamlet* throughout the fifties, sixties and seventies and may well explain why *Fatherless* was relatively unstaged in the USSR for such a long time. They remain a cancerous problem in Russia to this day.

By demolishing the myth of the *bezvremen'e* in his first book, Gromov was helping his readers connect with their true national past; he was restoring for them their historical memory and continuity; he was rebuilding the 'backbone' of the two centuries which Mandel'shtam claimed in his poem 'My Times' ('Vek') had been smashed by Bolshevism. Gromov's interpretation of 'The Steppe' then proceeded to show his readers the *full* perspective of Russian history that they should acquire, as Egorushka absorbs it through his senses and imagination on his journey. In his last thoughts on *The Cherry Orchard*, Gromov added the vital Russian element of beauty to his vision of his country's past and future growth.

An almost incidental effect of Gromov's investigation of the theme 'Chekhov and Dostoevskii' was to debunk the Russian intelligentsia's deeply held and historically disastrous view that the prime movers of Russian life and literature were 'ideas'. In his exposition of 'The Black Monk' he suggested that a 19th-century obsession with 'ideas' was the psychopathic progenitor of 20th-century fascism on the right and left, in which he clearly included Leninism-Stalinism. The primacy of the 'idea' is still a live issue in Russia. Even as I write Russian intellectuals are debating what *ideology* is needed to 'fill the vacuum' left by Soviet *ideology*.

Most important of all, though, Gromov's work on Chekhov and Dostoevskii is a blow against Russian monologism. There has been a long tradition in Russia of 'either-or' where preference among the literary classics is concerned: Pushkin *or* Gogol', Tolstoi *or* Dostoevskii, Dostoevskii *or* Chekhov, Pasternak *or* Mandel'shtam, and so on. Underlying it, evidently, is the assumption, or the desire to believe, that only one writer at a time can 'speak the truth' and is therefore qualified to be one's 'teacher', 'prophet' or authority on everything. The attitude particularly afflicted the intelligentsia in the 1890s when, as Gromov shows, Dostoevskii began to be accorded guru status. The supposedly fundamental antithesis 'Dostoevskii/Chekhov' was worked up by Russian intellectuals after Chekhov's death and has survived to our day.[75] Therefore when Gromov demonstrated that Chekhov was influenced by certain Dostoevskii texts, that there was much in common between these two great writers, and that it was a question of accepting Dostoevskii *and* Chekhov, he was deconstructing an 'exclusive' approach that had bedevilled Russian literary intellectuals for nearly a century. He was entering a powerful plea for the dialogue and pluralism that late 20th-century Russia needed as much in the cultural sphere as in the political. He was arguing for a rich, inclusive, polyphonic view of Russian literature rather than a monologic, divisive and impoverishing one.

Finally, in denying that *any* writer is a 'teacher of life' Gromov was tackling one of the most cherished delusions of pre-revolutionary and Soviet readers, one excoriated by writers from Pushkin to Bunin:

> Святая, наивная, державная вера во всемогущество книжного слова. Пережили татарское иго, победили Наполеона; но сколько пришлось вынести из-за тургеневских женщин, из-за литературных мечтаний и снов... Вред искусства, — заметил Толстой, — в том, что оно наполняет жизнь **подобием** жизни. [**26**, 5]

> Мы более или менее соглашаемся, что литература — не совсем жизнь, но с тем, что литература — **совсем** не жизнь, мы согласиться не в состоянии. [**29**, 376]

Gromov's writing on Chekhov is impregnated with 'interest in man, society and civilization' in the best Russian tradition, and this is one reason why his books have appealed to a much wider readership than 'Chekhov buffs'.

To sum up, of the seven constituents of the English literary-critical tradition that I have discussed here in a highly selective and simplified fashion, Gromov's work contains only three. He does make us 'see' important works of Chekhov differently, even if we sometimes feel that his interpretations are so one-sided that we have to reintegrate them into a more balanced understanding of the works as wholes. Moreover what he would probably regard as his greatest contribution to 'seeing' Chekhov differently, namely his claim that *Fatherless* is the seed from which 'all' subsequent Chekhov grew, does not change the way we see the *work* so much as the way we see Chekhov's development over time. The depth of Gromov's interest in Chekhov is unquestionable, however, as is his ability to communicate it and to relate certain issues of Chekhov's writing to the key spiritual issues of late 20th-century Russia (especially conscience) and the problems of the wider world (especially ecological disaster).

The requirements of English literary criticism that I have suggested Gromov does not meet are: synchronic experience of discrete works, analysis, detailed comparison, and judgement. His avoidance of these processes is exemplified by his handling of *Fatherless*. Although we can be sure that he 'Aesopically' related its theme to the Russia of his own day, he saw the play in overwhelmingly historical terms – as a study in the generation gap of the late 1870s 's glubokim istoricheskim podtekstom' [**26**, 65].[76] Although he examined the play's characters one by one [**5**, 12–28], he did this essentially from the point of view of how they fitted into the 'fathers/children' scheme of that period; he did not analyse, for instance, their interpersonal, sexual and ethical lives as individuals. There is no sense in his treatment that these characters might have a tantalizingly half-achieved synchronic life of their own in a theatre. Gromov does not subject the language of the play to more than superficial analysis. He claims that in each of the examples he considers 'zalozhen tochnyi priznak kharaktera' [**5**, 30], but his examples display less characterological differentiation than a strained aphoristic sameness, and I would suggest that the latter verbal quality is what he should have examined. Above all, Gromov does not analyse the possession of 'conscience' in Platonov's case; he is uncritical towards him in several senses. Instead of detailed comparison of, say, the language of *Fatherless* with that of *Ivanov*, or stagecraft and the creation of character in *Fatherless* and *Three Sisters*, Gromov presents juxtapositions of passages from *Fatherless* and other works [**5**, 32–33; **26**, 72–73] that merely display similarity: 'sootvetstviia' [**29**, 92] that are left to speak for themselves but which without analytical comparison say very little.

As we saw, actual critical judgment of *Fatherless* as a work of dramatic art is minimal in Gromov's writing about it. In effect he presents it as a highly tendentious work, so to speak an 'ideofact', born of the young Chekhov's ambition to jump onto the Russian literary *engagement* bandwagon by writing an 'idea-soaked' epic drama about the 'condition of Russia'. This is a very interesting focus, as it shows what notions of significance in literature Chekhov had to shed before he could write the still relatively 'topical' *Ivanov*, let alone become the Chekhov of his last four plays. But Gromov does not critically evaluate this focus any further. On the contrary, he leaves us with the remythologised image of a 'serious' young writer *s ideiami* who had produced a socio-political-economic masterpiece, rather than a 'nevinnaia lozh'' as Aleksandr Chekhov called it.[77] Finally, to claim as Gromov does that writing *Fatherless* was 'incomparably' more formative for Chekhov than the experience of contributing to the humorous press 'in these years' [**26**, 74] is splendidly declarative but lacking in critical perspective. It is not difficult to show that the young Chekhov's exposure to a real literary market, to its constraints of deadline, brevity, genre, technique, subject-matter and (of a sort) taste, saved him from attempting to perpetuate the very indulgencies that *Fatherless* suffers from and the nature of which Chekhov presumably acknowledged by concealing its manuscript.[78]

It seems fair to say, then, that in English terms Gromov is not a very good literary critic. He simply is not 'critical' enough. Philosophically he is not 'critical' because he presents theories about influences upon Chekhov, the significance of *Fatherless* in Chekhov's creative development, or features of Chekhov's biography and texts, that he does not test, that are often not capable of being tested, that simply have to be believed, and that occasionally resemble conspiracy theories. Literarily, his approach is predominantly historical, unanalytical, not genuinely comparative, and shows no inclination to pursue 'true judgment' or even qualitative discrimination. It is difficult to imagine an academic press in the Anglo-Saxon world today accepting either of Gromov's books, with their seamless blend of biography and literary-historical speculation, as contributions to literary *criticism*.

Yet on its own this conclusion is patently absurd: Gromov is not, and never can be, an English critic! It is legitimate, I think, to evaluate him within our own critical context, but we must also attempt to place ourselves in *Gromov's* critical context and evaluate him within that.

Gromov satisfies most of the requirements of the Russian literary-critical tradition to the highest degree. He is original, bold, and sure of his opinions. He undermined the Soviet orthodoxy about Chekhov with his early articles, then demolished it completely with a few perfectly aimed blows in his books. He is exhilarating for Russians to read. On the one hand his discoveries about Chekhov's earliest publications bespeak a brilliantly meticulous and logical mind, on the other his critical hypotheses are notable for their imaginativeness, their creative élan. His criticism is firmly set in an historical perspective, as has been usual in Russia since the 19th century, and he is an exponent of 'historical poetics' as developed by A.N. Veselovskii (1838–1906), one of the 'philologists' of the old school whom he admired most. Yet Gromov also concentrates on the *image* in Chekhov (almost 'icon' in the case of *The Cherry Orchard*), linking it with psychology and acknowledging here a debt to another 'philologist', A.A. Potebnia (1835–91). Gromov's reading is catholic, his knowledge of Russian literature encyclopaedic. He can therefore relate works, facts and ideas into fresh, cross-cultural patterns of the kind that have appealed to Russian readers of literary criticism from at least the late 19th century to Bakhtin. His stress upon synthesis, and his great gift for it, are not at all new to the Russian tradition. The patterns that he creates with words and evidence are appreciated in a Russian context more for their aesthetic rightness ('beauty') than their critical rigour or logical cohesion. Above all, from the Russian point of view, Gromov is 'committed' to his subject, he 'loves' it, and he relates it to the living concerns of ordinary Russians at the end of the Communist era and beyond. He writes about Chekhov in a way that makes Chekhov 'matter' to Russians; he, Gromov, therefore 'matters' to them as well. As a Russian critic he is mainstream and very good indeed. I believe we can say that he is not only the greatest Chekhov scholar Russia has produced, but a major 20th-century Russian literary critic in his own right.

Clearly, what at the beginning of this section was referred to as 'the fact of difference' is very considerable indeed between Gromov as an 'English' critic and as a 'Russian' one. If this essay demonstrates anything, however, I hope it is that a dialogue between the two critical cultures can be revealing and fruitful. In general terms it can at least lend us a new 'horizon' and introduce us to a new way of 'seeing'. More specifically, Gromov's 'metaphysical' and 'synthetic' approach to literary interpretation may act as a healthy antidote to the western tendency to lose ourselves in analytical mazes. For the disturbing fact to an English critical mind, perhaps, is that even when Gromov's literary hypotheses are neither 'verifiable' nor 'falsifiable' they prove richly suggestive, useful, and therefore plausible as *working hypotheses* about Chekhov.

Viewed as a Russian critic, however, Gromov undoubtedly owes some of his success to the fact that he is an exciting writer of his native language. His style is clear, fluent, natural, almost colloquial, but in fact each sentence is highly crafted and self-contained; usually one cannot imagine adding a single word or taking one away. These qualities give his prose a ring of truth and authority. As we have seen, his sentences frequently acquire an aphoristic turn: 'Dialektika vremeni raskryvaetsia u Chekhova v kharakternom paradokse: rozhdaias' na svet, chelovek popadaet v proshloe' [**8**, 9], 'Istinnyi smysl kratkosti, konechno, v tom, chto ona parodiruet dolgoe chtenie' [**26**, 4]. The abiding impression is one of wit (*um*) and rhetorical assurance. When Gromov is allusive, sub-textual or Aesopic in the Russian tradition, one often senses a twinkle of irony (as when he uses the formula 'starye nedopetye pesni Gromova', ostensibly referring to the 'main hero' of 'Ward N° 6'). But he also has a very engaging sense of the ridiculous:

> Разумеется, ношение ранца не по форме и клетчатых панталон [As Chekhov is recorded as having done at school] — это еще не революция. [**4**, 133]

> можно впасть в крайность, уже проявившуюся во множестве работ о Чехове, где, например, на одной странице собраны все юмористические фамилии, встречающиеся в прозе ранних лет: и генеральша Жеребчикова, и купец Кашалотов, [...] и т.д., и т.д., и несть числа. В этом случае нельзя даже сказать, что мы пересолили — мы предлагаем читателю соль в чистом виде, выпарив ее, так сказать, из влаги юмора. В этом виде она неудобоварима. [**29**, 284]

His writing varies in tone from the limpid, deductive and documentary to the dramatic, lyrical, or smoulderingly irate; there is no 'single' tone and consequently little time for the reader to become bored. In his early writing Gromov seems influenced by the 'telegraphic' style of the Formalists (possibly via a previous biographer, Aleksandr Roskin, whose work he studied closely): he is given to rather portentous one-sentence paragraphs that sometimes fall flat ('Kutezhi studencheskikh let zakonchilis' dlia Aleksandra i Nikolaia neizlechimym alkogolizmom' [**7**, 170]). By his mature years he had become a master of very varied paragraph lengths. One could almost mark each of these periods with a musical tempo – another guarantee that the reader will be absorbed and borne along by what Gromov has to say. Whether consciously or unconsciously, he occasionally produces sentences that in their phonetic and rhythmic organisation gravitate towards verse: '**kak** rano **Ch**ekhov po**k**orilsia literature, **kak** rano privy**k** **k** odin**och**estvu, **k** str**og**omu, po**ch**ti in**och**es**k**omu raspo**ria**d**k**u, **k**ot**or**ym **ok**ruzhil i **og**ran**ich**il seb**ia**' [**29**, 40]. Into his own discourse he cuts passages of quotation from a multiplicity of sources, these passages are often 'free-standing', i.e. not introduced by Gromov (although of course in quotation marks), and he will jump to a new topic unexpectedly, leaving a 'lacuna' that exists as white paper, a row of asterisks, or a 'double-take' in the mind of the reader. As we have seen, Gromov relishes weaving *patterns* with his observations, evidence and quotations, rather than proceeding along a straight line of argument, and for Russians this enhances the pleasure of reading him. Altogether, there is a strong sense of creative 'play' about Gromov's writing; of a master with words 'playing' with tone, period, tempo, sound values and visual effect. His presentation of his themes is 'artistic'.

Unfortunately, this is again likely to produce difficulty for the educated English reader, who can accept creative writers writing literary criticism but is less comfortable with the idea of literary criticism being simultaneously creative writing. In Gromov's case it is complicated by the fact that some of his writing techniques are conspicuously Chekhovian. Reviewing Gromov's 1993 book, S.Iu. Nikolaeva observed: 'Kniga [...] prosta i slozhna odnovremenno. Prosta – potomu chto napisana legkim, sovershennym russkim iazykom (tak chto podchas lish' kavychki pozvoliaiut otdelit' slova Chekhova ot avtorskikh).'[79] By incorporating quotations from Chekhov into his own text as whole paragraphs without lead-ins from himself (e.g. [**26**, 10, 108, 150, 185–86, 194]), Gromov brings Chekhov's voice beguilingly close to his own. Sometimes one feels that the Chekhov quotations in *guillemets* are Gromov's interior monologue. Gromov himself practises the techniques of juxtaposition, 'lacunae', fragmentariness and 'blocks' of prose that he describes so well in Chekhov's hands [**26**, 187, 201]. As we noted, Gromov's essay on 'The Steppe' in his 1989 book seems itself to re-enact the circular motions of that narrative.[80] His 1993 essay on *The Cherry Orchard* is a complex design of theme and time reminiscent of Chekhov's longer stories. A feeling pervades Gromov's writing on Chekhov that he, Gromov, has attempted to identify himself as much as possible with Chekhov's own point of view, to meld himself in fact with his author to the point of occasionally producing pastiche. One is reminded of Roland Barthes on the difference between the 'unalloyed reader' and the critic: 'Le seul commentaire que pourrait produire un pur lecteur, et qui le resterait, c'est le pastiche [...]. Passer de la lecture à la critique, c'est changer de désir, c'est désirer non plus l'oeuvre, mais son propre langage.'[81] To the English reader it may appear that Gromov has got 'inside' Chekhov superlatively, but has not sufficiently come 'out' again to produce *criticism* in a language wholly his 'own'. In this sense Gromov may seem to lack the 'dissociative faculty', the ability not only to 'saturate' oneself in one's subject but to 'separate' oneself suddenly from it 'in appreciation of the highest creative work', which Eliot regarded as necessary in a true critic.[82] But to the Russian reader Gromov's self-identification with 'his' author is one of Gromov's greatest virtues. It proves clearly, on the page in his own writing, that Gromov 'loves' Chekhov. And this aspect of his writing is another source of Gromov's power as a populariser in Russia.

A very engaging authorial personality does indeed, in Chekhov's words, 'disclose itself' when we put together the parts of Gromov's writing that we have been able to look at in this essay. How his personality as an author compared with his personality as a real person, a man, I do not know, nor is it really relevant here. Nevertheless, it would seem useful to end this study by presenting those new facts about Gromov's biography that have emerged with the passing of Soviet power. It is now possible in Russia to communicate such things fairly freely. Gromov's many devoted students have begun to put their memories and appreciation into print.[83] I first attended a lecture of Gromov's myself in 1972. In 1981 I attended several and met him publicly and privately on nine occasions spread over a month. I will collate some of these facts and memories to supplement those contained in Peter Henry's excellent account of 1991.

As a teenager during the War, Gromov worked in the Urals as a locksmith and metal pattern-maker. This was not just a bread-and-butter job: he enjoyed it, he reached a high grade as a qualified metalworker, and continued to make things in metal and wood for the rest of his life. Perhaps it is not fanciful to relate his practical talent for fitting components together and shaping patterns, to his powers as a literary-critical synthesist. A graphic example of the latter is his role in the creation of Olesha's posthumous book *Write Something Every Day* (*Ni dnia bez strochki*). Olesha had left this in the form of a heap of scraps of paper (restaurant napkins etc) with text on, but no directions about how they related to each other and the order in which they were to be printed. Even Shklovskii, the appointed editor, could not fathom Olesha's 'system'. By chance, Gromov saw the material at Shklovskii's flat and was fired by the challenge. In the course of a night's work he cracked the *zamysel*, the idea behind this autobiography, and working at Shklovskii's over the next few days he succeeded in fitting all the pieces together. How, Olesha's widow asked Gromov, did he 'know'? 'On znal i ot Chekhova, slozhivshego svoi mir iz malen'kikh rasskazikov.'[84] Shklovskii acknowledged Gromov's vital contribution in his introduction to this popular book.[85]

In 1964, from having been head of the Literature Department at Taganrog College of Education, Gromov moved to Moscow to be with his new wife, Lidiia Dmitrievna Opul'skaia. He had no full-time job to go to. Despite his previous publications on Tolstoi and Chekhov having been singled out for praise in the central press, he was cold-shouldered by the Moscow *literaturoved* establishment. He began giving lectures paid by the hour at Moscow University. Thanks in some measure to Khrapchenko, in 1967 he joined the teaching staff at the Moscow Printing Institute, where he stayed until 1977. It was in the early Moscow years of relative unemployment that Gromov completed his systematic reading of Chekhov and the compilation of his 'catalogue'. The situation was saved, it seems, by Gromov's involvement in the new Complete Works, of which Opul'skaia was a moving spirit. As we have seen, Gromov's input to this monumental achievement was fundamental. It continued across three decades. Even so, we now know that it had its own precariousness, anomalies and ironies. Gromov worked 'vne tsekha', to one side of the IMLI team; his attributions of early Chekhov works were fiercely contested by some of them; and yet the head of the Institute itself, the Central Committee's Chekhov inquisitor G.P. Berdnikov, was successfully excluded from any significant role in the edition!

On 2 October 1972 I went to a lecture by Gromov in the 'old' Philological Faculty of Moscow University on 'Prospekt Marksa' (Mokhovaia). It was one of a special course given by him under the title 'Chekhov – khudozhnik'. The room was poky, dingy and dark. There were about six of us in the audience, which was probably a reflection of young Russians' interest in Chekhov at the time or their expectations of any 'Soviet' literature-lecturer saying something original. Gromov delivered his lecture seated at a table, with cards spread out in front of him on which he appeared to have written themes and quotations. With his groomed black hair, high forehead, dark eyes and sensuous mouth, he was strikingly handsome. It was immediately clear that he was on top of his subject, was weighing every word, and was delivering a revisionist if not subversive account of Chekhov generally. He gently set aside the image of Chekhov projected by certain memoirists and the famous Braz portrait in the Tret'iakov Gallery (see [**26**, 10–13, 18–21]) and introduced us to completely new, 'unofficial' facts about Chekhov. He broached Chekhov's 'ideino-khudozhestvennoe edinstvo' and 'esteticheskaia filosofiia' (I quote from notes made at the time), and deconstructed what he called the 'myth' that, because Chekhov 'never said what he was doing, compared with Tolstoi and Dostoevskii', Chekhov 'voobshche ne myslit'. Yet he seemed extremely ill at ease. Sitting right in front of us, he allowed himself far honester eye-contact than was usual at Soviet lectures. His eyes seemed watchful and mournful. He gave the impression, frankly, of a man who is hunted.

The contrast in 1981 was considerable. He was giving a course of lectures on the classics from Pushkin to Chekhov at the 'new' Philological Faculty of Moscow University on 'Lenin Hills' (Vorob'evy gory). The auditorium was light, airy, with raked seating full of students, and Gromov delivered his lectures standing near but not behind a lectern. He wore a dark, well-cut suit. He was confident but extremely controlled in his inflections and choice of words; very occasionally he would stammer. I noted in my diary that his now 'gray, long stiffish hair' was combed back over his head 'like Mozart's last portrait' and he 'kept squinting [*prishchurival*] Cossack-like eyes'. The first lecture I attended was a *tour de force* on Pushkin's lyrical poetry. It analysed the crucial role of the pair *svoboda/vol'nost'* in Pushkin's verse from his earliest years. There was nothing Soviet whatsoever about Gromov's treatment of his subject, although in the micro-historical context the latter was sensitive. At one point the phrase 'Umerennyi demokrat Iisus Khristos' featured. It was a masterly, poised performance, like the others on Lermontov and Gogol' that I attended, and at the end there was a ripple of applause.

By this time Gromov held a salaried post in the Philological Faculty, but only as a temporary lecturer. His name was nationally known as an editor of six volumes of the Complete Works, as the presenter of the most popular selection of Chekhov's stories [**8**, **12**, **13**, **14**, **15**], and for numerous articles in popular publications (e.g. [**6**] and [**7**]). The Soviet system was widely recognised within Russia itself to have entered a 'sclerotic' phase, and discreet heterodoxy was surprisingly rife. One could not escape the impression from his lectures that Gromov was on the side of the angels. In the public corridors of the university, therefore, he had an obvious following of bright, inquiring students. At the same time, he was justifiably wary of being seen in the company of foreigners. After a public lecture by his head of department, at which presumably all the staff were expected to be present, he darted about in an uncharacteristic manner that signalled he did not want to be approached. At our first meeting, once the formal business in the corridor was over he steered me into a side room, where his manner changed completely, to one of warmth and spontaneous enthusiasm:

> [He] amazed me by suggesting, in fact insisting, that the most important thing I could look at here ('even to hold in your hands will be enough') is MSS of *P'esa bez nazvaniia*, although this published twice (1923 and in PSSP). Then he explained that he thought the place of this work in Chekhov's development was really important (that, in fact, if it had been accepted and been a success, he'd never have been involved in the humorous magazines in the first place), that after this he made, as it were, a 'bol'shoi krug' *back* to theatre, that actresses, of course, never read plays, that Ermolova in late 1880s/early nineties at *obedy* still really did not know who Chekhov was, etc. [Diary, 3 April 1981]

This view, now so familiar to us from Gromov's books, shocked me more than a little. However, perhaps it is a sign of how accepted Gromov's line on *Fatherless* already was that the very next day Aleksandr Chudakov expressed himself to me in a manner 'almost identical to Gromov on the need to elucidate *P'esa bez nazvaniia*'.

In the security of his home Gromov was, as Peter Henry has written, a brilliant conversationalist; but of a distinctive kind. His descriptions of the decimation of his family in 1937, his childhood on a *stanitsa* near Rostov, and the deadness of the steppe in high summer, were vivid and profoundly moving even though they must have been well-honed (see the paragraphs beginning 'Tot, kto vyros ili khotia by byval v donskikh priazovskikh stepiakh' in [**26**, 162; **29**, 181; **30**, 188]). His reactions to 'political' topics were passionate and uncomplicated. He fulminated against the 'old men' editors who had censored sexual references from Chekhov's letters in the Complete Works, but also against Prime Minister Thatcher and President Carter whose policies towards the USSR in the wake of its invasion of Afghanistan were in his view leading to the 'breakdown of cultural-scientific links' and the cancellation of such events as an international Chekhov conference at Yale. 'Oni u vas ne ponimaiut igry', he commented sourly. What Russia needed was 'more jeans, more books', more of everything that the West produced.

Whenever the subject turned to Chekhov, however, Gromov visibly relaxed and brightened. He tended not so much to take up what you had said and qualify it, develop it, or play with it, i.e. actually 'converse', as respond with a counter-statement, possibly unrelated or on an entirely different work, that seemed to come from deep inside his brain. You felt that he had his own, completely integrated view of Chekhov, man and artist, which he delighted in revealing glimpses of to you in the hope (often realised) of surprising you, but which was not up for discussion. On the other hand, when I consulted him and his wife about dozens of specific problems of translation in Chekhov's early stories, it became a genuine, quickening dialogue. He would smile slyly, grin, or chuckle to himself, and quote with feeling other examples in Chekhov that set us all laughing and spluttering. It was our collaboration over these Chekhovian 'black marks on the page' that together with the overflowing hospitality of the Gromov household sealed our friendship.[86]

I was sorry, therefore, that on the last extended occasion I met Gromov, on 26 April 1981, he was in a dark and philosophic mood. He spoke as though I was leaving Russia for good, as though we would never meet again, as though all free communication would be impossible and too dangerous anyway. I now realize that he was in the grip of the kind of pan-historical vision of Russia that lies behind his meditations on 'The Steppe' and *The Cherry Orchard*. In Russia, he said, it was always impossible to think in terms of individuals, only generations... My abiding memory of him, then, is of a man with a great appetite and talent for life, humour, literature, words, plasticity, *style*, but who was almost fatalistically resigned to the reality of Russian life as he perceived it and had known it.

In 1987 emphysema and a denunciation by faculty heads who accused him of devoting his life to avenging his father's execution by attacking the Soviet system in all that he wrote and said, obliged Gromov to leave Moscow University. By all accounts it was a bitter blow to him. Yet posterity can only regard it as a blessing, for it enabled him to complete his last article [**28**] and his last three volumes [**29**; **30**; **31**]. He died in Moscow on 22 August 1990.

This essay has attempted to bring together some of what Chekhov called the 'slozhnye chasti' that can only be composed into a whole after an author has died. Where Gromov is concerned it is just a beginning. The essay has not touched at all on his writing about Lev Tolstoi, Aleksei Tolstoi, Russian poetry, or other areas of Russian literature in which, judging by his lecture courses, he was highly competent. He disliked c.v.'s and lists of publications, so it will be some time before a full Gromov bibliography reflecting his diverse activities and interests can be pieced together, let alone the publications themselves be read and digested. To evaluate critically a writer with Gromov's gift for synthesis presupposes, moreover, a very time-consuming process of analysis. Yet his reputation as a Chekhov scholar and a major Russian literary critic is, I believe, already secure. His creative, intuitive and imaginative hypotheses about Chekhov's writing will be appreciated and argued about far into the future; especially, perhaps, as they soar beyond Russia and impinge on other cultures.

SELECT BIBLIOGRAPHY

1 M.P. Gromov, 'O zhanrovoi prirode p'esy A.P. Chekhova "Vishnëvyi sad"', in *A.P. Chekhov – velikii khudozhnik slova. (Sbornik statei)*, edited by I.I. Beskrovainyi (Rostov n/D, Kn. izd., 1960), pp. 3–24

2 ------, 'Zabytyi chekhovskii geroi. (Peizazhi molodogo Chekhova)', in *A.P. Chekhov – velikii khudozhnik slova. (Sbornik statei)*, edited by I.I. Beskrovainyi (Rostov n/D, Kn. izd., 1960), pp. 59–83

3 ------, 'O zhanre p'esy A.P. Chekhova "Vishnëvyi sad"', *Nauchnye doklady vysshei shkoly. Filologicheskie nauki* (1960), N° 4, 72–81

4 ------, 'Tsenoiu molodosti', *Trudy Taganrogskogo pedagogicheskogo instituta*, 13 (1962), 125–43

5 ------, 'Pervaia p'esa Chekhova', in *A.P. Chekhov. Sbornik statei i materialov*, 3 (Rostov n/D, Kn. izd., 1963), pp. 5–35

6 A.N. Tolstoi, *Detstvo Nikity*, with an introduction by M.P.Gromov (Moscow, 'Khudozhestvennaia literatura', 1966), 126 pp.

7 M.P. Gromov, 'Anton Chekhov: pervaia publikatsiia, pervaia kniga', *Al'manakh 'Prometei'*, 2 (1967), 162–78

8 A.P. Chekhov, *Rasskazy*, selected and with a foreword by M.P. Gromov (Moscow, 'Khudozhestvennaia literatura', 1970), 535 pp.

9 M.P. Gromov, 'Povestvovanie Chekhova kak khudozhestvennaia sistema', in *Sovremennye problemy literaturovedeniia i iazykoznaniia: k 70-letiiu so dnia rozhdeniia akademika Mikhaila Borisovicha Khrapchenko*, edited by N.F. Bel'chikov (Moscow, 'Nauka', 1974), pp. 307–15

10 ------, 'Portret, obraz, tip', in *V tvorcheskoi laboratorii Chekhova*, edited by L.D. Opul'skaia, Z.S. Papernyi and S.E. Shatalov (Moscow, 'Nauka', 1974), pp. 142–61

11 ------'Vstupitel'naia stat'ia k primechaniiam' and 'Primechaniia', in PSSP (Works), 1 (Moscow, 'Nauka', 1974), pp. 550–57, 558–603

12 A.P. Chekhov, *Izbrannoe*, selected and with an introduction by M.P. Gromov (Moscow, 'Khudozhestvennaia literatura', 1974), 606 pp.

13 ------, *Izbrannoe. Povesti i rasskazy*, selected and with an introduction by M.P. Gromov (Moscow, 'Khudozhestvennaia literatura', 1975), 607 pp.

14 ------, *Izbrannoe*, selected and with a foreword by M.P. Gromov (Moscow, 'Meditsina', 1975), 606 pp.

15 ------, *Izbrannoe*, selected and with a foreword by M.P. Gromov (Moscow, 'Atomizdat', 1975), 606 pp.

16 M.P. Gromov, 'Primechaniia', in PSSP (Works), 3 (Moscow, 'Nauka',

1975), pp. 578, 585–89, 594–605
17 ------, 'Vstupitel'naia stat'ia k primechaniiam' and 'Primechaniia', in PSSP (Works), 4 (Moscow, 'Nauka', 1976), pp. 456–66, 467–522
18 ------, 'Skrytye tsitaty (Chekhov i Dostoevskii)', in *Chekhov i ego vremia*, edited by L.D. Opul'skaia, Z.S. Papernyi and S.E. Shatalov (Moscow, 'Nauka', 1977), pp. 39–52
19 ------, 'Kommentarii i primechaniia' ['The Steppe'], in PSSP (Works), 7 (Moscow, 'Nauka', 1977), pp. 626–45
20 ------, 'Kommentarii i primechaniia' ['A Man in a Case', 'Gooseberries', 'About Love'], in PSSP (Works), 10 (Moscow, 'Nauka', 1977), pp. 369–90
21 ------, 'Vstupitel'naia stat'ia k primechaniiam' and 'Kommentarii i primechaniia' [*Fatherless*, *On the Highway*, *Swan Song*, *The Bear*, *The Proposal*], in PSSP (Works), 11, (Moscow, 'Nauka', 1978), pp. 381–84, 388–92, 393–408, 426–40
22 ------, 'Talant i metod', *Vestnik MGU, Seriia 9, Filologiia* (1981), N° 1, 32–38
23 ------, 'Primechaniia' ['Dubia' etc], in PSSP (Works), 18 (Moscow, 'Nauka', 1982), pp. 235–39, 288–89, 295–97
24 ------, 'A.P. Chekhov v perepiske s sovremennikami', in *Perepiska A.P. Chekhova v dvukh tomakh*, edited by V.E. Vatsuro and others, compiled and with commentaries by M.P. Gromov, A.M. Dolotova and V.B. Kataev, 1 (Moscow, 'Khudozhestvennaia literatura', 1984), pp. 5–35
25 *'Kak serdtsu vyskazat' sebia...' Russkaia lirika ot Zhukovskogo do Bloka*, selected and with an introduction by M.P. Gromov (Moscow, 'Molodaia gvardiia', 1986), 525 pp.
26 M.P. Gromov, *Kniga o Chekhove* (Moscow, 'Sovremennik', 1989), 384 pp.
27 ------, *Tvorcheskii put' A.P. Chekhova. Kniga dlia uchitelei* (Moscow, 'Prosveshcheniie', 1991) [Thus announced in *Novye knigi SSSR*, 1990.]
28 ------, '"Pozhelanie zhizni napolniaiushcheisia smyslom i svobodoi". Tri pis'ma Borisa Pasternaka', *Literaturnaia gazeta*, 12 February 1992, N° 7 (5384), p. 6
29 ------, *Chekhov*, Seriia 'Zhizn' zamechatel'nykh liudei' (Moscow, 'Molodaia gvardiia', 1993), 396 pp.
30 ------, '"Step'" kak literaturnyi pamiatnik' and 'Primechaniia', in A.P. Chekhov, *Step'. Istoriia odnoi poezdki*, edited by I.G. Ptushkina (Moscow, 'Nauka', 1995), pp. 167–267, 277–87
31 ------, 'A.P. Chekhov v perepiske s sovremennikami', in *Perepiska A.P. Chekhova v trekh tomakh*, edited by V.E. Vatsuro and others, compiled and with commentaries by M.P. Gromov, A.M. Dolotova and V.B. Kataev, 1 (Moscow, 'Nasledie', 1996), pp. 5–40
32 ------, *Tropa k Chekhovu* (Moscow, 'Detskaia literatura', in press)

NOTES

1 'Bunin o Chekhove', *Iuzhnyi krai*, 2 July 1914 (N° 12141). (Reference cited from [**24**, 5].)

2 Peter Henry, 'Mikhail Petrovich Gromov, 1927–1990', *Slavonica*, 16 (Spring 1991), 153–54 (p. 154).

3 See Roland Barthes, *Le plaisir du texte* (Paris, Editions du Seuil, 1973), p. 66: 'Or le langage encratique (celui qui se produit et se répand sous la protection du pouvoir) est statutairement un langage de répétition.'

4 V.F. Frolova, *Izuchenie rasskaza Chekhova 'Kashtanka' v V klasse* (Moscow, Uchpedgiz, 1957), p. 3.

5 Compare F.M. Dostoevskii, *Polnoe sobranie sochinenii v tridtsati tomakh*, edited by V.G. Bazanov and others, 17, *Podrostok (Rukopisnye redaktsii)* (Leningrad, 'Nauka', 1976), pp. 142–43.

6 PSSP (Letters), 9, p. 166.

7 *Wild Honey; The Untitled Play by Anton Chekhov*, in a version by Michael Frayn (London and New York, Methuen, 1984), pp. xv–xvii.

8 Frayn, p. xiv.

9 Letter to Suvorin of 7 January 1889, PSSP (Letters), 3, p. 132.

10 Anatoly Smeliansky, *The Russian Theatre after Stalin* (Cambridge, CUP, 1999), p. 70.

11 A.P. Chudakov, *Poetika Chekhova* (Moscow, 'Nauka', 1971), p. 3.

12 'Zametki' [1920–74], in M.M. Bakhtin, *Literaturno-kriticheskie stat'i*, edited by S.G. Bocharov and V.V. Kozhinov (Moscow, 'Khudozhestvennaia literatura', 1986), p. 529.

13 See Marcus Aurelius, *Meditations*, translated by Maxwell Staniforth (Harmondsworth, Penguin Books, 1969), p. 65.

14 See PSSP (Works), 5, pp. 492, 612–13.

15 C.J.G. Turner, *Time and Temporal Structure in Chekhov*, Birmingham Slavonic Monographs, 22 (Birmingham, Department of Russian Language and Literature, University of Birmingham, 1994), p. 10.

16 W.H. Bruford, *Chekhov and his Russia. A Sociological Study* (London, Kegan Paul, Trench, Trubner and Co. Ltd., 1948), 233 pp. (republished by Routledge, London, 1998).

17 L.D. Gromova-Opul'skaia, pers. comm., 3 July 1997.

18 Chudakov, p. 274.

19 Chudakov, p. 3.

20 G. Berdnikov, 'O poetike Chekhova i printsipakh ee issledovaniia', *Voprosy literatury* (1972), N° 5, 124–41 (p. 128).

21 Bakhtin, p. 529.

22 PSSP (Works), 17, p. 51.

23 It is intriguing that Gromov does not include the pioneer of holistic therapy G.A. Zakhar'in (1829–97), whom Chekhov equated in medicine with Tolstoi. See V.B. Kataev,

Proza Chekhova: problemy interpretatsii (Moscow, Izd. Mosk. un-ta, 1979), pp. 89–95.

24 See, e.g., M.S. Gorbachev, *Perestroika i novoe myshlenie dlia nashei strany i dlia vsego mira* (Moscow, Izdatel'stvo politicheskoi literatury, 1987), pp. 148–50.

25 V.I. Lenin, *Polnoe sobranie sochinenii*, 5th edition, 12, edited by M.Ia. Pankratova (Moscow, Gosudarstvennoe izdanie politicheskoi literatury, 1960), p. 331.

26 I. Zil'bershtein, 'Lenin – chitatel' Chekhova', *Pravda*, 29 January 1935, N° 28 (6274), p. 7.

27 See, e.g., A.V. Lunacharskii, 'Chem mozhet byt' A.P. Chekhov dlia nas', *Pechat' i Revoliutsiia*, 4 (1924), 19–34; 'Chekhov i ego proizvedeniia kak obshchestvennoe iavlenie', in A.P. Chekhov, *Sobranie sochinenii*, edited by A.V. Lunacharskii, 1 (Moscow-Leningrad, GIZ, 1929), pp. 3–14.

28 See Viktor Shklovskii, *O teorii prozy* (Moscow-Leningrad, 'Krug', 1925), p. 161: 'Poniatie **siuzheta** slishkom chasto smeshivaiut s opisaniem sobytii – s tem, chto predlagaiu uslovno nazvat' **fabuloi**.'

29 Compare Chudakov, p. 188: 'Pod fabuloi my ponimaem, v sootvetstvii so slozhivsheisia eshche v 20-e gody terminologiei, sovokupnost' sobytii (epizodov) proizvedeniia. Eto otobrannyi pisatelem material. Siuzhet – organizatsiia, kompozitsiia etogo materiala.'

30 Ronald Hingley, *A New Life of Chekhov* (London, OUP, 1976), p. 94.

31 See G.N. Pospelov: 'Sushchestvuet tochka zreniia, kotoraia ne predstavliaetsia obosnovannoi, chto termin "fabula" izlishen, poskol'ku ves' diapazon ego znachenii pokryvaetsia poniatiem "siuzhet", "skhema siuzheta", "kompozitsiia siuzheta".' *Literaturnyi entsiklopedicheskii slovar'*, edited by V.M. Kozhevnikov and P.A. Nikolaev (Moscow, 'Sovetskaia entsiklopediia', 1987), p. 461, 'Fabula'.

32 The specific Russian-ness of 'The Steppe' stands out if we compare it with Egdon Heath in *The Return of the Native*. Hardy painstakingly establishes the Heath's historical, geographical, geological, ecological and ethnographic identity, it has its own 'aged highway', and it is a protagonist in the novel. But there is no 'search for truth' along this highway, nor does one feel Egdon Heath to be vitally linked with Britain's historical continuum and a hero's awareness of this continuum.

33 D.S. Mirsky, *A History of Russian Literature*, edited and abridged by Francis J. Whitfield (London, Routledge and Kegan Paul, 1964), p. 14.

34 See Nils Åke Nilsson, *Studies in Čechov's Narrative Technique. 'The Steppe' and 'The Bishop'*, Acta Universitatis Stockholmensis, Stockholm Slavic Studies, 2 (Stockholm, Almqvist and Wiksell, 1968), p . 25: 'In Čechov [...] the interplay between narrator and the chosen point of view is [...] actually sometimes rather fatal to the unity he was so eager to achieve. [...] Čechov does not always seem able to make up his mind who should tell the story – Egoruška through his view of events as they unfold themselves, or the narrator himself.'

35 Nilsson, p. 25.

36 The publication timescale naturally appears different. The standard work on literary influence in Chekhov, V.B. Kataev's *Literaturnye sviazi Chekhova* (Moscow, Izd-vo MGU, 1989), 261 pp., came out in the same year as Gromov's *Kniga o Chekhove* but contains very little on Dostoevskii. The first extended post-Gromov synchronic study appears to be E.A. Polotskaia's 'Chelovek v khudozhestvennom mire Dostoevskogo i Chekhova', in: E.A. Polotskaia, *O poetike Chekhova* (Moscow, 'Nasledie', 2000), pp. 135–92 (a re-presentation of an article first published in 1971).

37 Vl.I. Nemirovich-Danchenko, *Iz proshlogo* (Moscow, GIKhL, 1938), p. 31. The memoir was widely reprinted in the Soviet era.

38 Letter to E.M. Mukhina, 5 June 1905, in Innokentii Annenskii, *Knigi otrazhenii*, edited by B.F. Egorov and A.V. Fedorov (Moscow, 'Nauka', 1979), p. 460.

39 Connections had been made between Chekhov's and Dostoevskii's works by *western* scholars, for example Andrew Durkin, Ronald Hingley, Robert Louis Jackson and Donald Rayfield, but nothing as detailed as Gromov's inquiry had been carried out.

40 PSSP (Letters), 7, p. 315.

41 Donald Rayfield, 'Orchards and Gardens in Chekhov', *Slavonic and East European Review*, 67, N° 4 (October 1989), 530–45 (p. 537).

42 For a rigorous examination of the convergence between Nietzsche's and Hitler's 'ideas', see Ernst Tugendhat, 'Der Wille zur Macht: Macht und Anti-Egalitarismus bei Nietzsche und Hitler – Einspruch gegen den Versuch einer Verharmlosung', *Die Zeit*, 14 September 2000 (N° 38), pp. 51–52.

43 P.G. Pustovoit, 'Chekhovskie dni v Taganroge', *Nauchnye doklady vysshei shkoly. Filologicheskie nauki* 1960 (N° 3), 165–69 (p. 167).

44 For example, Gromov does not question the conventional wisdom that Stanislavskii and Nemirovich directed the first production as a 'drama' or 'tragedy'. In fact, Stanislavskii's production score 'manifests a lightness that suggests Stanislavsky had understood that Chekhov had written what he said he had – a comedy, even at times a farce. [...] The wonder is that the production ever acquired a reputation for tragic solemnity and tearfulness' – Nick Worrall, 'Stanislavsky's Production Score for Chekhov's *The Cherry Orchard* (1904): A Synoptic Overview', *Modern Drama*, 42, N° 4 (Winter 1999), 519–40 (p. 539).

45 V.G. Belinskii, *Polnoe sobranie sochinenii*, edited by N.F. Bel'chikov and others, 5, *Stat'i i retsenzii 1841–1844* (Moscow, Izd. AN SSSR, 1954), p. 596.

46 7 March 1901, PSSP (Letters), 9, p. 220.

47 Letter to M.P. Alekseeva (Lilina), 15 September 1903, PSSP (Letters), 11, p. 248.

48 See I.A. Bunin, *O Chekhove. Nezakonchennaia rukopis'* (New York, Izdatel'stvo imeni Chekhova, 1955), pp. 215–17.

49 T.S. Eliot, *After Strange Gods. A Primer of Modern Heresy* (London, Faber and Faber, 1934), p. 30.

50 When Chekhov said that 'The Student' was his 'favourite' story, was he speaking as its creator or as a reader? Gromov would have us believe the former and that Chekhov said it because the 'voploshchennaia v rasskaze mysl'' was particularly dear to him [**29**, 345]. How does Gromov know this? Was Chekhov that didactic? Chekhov's brother Ivan thought the story was Chekhov's 'favourite' simply because Chekhov considered it his 'naibolee otdelannoi [veshch'iu]' (PSSP (Works), 8, p. 507).

51 James Redmond, 'The Mind's Eye, the Worthy Scaffold, the Real Thing: How to Read a Shakespeare Play', in *Reading Plays: Interpretation and Reception*, edited by Hanna Scolnicov and Peter Holland (Cambridge, CUP, 1991), pp. 56–80 (p. 77).

52 Compare with the point made in note 44.

53 N.V. Gogol', *Polnoe sobranie sochinenii*, edited by N.F. Bel'chikov and others, 6, *Mertvye Dushi I* (Leningrad, Izd. AN SSSR, 1951), p. 246.

54 A phrase used by Catherine Merridale in 'English-language History and the Creation of Historical Paradigm', *History of the Human Sciences*, 9, N° 4 (November 1996), 81–98 (p. 83): 'the fact of difference is fundamental to the problem of cross-cultural historical dialogue'. The article examines difficulties in the post-1991 debate about Soviet history between western and Russian historians. It can usefully be compared with some of the problems of discussing Gromov as a scholar and critic.

[55] *Pis'ma A.P. Chekhovu ego brata Aleksandra Chekhova*, edited by I.S. Ezhov and I.K. Luppol (Moscow, Sotsekgiz, 1939), p. 50.

[56] Donald Rayfield, *Anton Chekhov. A Life* (London, HarperCollins, 1997), p. 340.

[57] F.M. Dostoevskii, *Polnoe sobranie sochinenii v tridtsati tomakh*, edited by V.G. Bazanov and others, 13, *Podrostok* (Leningrad, 'Nauka', 1975), p. 454.

[58] Respectively: M.L. Kalugina, 'Mikhail Petrovich Gromov (1927–1990)', in *Istoriko-literaturnye kursy: metodologiia, kontseptsii, problemy. (Materialy mezhvuzovskoi nauchnoi konferentsii 'Mirovaia literatura i sovremennoe universitetskoe obrazovanie')*, edited by R.L. Grinshtein (Moscow, Izdatel'stvo URAO, 1999), pp. 3–7 (p. 7) (also as '"Esli tebe kogda-nibud' ponadobitsia moia zhizn'..."', in *Mir filologii. Posviashchaetsia Lidii Dmitrievne Gromovoi-Opul'skoi*, edited by M.I. Shcherbakova and M.A. Mozharova (Moscow, 'Nasledie', 2000), pp. 176–80 (p. 180)), and R.E. Lapushin, 'Mikhail Gromov. Chekhov (Zhizn' zamechatel'nykh liudei). M., Molodaia gvardiia, 1993', *Nauchnye doklady vysshei shkoly. Filologicheskie nauki* 1994 (N° 2), 120–22 (p. 120).

[59] For example:

> Что касается г. Эттингера, то его "Думы и мысли" составлены совсем по-детски, говорить о них серьезно нельзя. [...] все эти "мысли и думы" не мои, а моих героев, и если какое-либо действующее лицо в моем рассказе или пьесе говорит, например, что надо убивать или красть, то это вовсе не значит, что г. Эттингер имеет право выдавать меня за проповедника убийства и кражи. (Letter to A.F. Marks, 23 October 1902, PSSP (Letters), 11, p. 64.)

[60] M.M. Bakhtin, 'K metodologii literaturovedeniia', in *Kontekst. 1974. Literaturno-teoreticheskie issledovaniia*, edited by N.K. Gei and others (Moscow, 'Nauka', 1975), p. 203.

[61] Karl R. Popper, *Conjectures and Refutations. The Growth of Scientific Knowledge* (London, Routledge and Kegan Paul, 1963), p. 50.

[62] John Casey, *The Language of Criticism* (London, Methuen & Co. Ltd, 1966), p. 140.

[63] F.R. Leavis, 'Criticism and Philosophy', in *The Common Pursuit* (Harmondsworth, Penguin Books, 1966), pp. 212–13.

[64] See, for example, T.S. Eliot, *The Sacred Wood. Essays in Poetry and Criticism* (London, Methuen & Co. Ltd, 1976), p. 37, and F.R. Leavis, *The Living Principle. 'English' as a Discipline of Thought* (London, Chatto & Windus, 1977), pp. 19, 35–36.

[65] A criticism well voiced by Lapushin, p. 120.

[66] See Smeliansky, pp. 102, 123, 221 (note 12).

[67] John Casey, 'Modern Charlatanism. III. Frozen Labyrinths: Roland Barthes', *The Cambridge Review*, 30 January 1976, 87–93 (p. 87).

[68] Eliot, *The Sacred Wood*, p. 37.

[69] Leavis, *The Living Principle*, pp. 19, 71–154.

[70] F.R. Leavis, 'Criticism and Philosophy', in *The Common Pursuit* (Harmondsworth, Penguin Books, 1966), p. 213. See also Leavis, *The Living Principle*, pp. 19, 35–36, 46–47.

[71] His principal objection to Soviet *chekhoved*'s was that they did not 'love' Chekhov. Compare Patrick Miles, 'O liubvi k tvortsu', in *Mir filologii. Posviashchaetsia Lidii Dmitrievne Gromovoi-Opul'skoi*, edited by M.I. Shcherbakova and M.A. Mozharova (Moscow, 'Nasledie', 2000), pp. 162–64.

[72] Eliot, *The Sacred Wood*, p. 37.

[73] Eliot, *The Sacred Wood*, pp. 37–38.

[74] F.R. Leavis, 'Sociology and Literature', in *The Common Pursuit* (Harmondsworth,

Penguin Books, 1966), p. 200.

75 The supposed mutual exclusiveness of Dostoevskii and Chekhov as elaborated by, for instance, Zinaida Gippius, was exported to the West by Russian intellectuals who left after 1917 and, particularly where combined with Russian Orthodoxy of a nostalgic type, has had a very long-running dissolvent effect on European and American university Slavonic departments. In Russia itself in the 20th century Dostoevskii's later novels were, for understandable reasons, read increasingly as theological texts.

76 It is interesting to note that the 'historical' view of *Fatherless* seems to have spread to Britain. See Benedict Nightingale, 'Angry Young Anton. Chekhov's Youthful Rant, *Platonov*, Foreshadowed the Russian Revolution', *The Times*, 'Times 2', 14 September 2001, p. 15 (review of a production of David Hare's version of *Fatherless* at the Almeida Theatre, London).

77 *Pis'ma A.P. Chekhovu ego brata Aleksandra Chekhova*, p. 50.

78 For instance, after working professionally in the humorous and daily press for nearly four years, Chekhov produced for his brother a list of desirable qualities in modern Russian artistic writing that is virtually the opposite of *Fatherless*: '1) otsutstvie prodlinnovennykh slovoizverzhenii politiko-sotsial'no-ekonomicheskogo svoistva; 2) ob"ektivnost' sploshnaia; 3) pravdivost' v opisanii deistvuiushchikh lits i predmetov; 4) sugubaia kratkost'; 5) smelost' i original'nost'; begi ot shablona; 6) serdechnost'.' (Letter to Aleksandr Chekhov, 10 May 1886, PSSP (Letters), 1, p. 242.) It is difficult to believe Chekhov would have reached these conclusions so soon if *Fatherless* had somehow been successfully staged at the Malyi and launched him on a career in the Russian theatre.

79 S.Iu. Nikolaeva, 'Anton Chekhov: "Liniia zhizni"', *Russkaia literatura* 1994 (N° 2), 277–80 (p. 280).

80 A Russian reviewer described this essay as 'uzhe pochti sotvorchestvo' – B.V. Averin, 'Issledovanie M.P. Gromova o Chekhove', *Russkaia literatura* 1990 (N° 2), 252–54 (p. 254).

81 Roland Barthes, *Critique et vérité* (Paris, Editions du Seuil, 1966), p. 79.

82 Eliot, *The Sacred Wood*, p. 37.

83 Andrei Lebedev, 'Chekhov glazami vnimatel'nogo chitatelia', *Russkaia mysl'*, 12–18 May 1994 (N° 4029), p. 13; S. Nikolaeva, 'K 70-letiiu M.P. Gromova (1927–1990)', in *Chekhoviana. Chekhov i ego okruzhenie*, edited by A.M. Turkov and others (Moscow, 'Nauka', 1996), pp. 390–92; M.L. Kalugina, 'Mikhail Petrovich Gromov (1927–1990)', in *Istoriko-literaturnye kursy: metodologiia, kontseptsii, problemy. (Materialy mezhvuzovskoi nauchnoi konferentsii 'Mirovaia literatura i sovremennoe universitetskoe obrazovanie')*, edited by R.L. Grinshtein (Moscow, Izdatel'stvo URAO, 1999), pp. 3–7 (also as '"Esli tebe kogda-nibud' ponadobitsia moia zhizn'..."', in *Mir filologii. Posviashchaetsia Lidii Dmitrievne Gromovoi-Opul'skoi*, edited by M.I. Shcherbakova and M.A. Mozharova (Moscow, 'Nasledie', 2000), pp. 176–80).

84 L.D. Gromova-Opul'skaia, pers. comm., 11 September 1992.

85 Iurii Olesha, *Ni dnia bez strochki. Iz zapisnykh knizhek* (Moscow, 'Sovetskaia Rossiia', 1965), p. 8.

86 See *Chekhov: The Early Stories 1883–88*, chosen and translated by Patrick Miles and Harvey Pitcher (London, John Murray, 1982), p. 8.

APPENDIX
English Versions of Russian Titles

'A Boring Story'	'Skuchnaia istoriia'
'About Love'	'O liubvi'
'A Man in a Case'	'Chelovek v futliare'
A Nest of Gentlefolk	*Dvorianskoe gnezdo*
Anna Karenina	*Anna Karenina*
'A Terrorist's Tale'	'Rasskaz neizvestnogo cheloveka'
'Betrothed'	'Nevesta'
Crime and Punishment	*Prestuplenie i nakazanie*
Dead Souls	*Mertvye dushi*
'Dear Babkino's bright starlet!'	'Milogo Babkina iarkaia zvezdochka!'
'Dreams'	'Mechty'
'Easter Eve'	'Sviatoiu noch'iu'
'Fat and Thin'	'Tolstyi i tonkii'
Fatherless	*Bezottsovshchina*
'Fear'	'Strakh'
'Good People'	'Khoroshie liudi'
'Gooseberries'	'Kryzhovnik'
'Happiness'	'Schast'e'
'His Sister'	'Sestra'
'In the Ravine'	'V ovrage'
Ivanov	*Ivanov*
'Kashtanka the Dog'	'Kashtanka'
'Letter to a Learned Neighbour'	'Pis'mo k uchenomu sosedu'
'Light Breathing'	'Legkoe dykhanie'
My Contemporary's History	*Istoriia moego sovremennika*
'My Times'	'Vek'
'Naden'ka X's Holiday Homework'	'Kanikuliarnye raboty institutki Naden'ki N'
'Neighbours'	'Sosedi'
'On Official Business'	'Po delam sluzhby'
On the Highway	*Na bol'shoi doroge*
Swan Song	*Lebedinaia pesnia*
Tales of Melpomene	*Skazki Mel'pomeny*
'Taras Bul'ba'	'Taras Bul'ba'
The Adolescent	*Podrostok*
The Bear	*Medved'*
'The Bishop'	'Arkhierei'

'The Black Monk'	'Chernyi monakh'
The Cherry Orchard	*Vishnëvyi sad*
'The Death of a Civil Servant'	'Smert' chinovnika'
'The Duel'	'Duel''
'The Flying Islands'	'Letaiushchie ostrova'
'The Head Gardener's Tale'	'Rasskaz starshego sadovnika'
The Karamazov Brothers	*Brat'ia Karamazovy*
'The Lady with the Little Dog'	'Dama s sobachkoi'
'The Little Joke'	'Shutochka'
The Lower Depths	*Na dne*
The Proposal	*Predlozhenie*
'The Reed-Pipe'	'Svirel''
'The Steppe'	'Step''
'The Student'	'Student'
'The Village of Stepanchikovo and its Inhabitants'	'Selo Stepanchikovo i ego obitateli'
'The Wife'	'Zhena'
The Wood Demon	*Leshii*
'Thieves'	'Vory'
Three Sisters	*Tri sestry*
Uncle Vania	*Diadia Vania*
'Under Way'	'Na puti'
'Ward N° 6'	'Palata N° 6'
What Is To Be Done? (Tales about new people)	*Chto delat'? (Iz rasskazov o novykh liudiakh)*
'Who's to Pay'	'Komu platit''
Woe from Wit	*Gore ot uma*
Write Something Every Day	*Ni dnia bez strochki*